THE
POLITICAL THEORY
OF POSSESSIVE
INDIVIDUALISM

Hobbes to Locke

BY

C. B. MACPHERSON

PROFESSOR OF POLITICAL SCIENCE
UNIVERSITY OF TORONTO

OXFORD NEW YORK TORONTO MELBOURNE
OXFORD UNIVERSITY PRESS

Oxford Univeristy Press, Walton Street, Oxford OX2 6DP

OXFORD LONDON GLASGOW NEW YORK
TORONTO MELBOURNE WELLINGTON
KUALA LUMPUR SINGAPORE JAKARTA HONG KONG
TOKYO DELHI BOMBAY CALCUTTA MADRAS KARACHI
NAIROBI DAR ES SALAAM CAPE TOWN

ISBN 0 19 881084 9

© *Oxford University Press 1962*

First published by the Clarendon Press 1962
First issued as an Oxford University Press paperback 1964
Eighth impression 1979

Reproduced, printed and bound in Great Britain by
Cox & Wyman Ltd, London, Reading and Fakenham

FOR
SUSAN
STEPHEN
SHEILA

PREFACE

SOME time ago I suggested that English political thought from the seventeenth to the nineteenth centuries had an underlying unity which deserved notice. I called the unifying assumption 'possessive individualism' and suggested that central difficulties of liberal-democratic thought from John Stuart Mill to the present might be better understood if they were seen to have been set by the persistence and deep-rootedness of that assumption.[1] The notion of possessive individualism promised also to yield a fresh understanding of the main seventeenth-century political theories, in some cases resolving unsettled problems of their meaning.

The present work, which pursues that promise, has grown over several years. The study of Locke establishes, I hope, a reading of his theory of property right which alters the general view of his political theory. Parts of that study, which was the first to be done, were published in two articles in 1951 and 1954. I have not found it necessary to alter or add substantially to what I then said, though I have added references to some subsequent work on Locke. The study of Hobbes suggests that prevalent treatments of his political theory leave a good deal to be understood, and offers an alternative interpretation. The study of Leveller theory undertakes to correct a substantive error in the standard treatments, and explores the implications of the possessive aspect of their notion of freedom. The study of Harrington seeks to disengage his theory from the controversy over the gentry and to show that it is better understood as having bourgeois roots. Internal contradictions, especially in Locke's and Harrington's theories, which had hitherto gone unnoticed or been too easily dismissed, have been examined and used as clues to the thinker's implicit assumptions; so treated, the

[1] *Cambridge Journal,* vii. 560–8 (June 1954).

contradictions pointed to a fuller understanding of the whole theory.

Each study thus contributes, I hope, to a more adequate, and some of them to a more accurate, understanding of seventeenth-century English political thought. Together they may be thought to establish the usefulness of the notion of possessive individualism as a central assumption of liberal political theory.

Acknowledgement is made to the editors of the *Western Political Quarterly* for permission to use material first published in its pages as two articles, 'Locke on Capitalist Appropriation', December 1951, and 'The Social Bearing of Locke's Political Theory', March 1954; and to the editors of *Past & Present* for permission to use the material on Harrington, which appeared in its April 1960 issue.

Friends and colleagues with whom I have discussed most of the ideas here presented have saved me from some enthusiasms. They will not wish to be thanked specifically: some of them have been more helpful than they know. So have my students, who have made me aware of some difficulties in the subject-matter and encouraged me to think they could be overcome.

The paths of scholarship are smoothed in different fashions in different centuries: I may be permitted to record my thanks to the Nuffield Foundation, the Canada Council, and my own university, who have been pleased to think my studies something, and otherwise to oblige me with real testimonies of their good opinion.

C. B. MACPHERSON

University of Toronto
June 30, 1961

CONTENTS

I. INTRODUCTION   1

  1. The Roots of Liberal-Democratic Theory   1

  2. Problems of Interpretation   4

II. HOBBES: THE POLITICAL OBLIGATION OF THE MARKET   9

  1. Philosophy and Political Theory   9

  2. Human Nature and the State of Nature   17

    (i) Abstraction from Society   17

    (ii) The State of Nature   19

    (iii) From Physiological to Social Motion   29

  3. Models of Society: 46

    (i) The Use of Models   46

    (ii) Customary or Status Society   49

    (iii) Simple Market Society   51

    (iv) Possessive Market Society   53

    (v) Hobbes and the Possessive Model   61

    (vi) The Inadequacy of the State of Nature   68

  4. Political Obligation   70

    (i) From Motivation to Obligation   70

    (ii) Moral or Prudential Obligation?   72

    (iii) The Postulate of Equality   74

    (iv) Morality, Science, and the Market   78

    (v) The Presumption of Obligation from Fact   81

  5. Penetration and Limits of Hobbes's Political Theory   87

    (i) Historical Prerequisites of the Deduction   87

    (ii) The Self-perpetuating Sovereign   90

    (iii) Congruence of Sovereignty and Market Society   95

    (iv) Some Objections Reconsidered   100

III. THE LEVELLERS: FRANCHISE AND FREEDOM   107

  1. The Problem of the Franchise   107

  2. Types of Franchise   111

3. The Record 117
   (i) The Chronology 117
   (ii) Putney and After 120
   (iii) Before Putney 129
   (iv) Summing-up 136
4. Theoretical Implications 137
   (i) The Property in One's Person 137
   (ii) The Deduction of Rights and the Grounds for Exclusion 142
   (iii) Levellers' and Independents' Individualism 148
   (iv) Limits and Direction of the Levellers' Individualism 154

IV. HARRINGTON: THE OPPORTUNITY STATE 160
1. Unexamined Ambiguities 160
2. The Balance and the Gentry 162
3. The Bourgeois Society 174
4. The Equal Commonwealth and the Equal Agrarian 182
5. The Self-Cancelling Balance Principle 188
6. Harrington's Stature 191

V. LOCKE: THE POLITICAL THEORY OF APPROPRIATION 194
1. Interpretations 194
2. The Theory of Property Right 197
   (i) Locke's Purpose 197
   (ii) The Initial Limited Right 199
   (iii) The Limitations Transcended 203
     (a) The spoilage limitation 204
     (b) The sufficiency limitation 211
     (c) The supposed labour limitation 214
   (iv) Locke's Achievement 220
3. Class Differentials in Natural Rights and Rationality 221
   (i) Locke's Assumption of the Differentials in Seventeenth-Century England 222
   (ii) Differential Rights and Rationality Generalized 229
     (a) Differential rights 230
     (b) Differential rationality 232
4. The Ambiguous State of Nature 238

5. The Ambiguous Civil Society   247

6. Unsettled Problems Reconsidered   251

   (i) The Joint-stock Theory   251

   (ii) Majority Rule v. Property Right   252

   (iii) The Equation of Individual and Majority Consent   252

   (iv) Individualism v. Collectivism   255

   (v) Locke's Constitutionalism   257

VI. POSSESSIVE INDIVIDUALISM AND LIBERAL
    DEMOCRACY   263

   1. The Seventeenth-Century Foundations   263

   2. The Twentieth-Century Dilemma   271

APPENDIX
   Social Classes and Franchise Classes in England, *circa* 1648   279

NOTES   293

WORKS AND EDITIONS CITED   302

INDEX   305

I

INTRODUCTION

1. *The Roots of Liberal-Democratic Theory*

A GREAT deal has been written in recent years about the difficulty of finding a firm theoretical basis for the liberal-democratic state. As the difficulty persists, it seems worth inquiring whether it may not lie as much in the roots of the liberal tradition as in any subsequent growth. For such an inquiry, the roots may properly be taken to be in the political theory and practice of the English seventeenth century. It was then, in the course of a protracted struggle in parliament, a civil war, a series of republican experiments, a restoration of the monarchy, and a final constitutional revolution, that the principles which were to become basic to liberal democracy were all developed, though not with equal success at the time. And it is clear that an essential ingredient, both of the practical struggle and of the theoretical justifications, was a new belief in the value and the rights of the individual.

Whether the individualism of the seventeenth century is deplored as having undermined the Christian natural law tradition, or applauded as having opened new vistas of freedom and progress, its importance is not disputed. Nor is it doubted that individualism has been an outstanding characteristic of the whole subsequent liberal tradition. Individualism, as a basic theoretical position, starts at least as far back as Hobbes. Although his conclusion can scarcely be called liberal, his postulates were highly individualistic. Discarding traditional concepts of society, justice, and natural law, he deduced political rights and obligation from the interest and will of dissociated individuals. Individualism of another sort, emphasizing the equal moral worth of every human being, was clearly fundamental in Puritan political thinking. And individualism has a large, if ambiguous, place in Locke's political theory. All these theories were closely related to the struggle for a more liberal state. The Puritan theories and Locke's, between them, provided its main justification. Even the utilitarian doctrine which seemed to supersede them in the eighteenth and nineteenth centuries is at bottom only a restatement of the individualist principles which were worked out in the seventeenth century: Bentham built on Hobbes.

One would not expect fundamental political principles of the seventeenth century to be entirely sufficient for a changed and more complex twentieth-century world. But one might expect that they could still be built upon, if they were as solid as they seemed, that is, if they corresponded as well as they seemed to do to the needs, aspirations, and capacities of modern man. This expectation has not been fulfilled. The foundations have cracked and tilted. If they are not to be abandoned, they need to be repaired.

What kind of fundamental repair should be attempted must depend on the diagnosis of the weakness. There has been no lack of diagnoses. Ever since John Stuart Mill's attack on Bentham's utilitarianism, which had by then become the embodiment of political individualism, the weakness of liberal individualism has been more or less identified with Bentham's narrowly selfish, narrowly rationalist, version of it. The Benthamite assumption that man in his political relations was and should be treated as a calculator of his own interests, and that this exhausted his nature as political man, has been seen as a perversion of the fundamental liberal insights of an earlier tradition.

On this sort of diagnosis, the repair that was needed was one that would bring back a sense of the moral worth of the individual, and combine it again with a sense of the moral value of community, which had been present in some measure in the Puritan and Lockean theory. In this way it might be hoped to get back to what seemed the desirable values of individualism while discarding its excesses. The many attempts to do this, ranging, since Mill, from T. H. Green's idealism through many kinds of modern pluralism, have all run into serious difficulty, so much so that it is worth reconsidering the diagnosis.

The present study is an attempt to do this. It suggests that the difficulties of modern liberal-democratic theory lie deeper than had been thought, that the original seventeenth-century individualism contained the central difficulty, which lay in its possessive quality. Its possessive quality is found in its conception of the individual as essentially the proprietor of his own person or capacities, owing nothing to society for them. The individual was seen neither as a moral whole, nor as part of a larger social whole, but as an owner of himself. The relation of ownership, having become for more and more men the critically important relation determining their actual freedom and actual prospect of realizing their full potentialities, was read back into the nature of the individual. The individual, it was thought, is free inasmuch as he is proprietor of his person and capacities. The human essence is freedom from dependence on the wills of others, and freedom is a function of possession. Society becomes a lot of free equal individuals related to each other as proprietors of their own capacities and of what they have acquired by their exercise. Society consists of relations of exchange between proprietors. Political society becomes a calculated device for the protection of this property and for the maintenance of an orderly relation of exchange.

It cannot be said that the seventeenth-century concepts of freedom, rights, obligation, and justice are all entirely derived from this concept of possession, but it can be shown that they were powerfully shaped by it. We shall see that possessive assumptions are present not only in the two main systematic theories of political obligation (Hobbes's and Locke's) but also, where they might be least expected, in the theories of the radical Levellers and the gentry-minded

Harrington. I shall argue that these assumptions, which do correspond substantially to the actual relations of a market society, were what gave liberal theory its strength in the seventeenth century, but that they became the source of its weakness in the nineteenth, when the development of the market society destroyed certain prerequisites for deriving a liberal theory from possessive assumptions, while yet the society conformed so closely to those assumptions that they could not be abandoned. They have not been abandoned yet, nor can they be while market relations prevail. When we see how deeply they are embedded in the original theory we shall understand their persistence; when their persistence is recognized we can consider how far it is responsible for the difficulties of liberal-democratic theory in our own time.

2. *Problems of Interpretation*

The social assumptions whose importance in seventeenth-century political theory I have sought to establish have not generally been clearly identified and, therefore, I believe, have not generally been given sufficient weight. Since most of them appear in the theories as uncertain mixtures of assumptions about fact and assumptions about right, they tend to be beneath or beyond the notice of both philosophical and historical critics. And these social assumptions can easily be overlooked, or undervalued, because they are sometimes not explicit, or not fully formulated, in the theories themselves. This raises a general problem of interpretation.

To say that a theorist has failed to state some of his assumptions clearly is of course to presume that he was using some assumptions beyond those he has explicitly formulated. This presumption cannot be certainly established. It cannot be established merely by showing that some unstated assumptions are logically required (as they commonly are) to produce the theory's conclusions; one would have also to suppose that the theorist was a strictly logical thinker. This supposition is unwise. While political theorists do try to persuade their readers by some sort of reasoned argument, the requirements of political persuasion and of logic are not always identical. Besides, a thinker of a previous century may not have had the same notion of logic that we have.

But while the presumption that a theorist was using assumptions beyond those he explicitly formulated cannot be certainly established, it is still a fairly strong one. It would be surprising if political theorists did always state all their assumptions clearly. Two probable reasons for their not doing so are fairly obvious.

First, where a writer can take it for granted that his readers will share some of his assumptions, he will see no need to set these out at the points in his argument where we, who do not share those assumptions automatically, think they should have been stated to make the argument complete. For example, it was a common assumption in the seventeenth century that the labouring class is a class apart, scarcely if at all to be counted as part of civil society. We should not be justified in imputing that assumption to a seventeenth-century theorist simply on the ground that his conclusion does not follow without it and does follow with it. For it is possible that some other assumption could be found which would produce his conclusion, and that that other assumption ought rather to be imputed. But when an assumption not only meets the two conditions (*a*) that it was common enough that a writer could take it for granted in his readers, and (*b*) that it fills a gap in his argument, but moreover is mentioned or used by the writer in some context other than the one in which we think it is required, the probability that he was making the assumption throughout his argument becomes too strong to be overlooked. It may well be more misleading for us to exclude it than to admit it. We shall be noticing several instances of assumptions which are quite essential to a theory being mentioned casually, as if hardly worth stating,[1] or revealed incidentally in the course of an argument about something else.[2]

A second reason for a theorist's failure to state an assumption clearly is that he may not be clearly aware of it. It would be strange indeed if a thinker did not sometimes carry over into his premisses some general assumptions about the nature of man or of society, shaped by his living in his own society, without being fully aware that he was doing so. No man formulates all that is in his mind; few formulate all that may later be seen to be relevant to their problems. What they leave unformulated may nevertheless pervade their thinking. The possibility that such implicit assumptions are present should not be overlooked. They should not be imputed merely on the ground that they seem to be logically required by the author's argument. But when such assumptions do make sense of the argument (or more sense than can otherwise be made of it), and are ones that we can now see might readily have arisen from that thinker's experience of his own society, and when, moreover, they are repeatedly implied in various of his incidental arguments,[3] the probability that he was using such assumptions is sufficient to entitle us to admit them.

There is of course some risk in reading into an author's work any assumptions he did not clearly state. However strong the presumption that he was taking some assumptions for granted, or that he held some without being aware of them, we cannot be certain that we have got them right. But it is less risky to make the attempt than to avoid it on principle. If we admit only assumptions which meet the tests just mentioned, we may at least hope to avoid the all-too-frequent course of imputing unconsciously assumptions

[1] e.g. the Levellers' assumption that servants are rightly excluded from the franchise (below, pp. 122 ff.), and Locke's assumption that the labour of my servant is my labour (below, p. 215).

[2] e.g. Locke's assumption that the labouring poor are incapable of rational obligation (below, p. 224).

[3] e.g. Harrington's assumption that market relations prevail in his gentry-led society (below, pp. 175–81), and Locke's two contradictory conceptions of society (below, pp. 243 ff.).

which we take for granted but which a writer of an earlier century would not have done.

There may be other reasons, besides the two already noticed, why a thinker has not clearly stated all the assumptions he is using. He may have deliberately concealed or disguised some of them, either from fear of offending the readers whom he wanted to convert to his conclusions, or from fear of persecution. Political theory was a dangerous trade in the seventeenth century. And even apart from personal danger, a cautious theorist who had reached an intellectual position which was a decisive break with the received tradition might well think that some subterfuge was needed to carry his readers with him. Explanations of this sort have been increasingly offered by recent scholars, especially to account for the confusions in Locke's theory.[1] The possibility, and in Locke's case the probability, of some measure of concealment of assumptions, cannot be neglected. But it has seemed to me that the concealment hypothesis cannot, even in Locke's case, explain all that has to be explained, and that it is an unsatisfactory alternative to the hypothesis that some social assumptions have been left imperfectly stated, or implicit, for one of the reasons I have suggested.

A general remark may be made finally about the question of logical consistency in political theories. My point of departure in each of the following studies is some real or supposed inconsistency in a theoretical structure. I have found it a fruitful hypothesis that each of the thinkers intended to be consistent, or (which comes to the same thing) was consistent within the limits of his vision. But it should be noticed that this is far from being a hypothesis that each of the theories is, when properly understood, consistent. Sometimes, indeed, the result has been to show that what appears to be an inconsistency is not so when we recognize the

---

[1] e.g. by Leo Strauss, *Natural Right and History* (Chicago, 1953), pp. 206–11, 246–7; R. L. Cox, *Locke on War and Peace* (Oxford, 1960), discussed below, p. 197, n. 2; and Note R, p. 300.

existence of an implicit or imperfectly stated assumption which had hitherto been overlooked or not given enough weight. But more often the result has been to show that the theory is in some respects strictly inconsistent, even (or especially) when its implicit assumptions have been given full weight. What the analysis achieves then is not a resolution of logical inconsistencies but an explanation of how the theorist could have been unconscious of them.

The question of consistency is in any case a secondary one. The hypothesis of intended consistency is no more than a useful approach. When we find inconsistent positions being taken in a single sentence (e.g. in a Leveller statement that since *all persons* have an equitable right to a voice in elections, therefore the franchise should be given to all men except servants and beggars[1]) we are entitled to ask whether any assumptions the writer may then have had in mind can account for such statements, and we should be unwise not to look about for evidence of there being such assumptions. The presence of apparently clear inconsistency is to be treated as a clue to inadequately stated assumptions. The hypothesis that a thinker was consistent within the limits of his vision is useful less as a way of resolving inconsistencies than as a pointer to the direction and limits of his vision, which may then be established by other evidence.

[1] John Harris, *The Grand Designe*, quoted below, p. 125.

II

HOBBES: THE POLITICAL OBLIGATION OF THE MARKET

1. *Philosophy and Political Theory*

HOBBES is widely, and rightly, regarded as the most formidable of English political theorists; formidable not because he is difficult to understand but because his doctrine is at once so clear, so sweeping, and so disliked. His postulates about the nature of man are unflattering, his political conclusions are illiberal, and his logic appears to deny us any way out. But clear as his theory is in comparison with most others, its unusual breadth and depth has left it open to criticism of many kinds. It has been attacked repeatedly on theological, philosophical, and pragmatic political grounds. Yet it has survived, and with added lustre. Direct attack having left it vigorous and perennially fascinating, it has been interpreted, re-interpreted, and even nowadays completely reconstructed.

It might seem that nothing more could usefully be said. Yet the interpretations now most widely accepted and most influential leave something to be desired. Most of them have proceeded by breaking up what Hobbes had presented as a monolithic structure. Sometimes this has been done to discredit the whole theory, but more often to rescue a substantial part of it from what were thought to be fatal weaknesses in other parts. There can be no objection to probing an apparent monolith, and if the probe reveals that the structure is not genuine this fact should be recorded and demonstrated. But as often as this has been done to Hobbes, the results have been inconclusive, and it may be doubted whether the process has furthered the understanding of Hobbes's theory.

The first wedge was driven in between Hobbes's philosophic materialism and his political theory. Some of the best-known students of Hobbes have taken the view that his political theory was not derived from his materialism or decisively affected by his concept of science; this view reached its culmination in the influential study published by Strauss in 1936.[1] This line of interpretation, however, did not require any very extensive revision of Hobbes's political theory. For while Hobbes had spoken of the possibility of deducing his psychological principles (and hence his political theory) from the geometrical and physical first principles of matter and motion,[2] he did not in fact try to make any such deduction. He pointed out that the psychological principles from which a political science could be deduced need not themselves be deduced from the laws of motion of material but could be reached directly by self-observation, and this was the method he used.[3] Hence to set aside Hobbes's materialism is not necessarily to undermine his political theory, although I shall argue[4] that the political theory requires the materialism for another reason.

More recently a new wedge has been driven, this time between Hobbes's psychological principles and his political theory, and this has had the more far-reaching consequence of requiring a virtual reconstruction of the political theory. The new view was put forward by A. E. Taylor in 1938.[5] Hobbes's theory of political obligation, it was argued, had no logically necessary connexion with his propositions about the psychological nature of man. This view has been widely accepted. Since its publication, outstanding students of Hobbes have tried to construct out of Hobbes's writings a theory they could regard as logically coherent and as being what Hobbes really meant. To do so they have had to set aside Hobbes's own statements that he was deducing his

---

[1] G. C. Robertson, *Hobbes* (1886); John Laird, *Hobbes* (1934); Leo Strauss, *The Political Philosophy of Hobbes, Its Basis and Genesis* (Oxford, 1936).

[2] *Elements of Philosophy* (*English Works*, ed. Molesworth, i. 74).

[3] Ibid., pp. 73, 74; cf. *Leviathan*, Intro.   [4] Below, pp. 78–79.

[5] A. E. Taylor, 'The Ethical Doctrine of Hobbes', *Philosophy*, xiii (1938).

political theory from his premisses about human nature,[1] and to find some other basis in Hobbes for the theory of political obligation.

Thus Oakeshott, after disarmingly remarking that we should not expect a coherence in Hobbes's moral thinking which is foreign to the ideas of any seventeenth-century writer, and that we should not attempt to create such a coherence by extracting some consistent doctrine from his writings, rejects, as just such an erroneous extraction, the theory of political obligation in terms of self-interest, and goes on to offer an interpretation which will give 'as coherent a view as is consistent with all of what Hobbes actually wrote'.[2] This view is that Hobbes's political obligation is a mixture of physical obligation (submission to the superior force of the sovereign), rational obligation, which prevents a man from willing an action the probable consequences of which he rationally perceives to be likely to be harmful to himself (which is based on self-interest), and moral obligation, which is created by the voluntary act of authorizing the sovereign, and consists of obedience to the commands of the authorized sovereign (which is not based on self-interest).[3]

This degree of coherence has not satisfied other scholars. Warrender, sharing the view that Hobbes's theory of political obligation is not sufficiently based on self-interest, rejects Oakeshott's cautionary admonitions and constructs from Hobbes a highly coherent theory of obligation, in which political obligation is moral obligation and is deduced not from the postulates about man's nature but from the will or command of God, or from a body of natural law which bears its own authority.[4] This construction has in turn been found unsatisfactory by other critics ; its very

[1] *Rudiments*, Ep. Ded., p. 5, and Preface, pp. 11, 13; *Elements of Law*, Ep. Ded., p. xvii, and chap. i, sect. 1; *Leviathan*, Review and Conclusion, p. 554. For details of these three works, and editions used, see Note A, p. 293.

[2] M. Oakeshott, Introduction to his edition of *Leviathan* (Oxford, 1947), p. lviii.

[3] Op. cit., pp. lix–lxi.

[4] Howard Warrender, *The Political Philosophy of Hobbes* (Oxford, 1957), and *Political Studies*, viii. 1 (Feb. 1960), 48–57. Cf. Note D, p. 294.

excellence and thoroughness in developing the implications of the Taylor thesis has led to the whole thesis being called into question.[1]

But if we reject the Taylor thesis and return to the traditional view that Hobbes was deducing his theory of political obligation from postulates about human nature which he held to be self-evident to any thoughtful observer, we are faced again with the old difficulties which the Taylor thesis had the merit of avoiding or resolving. Two difficulties particularly may be noticed.

First, Hobbes's theory of human nature has seemed so unacceptable, at least as the universal theory Hobbes claimed it to be, that unless the political theory could be logically detached from it, the political theory did not seem to be worth serious consideration; yet the political theory continues to haunt Hobbes's critics as worth serious consideration. Hobbes's theory of human nature is indeed difficult to accept entire. Apart from the fact that it is apt to arouse strong emotional resentment, and so to be rejected out of hand, it may be rejected on various reasoned grounds. Its mechanical materialism may be held to be untenable. Or it may be rejected empirically: if the theory of human nature were valid, then (granting, as such critics generally do freely grant, that Hobbes's deduction was good) the political conclusions he drew should have been acceptable to the men for and about whom he was writing, whereas in fact they never have been accepted. It is probably because Hobbes's theory of human nature is considered to be untenable (for one or another of such reasons), while yet his prowess as a thinker is admired and his conclusions are uneasily felt to have considerable force, that searches are made for some other basis for his conclusions about political obligation. But admiration for Hobbes as a thinker need not drive us to such lengths.

This difficulty, I shall suggest, can be disposed of without going to the extreme of jettisoning Hobbes's theory of

[1] Notably by Stuart M. Brown, Jr., 'Hobbes: The Taylor Thesis', *Philosophical Review*, lxviii. 3 (July 1959).

human nature or denying its essential place in his deductive system. When we see his theory of human nature as a reflection of his insight into the behaviour of men towards each other in a specific kind of society, we can see why Hobbes thought his propositions about human nature would be self-evident to all honest contemporary observers once he had set them out 'orderly and perspicuously'. We can see also that, while his propositions are not universally valid, they are more nearly valid for his and our time than is allowed by those who must have all or nothing and who therefore reject whatever cannot be shown to be universally valid. Nor is there any difficulty in showing why his propositions, in spite of their high degree of accuracy and adequacy, were not acceptable to his contemporaries.[1] In short, when Hobbes's universal claims are reduced to an historical measure, there is no need to divorce his theory of human nature from his political theory in order to rescue the latter; both theories are seen to have a specific historical validity, and to be consistent with each other.

A second difficulty with the traditional view is that it presents Hobbes as having committed what is now said to be a grave logical error, namely, as having tried to deduce moral obligation from empirical postulates of fact. The core of his theory of human nature is undoubtedly a series of postulates of supposed fact. And the political theory is certainly presented in terms of moral obligation. If the political theory was intended to be a strict deduction from the theory of human nature, Hobbes is convicted of having deduced what ought to be from what is; convicted, because it is now held that it is logically improper to deduce ought from is. To rescue Hobbes from this position it has seemed necessary to detach his theory of obligation from his theory of human nature and to find some other basis for the former, or else to deny that his theory of obligation is (as Hobbes thought it was) a moral rather than merely a prudential theory of obligation.

[1] See below, Sect. 5, ii.

But here, as with the first difficulty, an historical view of Hobbes's thought may show us that it is not necessary to go to such extremes. Why should we impose on Hobbes logical canons which are post-Hobbesian? It may be said that we must still do so if we are to satisfy ourselves to what extent his political theory is logically sound and can properly be built upon today. But the rule that obligation cannot be deduced from fact is itself historically questionable. I shall suggest[1] that when Hobbes's historically conditioned assumptions are given adequate recognition there is some reason to think that Hobbes had struck through several layers of philosophical confusion and hit on a relation between fact and obligation which has as good or better a logical standing than the modern rule. I shall argue that his penetrating vision into his own society enabled him to make a philosophic leap which, because of the demands society then made on political philosophy, was not taken up, and was soon lost sight of. Here, without anticipating the argument, it need only be said that in view of the difficulties we have seen to be involved in imposing post-Hobbesian logical requirements on Hobbes, there is a *prima facie* case for turning to social and historical considerations when we confront problems of Hobbes's logical consistency or adequacy.

We shall perhaps be told that logical and historical enquiries are each autonomous and that no historical interpretation, however acceptable, can affect the question of a theory's consistency and logical adequacy. It is true enough that no amount of historical evidence or conjecture about an author's motives or idiosyncrasies can be expected to contribute to a judgement of the logical adequacy of his system; though even that sort of historical inquiry, by drawing attention to the purpose for which and the audience to which he was writing, may save us from attributing to him philosophical questions he was not asking, and from searching his work for answers he was not seeking. The sort of historical interpretation I have in mind, however, is not con-

[1] Below, Sects. 4, v and 5, i.

cerned with motives. It considers historically the probable
content of unstated or unclear assumptions that are contained or necessarily implied in the theory itself. I see no
reason to fence this off from philosophical inquiry. There has
indeed been an increasingly sharp division of labour between
philosophers and political theorists in recent years, especially
since philosophers have turned to linguistic analysis. This
has reached the point where it can seriously be proposed by
the most able recent philosophic writer about Hobbes, that
historical considerations are irrelevant to the establishment
of Hobbes's meaning: 'the problem of how Hobbes's theory
originated or how it is to be explained' is put in a separate
compartment from 'the prior question of what his theory
is'.[1] But to call this the prior question is to beg the question.
It may equally well be that one cannot establish what the
theory is without making historical as well as logical conjec-
tures about Hobbes's unclear or unstated assumptions. In
any case, it seems worth trying whether an inquiry at once
logical and historical can throw a different light on Hobbes's
theory, and can bring out essentials of it that have been left
in the shadows by the prevailing sorts of logical analysis.

In the inquiry which follows I start by assuming that
Hobbes was trying to do what he said he was doing, i.e.
deducing political obligation from the supposed or observed
facts of man's nature. Instead of putting his theory immediately to post-Hobbesian tests of logical consistency in the
matter of *ought* and *is*, and then trying to construct from his
writings a theory which will pass the tests, or excusing him
on the ground that no seventeenth-century thinker should
be put to such tests, and then making out the best case one
can for him as a thinker handicapped by the philosophical
shortcomings of his time, I set aside temporarily the question
of these tests and move directly to the social content of some
of his assumptions.

In Section 2 I show that the argument from the physiological nature of man to men's necessary behaviour towards

[1] Warrender, op. cit., pp. viii–ix.

each other, from which behaviour the need for a sovereign follows, is not the simple deduction from physiological postulates that it is often taken to be, but that it is consistent only with a certain model of society. I believe that Hobbes's argument from the physiological to the social motion of man is often seen less clearly than it might be because it is usually taken as culminating in the hypothetical state of nature, which itself is often not clearly understood. I therefore proceed by trying to put the state of nature in focus, first by showing that it is about social, not natural men, and then by showing that it is in any case not the culminating point of the argument from physiology to the behaviour of men towards each other, but that before Hobbes uses the state of nature hypothesis at all he has developed a theory of the necessary relations of men *in society* (which is later reproduced with variations in the state of nature hypothesis). I then show that his theory of the necessary relations of men in society requires the assumption of a certain kind of society. The question, how far back in his argument from the physiological to the social motion of man he put the necessary social assumptions, is less important than the other question, with what kind of society is the social motion at which he arrives consistent? Both questions, however, are worth consideration. The first admits of more than one answer, depending on one's reading of some possibly inconsistent statements by Hobbes about what is innate and what is acquired in man's nature. This difficulty is noticed, and the reasons for preferring one reading are given. The second question is then shown to admit of only one answer on either reading of the passages relevant to the first question.

Having thus shown that Hobbes's theory of the social motion of man requires the assumption of a certain kind of society, I examine (in Section 3) some models of society, in order to demonstrate more precisely what kind of society is required. I argue that Hobbes did more or less consciously construct such a model, and that the model did correspond in large measure to seventeenth-century English society.

The recognition of Hobbes's social assumptions, and of the consequent completeness of his deduction of men's need for a sovereign, does not in itself dispose of the philosophic question whether the political obligation whose necessity Hobbes has thus demonstrated is properly moral obligation or merely expedient and prudential obligation, but it does put that question in a different perspective.

I then argue, in Section 4, that, in the light of Hobbes's assumptions, his deduction of obligation from fact must be allowed a logical validity as well as a striking novelty. It is argued that because of the assumption he made about the nature of society, which he saw as a series of competitive relations between naturally dissociated and independently self-moving individuals, with no natural order of subordination, he was able to deduce a moral obligation from the supposed facts, without importing hierarchical moral values or teleological principles; that his materialism was an integral part of that deduction; and that the deduction of obligation directly from the supposed facts about the nature of man and the necessary relations between men is not illogical in principle but requires conditions which were not clearly satisfied before Hobbes's time.

In Section 5 I conclude, from a reconsideration of Hobbes's originality, and of the reasons for his doctrine being so generally unacceptable, that he was much less in error, and that his theory has a much greater relevance to modern society, than is usually allowed.

2. *Human Nature and the State of Nature*

i. *Abstraction from society*

It is commonly said or assumed, by those who take the traditional view of Hobbes, that his psychological propositions are about man as such, man completely abstracted from society, and that those propositions contain all that is needed for his deduction of the necessity of the sovereign state. But there is a serious oversimplification in this view. If by his psychological propositions we mean those propositions about sense, imagination, memory, reason, appetite, and aversion, in which Hobbes describes the human being as a system of self-moving, self-guided matter in motion (i.e. the propositions with which Hobbes opens the argument of *Leviathan*, and which might be said to be about man as such, completely abstracted from society), then Hobbes's psychological propositions do not contain all that is needed for the deduction of the necessity of the sovereign state. If on the other hand we use the term psychological propositions to include Hobbes's statement of the necessary behaviour of men towards each other in any society (viz. that all men seek ever more power over others), or his similar statement of their behaviour in the hypothetical absence of any society (i.e. in the state of nature), then the psychological propositions do contain all that is needed for the deduction of the necessity of a sovereign, but they are not about the human animal as such; some assumptions about the behaviour of men in civilized society had to be added. You can move from the universal struggle for power in society, or from the state of nature, to the necessity of the sovereign without further assumptions, but you cannot move from man as a mechanical system to the universal struggle for power, or to the state of nature, without further assumptions. And the further assumptions are, I shall argue, tenable only about the relations prevailing between men in a certain kind of society, although Hobbes assumed they were universally valid. This is an unfamiliar view of Hobbes and requires further explanation.

I shall develop it in two ways. I shall show first (in Section 2, ii) that Hobbes's state of nature or 'natural condition of mankind' is not about 'natural' man as opposed to civilized man but is about men whose desires are specifically civilized; that the state of nature is the hypothetical condition in which men as they now are, with natures formed by living in civilized society, would necessarily find themselves if there were no common power able to overawe them all. The evidence for this is contained in Hobbes's description of the state of nature.

Secondly, I shall examine (in Section 2, iii) the chain of deduction from the beginning, and show that the psychological analysis, which begins (or appears to begin) as an analysis of the nature of men in complete abstraction from society, soon becomes an analysis of men in established social relationships; that certain social assumptions have to be made in order to establish that all men in society seek ever more power over others (and even to establish the behaviour of men in the hypothetical state of nature), and hence to establish the necessity of the sovereign; and (in Section 3) that the necessary social assumptions are valid only for a specific kind of society.

ii. *The state of nature*

In all three of Hobbes's constructions of his political theory[1] the step immediately preceding the demonstration of the need for a sovereign able to overawe every individual is the state of nature, or natural condition of mankind. The state of nature depicts the way in which men, being what they are, would necessarily behave if there were no authority to enforce law or contract. Given the appetitive and deliberative nature of man (which in the *Elements* and in *Leviathan* is set out in the earlier chapters, and which in the *Rudiments* is disclosed by a swift analysis of men's behaviour in contemporary society), this is the way they would necessarily behave if law-enforcement and contract-enforcement were entirely removed. This behaviour would necessarily be an incessant struggle of every man with every man, a struggle of each for power over others. Hobbes's point, of course, is to show that this condition would necessarily thwart every man's desire for 'commodious living' and for avoidance of violent death, that therefore every reasonable man should do whatever must be done to guard against this condition, and

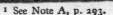
[1] See Note A, p. 293.

that nothing short of every man acknowledging an absolute sovereign power is sufficient to guard against it.

Hobbes's state of nature, as is generally recognized, is a logical not an historical hypothesis. It is an 'Inference, made from the Passions'; it describes 'what manner of life there would be, where there were no common Power to feare'.[1] Hobbes did not argue that the existing imperfectly sovereign state had originated by agreement between men who had previously been in an actual state of nature. On the contrary, he believed that a state of nature never did generally prevail over all the world (although he thought a close approximation to it existed among 'the savage people in many places of *America*'),[2] and he was clear that most existing sovereign states had had their origin not in compact but in conquest ('there is scarce a Common-wealth in the world, whose beginnings can in conscience be justified').[3] Nor did he argue that a perfect or completely sovereign state could be established only by agreement between men who were in an actual state of nature. He could not very well argue that, for his whole purpose in writing was to persuade men who now lived in imperfectly sovereign states (i.e. by definition, not in a state of nature) that they could and should acknowledge a complete obligation to a sovereign, and so should move themselves into a perfectly sovereign state. What he could, and did, argue was that to have a completely sovereign state men must act *as if* they had moved out of a state of nature by agreement.

The requisite sovereign power might come into existence in either of two ways: by some man or body of men conquering and subduing the inhabitants (sovereignty by acquisition) or by men agreeing by contract with each other to transfer all their natural powers to some man or body of men (sovereignty by institution).[4] It made no difference which way the sovereignty was established, as long as the

[1] *Leviathan*, ch. 13, p. 97.
[2] Ibid.
[3] *Leviathan*, Review and Conclusion, p. 551.
[4] *Leviathan*, ch. 17, p. 132.

sovereignty was acknowledged by all the citizens. It was enough if they acknowledged a *de facto* ruler or ruling assembly, and gave to it the full measure of obedience they would logically be obliged to give if they had voluntarily transferred to it the natural rights which they would have had in the hypothetical state of nature. In other words, all that is necessary is that they should act as if they had transferred their natural rights to a sovereign which they could have established by covenant with each other if they had ever lived in a state of nature.

When Hobbes comes to deduce the necessary rights of the sovereign and obligation of the subjects, he finds it convenient to speak of the covenant as an agreement actually made, or to be made, at a given point in time. By doing so, he avoids having to put his argument continually in conditional terms. Instead of the awkwardness of saying repeatedly 'if men had made such a covenant it would follow that . . .' he is able to say, throughout chapter 18 of *Leviathan*, 'because they have covenanted, it follows that . . .'. Yet before he does this he is careful to say that no such covenant need actually be made in order to establish the requisite sovereign power. The sovereign by acquisition has the same rights (and his subjects the same obligations), as the sovereign by institution.

Hobbes's state of nature is, then, a logical hypothesis. The fact that the state of nature is a logical and not an historical hypothesis is generally understood, and it would scarcely have required attention here had it not apparently led sometimes to a false inference. It seems often to be assumed that since the state of nature was not an historical hypothesis it must have been a logical hypothesis reached by setting aside completely the historically acquired characteristics of men. If it was not about primitive men it must have been about natural as contrasted with civilized men. But this does not follow. The state of nature was for Hobbes a condition logically prior to the establishment of a perfect (i.e. completely sovereign) civil society; what he deduced from the state of nature was the need for men to acknowledge the perfectly sovereign state instead of the imperfectly sovereign states they now had. He was therefore able to draw on his understanding of the historically acquired nature of men in existing civil societies in order to get his deductions about the state of nature. His 'inference made from the passions' could be made from the passions of existing men, passions shaped by civilized living. His inferences were so made. His state of nature is a statement of the behaviour to which men as they now are, men who live in civilized societies and have the desires of civilized men, would be led if all law and contract enforcement (i.e. even the present imperfect enforcement) were removed. To get the state of nature, Hobbes has set aside law, but not the socially acquired behaviour and desires of men.

The reason why this is so generally overlooked is, I think, that Hobbes's model of *society*, which he developed before he introduced the hypothetical state of nature, was itself almost as fragmented as his state of nature. His model of society contained a similar incessant competitive struggle of each for power over others, though within a framework of law and order. The behaviour of men in Hobbes's model of society[1] is, so to speak, so anti-social, that when he carries this behaviour into his hypothetical state of nature, it is there easily mistaken for a statement of the behaviour of non-social men. But it is a statement of the behaviour of social, civilized men. That this is so can be seen in a number of ways.

The most evident indication, though not in itself a decisive one, is that Hobbes offers, as a confirmation of the 'natural' tendency of men to invade and destroy each other, the observable behaviour of men in present civil society.

It may seem strange to some man, that has not well weighed these things; that Nature should thus [i.e. as in the state of nature] dissociate, and render men apt to invade, and destroy one another: and he may therefore, not trusting to this Inference, made from the Passions,

[1] See below, Sects. 2, iii and 3.

desire perhaps to have the same confirmed by Experience. Let him therefore consider with himselfe, when taking a journey, he armes himselfe, and seeks to go well accompanied; when going to sleep, he locks his dores; when even in his house he locks his chests; and this when he knowes there bee Lawes, and publike Officers, armed, to revenge all injuries shall bee done him; what opinion he has of his fellow subjects, when he rides armed; of his fellow Citizens, when he locks his dores; and of his children, and servants, when he locks his chests.[1]

And again, immediately after saying that a state of nature never generally existed:

Howsoever, it may be perceived what manner of life there would be, where there were no common Power to feare; by the manner of life, which men that have formerly lived under a peacefull government, use to degenerate into, in a civill Warre.[2]

The 'natural' behaviour of men, the behaviour to which they are necessarily led by their passions, can be seen, approximated at least, in the behaviour of civilized men who live under civil government, and of civilized men who, having lived under civil government, find themselves in civil war. And the reason that this observable behaviour of civilized men confirms the 'inference made from the passions' is that the inference was from the passions of civilized men.

A more decisive evidence that the state of nature is a statement of the behaviour to which specifically civilized men would be led if even the present imperfect sovereign were removed, is that the full state of nature is in fact reached by successive degrees of abstraction from civilized society. This is often lost sight of. Hobbes's picture of the full state of nature is clearly the negation of civilized society: no industry, no culture of the earth, no navigation, no commodious building, no arts, no letters, no society, 'and the life of man, solitary, poore, nasty, brutish, and short'. The picture is so impressive that we are apt to forget how Hobbes demonstrates its necessity. He deduces it from the appetites

[1] *Leviathan*, ch. 13, p. 97; cf. *Rudiments*, Preface, p. 11.
[2] *Leviathan*, ch. 13, pp. 97–98.

of men who are civilized in that they desire not merely to live but to live well or commodiously. Of the 'three principal causes of quarrel' that Hobbes finds 'in the nature of man', which together would put men into this brutish state of nature, if there were no power able to overawe them all, the first two (Competition and Diffidence) arise out of men's desire to live well.

It is the man who would 'plant, sow, build, or possesse a convenient Seat'[1] who must expect to be invaded and dispossessed by others seeking to enjoy the fruits of his labour (which invasion is the substance of the 'competition' Hobbes sees in the state of nature). And it is the holder of such cultivated land and convenient buildings who becomes fearful or diffident and must seek to secure himself by subduing as many of his potential invaders as possible, that is, 'by force, or wiles, to master the persons of all men he can, so long, till he see no other power great enough to endanger him'. Even the man 'that otherwise would be glad to be at ease within modest bounds' must increase his power by invading others if he is to have a chance of resisting the invasion of others. In short, the matter about which competition and diffidence would lead to a war of each with all, is the civilized matter of cultivated land and 'convenient seats'.

Even the third cause of quarrel (which Hobbes calls Glory) is more typical of men whose scale of values has been acquired by living in civilized society than of 'natural' men: it is that

> every man looketh that his companion should value him, at the same rate he sets upon himselfe: And upon all signes of contempt, or undervaluing, naturally endeavours, as far as he dares (which amongst them that have no common power to keep them in quiet, is far enough to make them destroy each other,) to extort a greater value from his contemners, by dommage; and from others, by the example.[2]

All three of the causes of quarrel are presented as factors operating in any kind of society, but becoming destructive

---

[1] *Leviathan*, ch. 13, p. 95.
[2] Ibid. pp. 95–96.

only when there is no common power to hold them in check. Competition, diffidence, and glory, far from being characteristic only of the brutish state of nature, are the factors in present civil society which would turn civil society into that brutish condition if there were no common power. Competition, diffidence, and glory are 'natural' dispositions of men in civil society. 'Natural' for Hobbes is not the opposite of social or civil. 'The naturall condition of mankind' covers the whole chapter in *Leviathan* in which Hobbes moves from the present dispositions of men to the brutish condition. The natural condition of mankind is within men now, not set apart in some distant time or place.

If the term 'state of nature' were not so firmly entrenched in the literature about Hobbes it would be helpful to discard it entirely and keep to such another term as 'the natural condition of mankind', which is more readily seen to be something within men. Hobbes himself rarely used 'state of nature'. In the *Elements* his chapter is entitled 'Of the condition of men in mere nature'.[1] It opens with the statement that, having previously described the whole of man's natural powers of body and mind, he will now 'consider in what estate of security this our nature hath placed us', and he proceeds to describe the 'natural' condition of men in all circumstances, i.e. their natural equality, vanity, and appetites, without using any particular phrase for this condition. He then shows that this would necessarily lead to the brutish condition if a common power were absent, and uses 'estate of war' to describe that condition. Similarly, in *Leviathan* he uses 'the natural condition of mankind' for his chapter title; opens with a discussion of the natural condition of men in all circumstances (their natural equality, competition, diffidence, and vanity), by which he finds 'in the nature of man' the three causes of quarrel, without using any particular phrase for this condition; then shows that if men have no common power over them they must be in the brutish condition, which he calls the 'time or condition of war'.

[1] *Elements*, part i, ch. 14; title on p. xv.

In both these treatments, where he avoids 'state of nature', and especially in *Leviathan*, it is possible to distinguish between the natural condition of man (i.e. the condition in which men are or tend to be in all circumstances, in or out of civil society, because of their natures), and the state of war (i.e. the condition that would follow if there were no common power, or which does follow if the common power is removed by hypothesis). In the *Rudiments*, however, where he does use 'state of nature',[1] he uses it indifferently to describe both conditions, and the distinction between them is lost. And because this distinction is lost, the hypothetical character of the state of war (which is maintained, though precariously, in the *Elements* and *Leviathan*) is lost in the *Rudiments*, where the state of nature, identified with the state of war, is said to have been 'the natural state of men, before they entered into society'.[2]

Yet there can be little doubt that in the *Rudiments*, as in the other two works, the state of nature is a logical abstraction drawn from the behaviour of men in civilized society. Indeed it is even clearer in the *Rudiments* than in the other two treatments that Hobbes has got at the 'natural' proclivities of men by looking just below the surface of contemporary society, and that the state of nature is a two-stage logical abstraction in which man's natural proclivities are first disengaged from their civil setting and then carried to their logical conclusion in the state of war. For the *Rudiments*, omitting the whole physio-psychological analysis of man as a system of matter in motion, opens with a brilliant dissection of men's behaviour in contemporary society, which reveals their 'natural' proclivities, and moves directly to the deduction of the necessary outcome in a state of war if there were no sovereign.

How, by what advice, men do meet, will be best known by observing those things which they do when they are met. For if they meet for traffic, it is plain every man regards not his fellow, but his business; if

---

[1] *Rudiments*, Preface, p. 13, ch. 1, sects. 4, 10, 15; cf. ch. 8, sect. 1.
[2] Ibid., sect. 12; cf. sect. 13.

to discharge some office, a certain market-friendship is begotten, which hath more of jealousy in it than true love, and whence factions sometimes may arise, but good will[1] never; if for pleasure, and recreation of mind, every man is wont to please himself most with those things which stir up laughter, whence he may (according to the nature of that which is ridiculous) by comparison of another man's defects and infirmities, pass the more current in his own opinion; and although this be sometimes innocent and without offence, yet it is manifest they are not so much delighted with the society, as their own vain glory. But for the most part, in these kinds of meetings, we wound the absent; their whole life, sayings, actions are examined, judged, condemned; nay, it is very rare, but some present receive a fling before they part, so as his reason was not ill, who was wont always at parting to go out last. And these are indeed the true delights of society, unto which we are carried by nature, that is, by those passions which are incident to all creatures. . . . So clear is it by experience to all men who a little more narrowly consider human affairs, that all free congress ariseth either from mutual poverty, or from vain glory, whence the parties met, endeavour to carry with them either some benefit, or to leave behind them that same εὐδοκιμεῖν some esteem and honour with those, with whom they have been conversant. The same is also collected by reason out of the definitions themselves, of will, good, honour, profitable.[2]

The nature of man is thus got primarily from observation of contemporary society, and incidentally confirmed by examining definitions.

It is from this analysis of the nature of man in society that Hobbes deduces the necessary tendency towards a state of war. He deduces it by temporarily setting aside fear, i.e. fear both of a sovereign and of other individuals. Take men as they now are, remove the fear of unpleasant or fatal consequences of their actions to themselves, and their present natural proclivities would lead directly to the state of war. The dissection of men's behaviour in present society shows that all society 'is either for gain, or for glory; that is, not so much for love of our fellows, as for the love of ourselves'. Since gain and glory 'may be better attained to by dominion,

---

[1] i.e. goodwill: 'benevolentia' in Latin version.
[2] Ibid., sect. 2, pp. 22–24.

than by the society of others: I hope no body will doubt but
that men would much more greedily be carried by nature,
if all fear were removed, to obtain dominion, than to gain
society'.[1]

Thus, if by hypothesis one removes all fear (fear both of a
sovereign and of other individuals), the full state of nature
(the state of war) follows. But the full state of nature is a
condition in which fear of other individuals must be omnipresent. Bring back into consideration, therefore, the fear of
other individuals (which is in fact never absent) and this
fear is shown to be heightened by the absence of a sovereign.
It follows that the full state of nature, or state of war, contradicts man's (desirous and fearful) nature. 'And so it happens,
that through fear of each other we think it fit to rid ourselves
of this condition, and to get some fellows', by setting up or
acknowledging a sovereign able to protect us.[2]

Thus in the *Rudiments* the state of war is a hypothetical
condition, got by a purely logical abstraction. Yet in calling
this hypothetical condition 'the state of nature' Hobbes
makes it easy to misread it either as a condition historically
prior to civil society or as a hypothetical condition deduced
from men's 'natural' characteristics considered entirely apart
from their socially acquired characteristics.

The trouble with Hobbes's concept of a state of nature is
that it tends to telescope two different conditions: the condition of antipathy and competition in which men are said to
find themselves all the time because of their natures, and the
brutish condition of war. The likelihood of this telescoping
appears to be greater when the term 'state of nature' is used
(as in the *Rudiments*) than when it is avoided, but the telescoping is never entirely absent. However, by holding steadily
to the fact that the men who would fall into the state of war
if there were no common power are civilized men, with civilized desires for convenient living and civilized tastes for
feeling superior, we can avoid the error of treating Hobbes's
state of nature as an analysis either of primitive man or of

---

[1] *Rudiments*, ch. 1, sect. 2, p. 24.   [2] Ibid., sects. 13–14, pp. 29–30.

man considered apart from all his socially acquired characteristics.

A third demonstration that Hobbes's state of nature does not set aside contemporary man's socially acquired characteristics but simply law- and contract-enforcement, or fear of a sovereign (and, temporarily, as we have just seen in the *Rudiments*, fear of other individuals), is provided by noticing what it is that Hobbes's man would lack, and would compellingly feel the lack of, in the full brutish state of nature. What he would lack is precisely all the goods of civilized living: property, industry, commerce, the sciences, arts, and letters, as well as security for his life. To be without these goods is contrary to man's nature. It is because of the lack of these goods that Hobbes's natural man is driven to seek a way out of the state of nature. 'The Passions that encline [natural] men to Peace, are Feare of Death; Desire of such things as are necessary to commodious living; and a Hope by their Industry to obtain them'.[1] The passion for commodious living is a passion of Hobbes's natural man. Natural man is civilized man with only the restraint of law removed.

iii. *From physiological to social motion*

We have seen that Hobbes's state of nature is a description neither of the necessary behaviour of primitive men (though primitive men approximate to it more nearly than do men under established civil governments) nor of the necessary behaviour of the human animal stripped of all his socially acquired appetites. The state of nature is a deduction from the appetites and other faculties not of man as such but of civilized men.

We now turn to examine Hobbes's chain of deduction from the beginning. The physiological and psychological analysis of the nature of man with which Hobbes opens the whole deductive argument in the *Elements* and in *Leviathan* begins as an analysis of the nature or motion of man con-

---

[1] *Leviathan*, ch. 13, p. 98.

sidered apart from established social relationships. It is, or appears to be, about man as such, not about civilized man. Yet since by the time the argument reaches the hypothetical state of nature it is about civilized man, the question is, where did civilization get into the argument?

The question might be thought to be unnecessary, since in a sense civilization was always there. Hobbes tells us himself that the psychological analysis is of contemporary man: 'whosoever looketh into himself, and considereth what he doth, when he does *think, opine, reason, hope, feare,* &c, and upon what grounds; he shall thereby read and know, what are the thoughts, and Passions of all other men, upon the like occasions', and the reader of *Leviathan* is invited to confirm Hobbes's reading of man with no more pains than 'onely to consider, if he also find not the same in himself. For this kind of Doctrine, admitteth no other Demonstration'.[1] And indeed the presumption is that it was the nature of civilized man that Hobbes was analysing from the beginning. For the resolutive-compositive method which he so admired in Galileo and which he took over,[2] was to resolve existing society into its simplest elements and then recompose those elements into a logical whole. The resolving, therefore, was of existing society into existing individuals, and of them in turn into the primary elements of their motion. Hobbes does not take us through the resolutive part of his thought, but starts us with the result of that and takes us through only the compositive part. The order of his thought was from man in society back to man as a mechanical system of matter in motion, and only then forward again to man's necessary social behaviour. But it is only the second half of this that he presents to his readers. And because he begins his presentation (in *Leviathan* and in the *Elements*) with the physiological and psychological analysis of man as a system of matter in motion, the reader is apt to forget that

[1] *Leviathan,* Intro., pp. 9, 10.
[2] On his use of this method see J. W. N. Watkins, 'Philosophy and Politics in Hobbes', *Philosophical Quarterly,* vol. v, no. 19 (1955), 125-46.

the whole construction had its source in Hobbes's thinking about civilized men.

In spite of this, it is still necessary to inquire where civilization got into Hobbes's construction. For in the resolutive-compositive method the resolutive stage proceeds not merely by breaking the phenomenon down into its simplest elements, but doing this with a considerable amount of abstraction. In that abstraction, something of the complex whole (in this case society and the nature of civilized man) may be set aside. And Hobbes has, or at least appears to have, set aside the specifically civilized characteristics of man in his opening presentation of the nature of man. So we must inquire how and where these got into his compositive stage. The inquiry is less needed in the *Rudiments*, for there Hobbes moves straight from his glimpse into contemporary society to the construction of the state of nature, without going at all into that higher degree of abstraction which comprises the initial psychological analysis in the *Elements* and *Leviathan*.

The man whom Hobbes presents in the opening chapters of *Leviathan* should be more readily intelligible to us than to Hobbes's contemporaries, for that man is very like an automated machine. It is not only self-moving but self-directing. It has, built into it, equipment by which it alters its motion in response to differences in the material it uses, and to the impact and even the expected impact of other matter on it. The first five chapters of *Leviathan* describe the items of this equipment: the senses, which receive the pressure of outside bodies, transmit them through the nerves to the brain and heart, which then deliver a counter-pressure; the imagination, or memory, which can recall past sense impressions and store up experience of them; the mechanism of 'Trayne of Thoughts' or 'Trayne of Imaginations', which hunts 'the causes, of some effect, present or past; or . . . the effects, of some present or past cause',[1] and which thus enables the mechanism to forecast the probable result of various possible

---

[1] *Leviathan*, ch. 3, p. 20.

actions it might take; language, which enables the machine to communicate and receive communications and to order its own reckonings; and reason, which by adding and subtracting names and the consequences of names can reach general propositions or rules for its own guidance.

Chapter 6 of *Leviathan* introduces the general direction or goal that is built in to the machine. The machine seeks to continue its own motion. It does this by moving towards things which it calculates are conducive to its continued motion and away from things not conducive. Motion towards is called appetite or desire, motion away from is called aversion. A few of the appetites and aversions, as for food, are built in to the machine, but most are acquired by 'Experience, and triall of their effects upon themselves, or other men'.[1] The acquired appetites and aversions are not always for the same things: they differ as between different machines (because they have different experiences), and within one machine at different times (because each one 'is in continuall mutation').[2] Whatever is the object of any machine's appetite it registers as good, and the objects of its aversion, evil. Each therefore seeks its own good and shuns its own evil.

All the states of mind and general dispositions of men, such as hope, despair, fear, courage, anger, confidence, diffidence, covetousness of riches, ambition for office or precedence, pusillanimity, magnanimity, love, jealousy, revengefulness, grief, pity, emulation, and envy, can be reduced to the action of the appetite for one's own good in various different circumstances.

Every man's actions are determined by his appetites and aversions, or rather by his calculation of the probable effects on the satisfaction of his appetites, of any action he might take.

When in the mind of man, Appetites, and Aversions, Hopes, and Feares, concerning one and the same thing, arise alternately; and

---

[1] *Leviathan*, ch. 6, p. 40.
[2] Ibid.

divers good and evill consequences of the doing, or omitting the thing propounded, come successively into our thoughts; so that sometimes we have an Appetite to it; sometimes an Aversion from it; sometimes Hope to be able to do it; sometimes Despaire, or Feare to attempt it; the whole summe of Desires, Aversions, Hopes and Fears, continued till the thing be either done, or thought impossible, is that we call DELIBERATION.[1]

All voluntary actions are determined by this process of deliberation. 'For a *Voluntary Act* is that, which proceedeth from the *Will*, and no other.' And *Will* '*is the last Appetite in Deliberating*'.[2] Finally, 'because Life it selfe is but Motion, and can never be without Desire, nor without Feare, no more than without Sense', each man must seek continual success in obtaining those things which he from time to time desires and will desire.[3]

Now in the whole of Hobbes's analysis so far, the only mention of the relation of one of these self-moving machines to others of them has been in the analysis of states of mind or general dispositions of men. Some of these (e.g. indignation, charity, covetousness, ambition, fortitude, liberality, jealousy, revengefulness, pity, cruelty, emulation, envy) Hobbes does explain as relations between men or as effects of relations between them. But the analysis of these states of mind is incidental to the main line of his deduction. It shows how a wide range of observable characteristics of men can be explained in terms of Hobbes's postulate that men are self-moving and self-directing appetitive machines, but this is rather an incidental confirmation of the original postulate than a stage in the main deduction from the nature of the mechanism to the necessary tendency of struggle of every man with every man.

The next propositions that are significant in the main deduction are in chapter 8, where in discussing intellectual virtues Hobbes makes two general statements from observation, one concerning the relations between men, and one

---

[1] *Leviathan*, ch. 6, p. 46.   [2] Ibid., p. 47.
[3] Ibid., p. 48.

concerning the differences between the passions of different men. The first is that men value everything by comparison with what others have: 'Vertue generally, in all sorts of subjects, is somewhat that is valued for eminence; and consisteth in comparison. For if all things were equally in all men, nothing would be prized.'[1] The second is that the difference between different men's wit (i.e. their ability to deal intelligently with the problems that confront them) is due chiefly to the different degree of their 'Desire of Power, of Riches, of Knowledge, and of Honour'. Some men have 'no great Passion for any of these things', some men have, and the difference of passions proceeds 'not onely from the difference of mens complexions; but also from their difference of customes, and education'.[2]

It is not until chapter 10, however, that Hobbes begins his serious analysis of the relations between these self-moving machines, and chapters 10 and 11 say almost all that Hobbes has to say about those relations. We have to notice that chapters 10 and 11 are about the relations between civilized men living in established societies, and that these two chapters contain all, or all but one, of the essential propositions from which Hobbes deduces in chapter 13 the necessity of war of every man against every man if a common power were removed. The only relevant necessary proposition not stated until chapter 13 is the natural equality of men, which is needed to show that the state of war could never end by any one man's victory over the rest.

In short, it is in chapters 10 and 11 that we find the main transition from man the machine by itself, to man the machine as a unit in a series of social relationships. And it is in these chapters that we shall expect to find such new postulates, stated or implied, as are needed for the deduction of the state of nature, and that we can see to what extent those postulates are drawn from the observed relations of men in a specific kind of society.

---

[1] *Leviathan*, ch. 8, p. 52.
[2] Ibid., p. 56.

The ground traversed in chapters 10 and 11 is substantially that between the neutral definition of power with which chapter 10 opens ('THE POWER *of a Man*, (to take it Universally,) is his present means, to obtain some future apparent Good'), and the conclusion early in chapter 11: 'So that in the first place, I put for a generall inclination of all mankind, a perpetuall and restlesse desire of Power after power, that ceaseth onely in Death',[1] power now being power over other men. It is this conclusion which leads directly to the state of war of chapter 13, when all political authority and law-enforcement are removed by hypothesis. The question is how Hobbes moves from the neutral definition of power to the desire of every man for ever more power over other men.

In *Leviathan*, immediately after the neutral definition of power, he classifies power as either original (or natural) or else instrumental, and asserts:

Naturall Power, is the eminence of the Faculties of Body, or Mind: as extraordinary Strength, Forme, Prudence, Arts, Eloquence, Liberality, Nobility. *Instrumentall* are those Powers, which acquired by these, or by fortune, are means and Instruments to acquire more: as Riches, Reputation, Friends, and the secret working of God, which men call Good Luck. For the nature of Power, is in this point, like to Fame, increasing as it proceeds; or like the motion of heavy bodies, which the further they go, make still the more hast.[2]

We notice that a man's natural power is defined not as his natural ability (strength, prudence, &c.) but as the *eminence* of his ability. It is the eminence of his ability over that of others that enables him to acquire instrumental powers (riches, reputation, friends, &c.). A man's power is not an absolute but a comparative quantity. It does not, as might be thought to have been implied in the first or neutral definition of power, consist of a man's personal capacities plus any further command over things that he can acquire by exercising those capacities; it consists of the excess of his personal capacities over those of other men, plus what he can

[1] Ibid., ch. 11, para. 2, p. 75.   [2] Ibid., ch. 10, p. 66.

acquire by that excess. A new postulate is implied in this redefinition of power, namely, that the capacity of every man to get what he wants is opposed by the capacity of every other man. This postulate is made explicitly in the parallel passage in the *Elements*. There, the power of a man to get something he wants is first defined as

the faculties of body and mind [and] such farther powers, as by them are acquired (viz.) riches, place of authority, friendship or favour, and good fortune. [This is followed by the statement:] And because the power of one man resisteth and hindereth the effects of the power of another: power simply is no more, but the excess of the power of one above that of another. For equal powers opposed, destroy one another; and such their opposition is called contention.[1]

Every man's power is opposed by the power of others, so universally that 'power simply' can be redefined as a comparative not an absolute quantity. This postulate of the opposition of individuals' powers is new: it is not contained in the previous propositions about man as a self-moving mechanism seeking to maintain or enhance his motion.[2]

If there were any doubt about the universality of the opposition of powers which Hobbes is stating in that postulate, it would be removed by his discussion of various specific kinds of power in society, and his analysis of valuing and honouring, which follow these definitions of power both in *Leviathan* and in the *Elements*. In *Leviathan*, the reason why such things as wealth and reputation are power is that they give defensive and offensive strength against others. Thus

. . . Riches joyned with liberality, is Power; because it procureth friends, and servants: Without liberality, not so; because in this case they defend not; but expose men to Envy, as a Prey. Reputation of power, is Power; because it draweth with it the adhaerence of those that need protection. . . . Also, what quality soever maketh a man beloved, or feared of many; or the reputation of such quality, is Power; because it is a means to have the assistance, and service of many.[3]

---

[1] *Elements*, part i, ch. 8, sect. 4, p. 26.
[2] It might be said to be implied in the earlier statement, already noted from ch. 8 of *Leviathan*, that the virtue of anything consists in its eminence, i.e. in comparison; but that statement also is not deducible from the physiological postulates.
[3] *Leviathan*, ch. 10, p. 66.

All the kinds of acquired power that Hobbes describes consist in defensive and offensive strength against others. And all of them consist in command over some of the powers of other men; they are all the product of the transfer of some men's powers to other men. Hobbes has in effect defined acquired power as ability to command the services of other men. A man's power over nature, his ability to transform nature by his own strength, intelligence, and knowledge is apparently put under the head of his original, not his acquired, power. The power of men associated to transform nature is neglected.

Hobbes's analysis of valuing and honouring, which follows the description of the kinds of power, fills out his picture of the relations of men in society. Transfers of power are assumed to be so usual that there is a market in power. A man's power is treated as a commodity, regular dealings in which establish market prices.

The *Value*, or WORTH of a man, is as of all other things, his Price; that is to say, so much as would be given for the use of his Power: and therefore is not absolute; but a thing dependant on the need and judgement of another. . . . And as in other things, so in men, not the seller, but the buyer determines the Price. For let a man (as most men do,) rate themselves at the highest Value they can; yet their true Value is no more than it is esteemed by others.[1]

The value men set on one another, in comparison with the value each sets on himself, is measured by the degree to which each is honoured or dishonoured by others, as shown by the positive or negative amount of deference accorded to him in various ways:

The manifestation of the Value we set on one another, is that which is commonly called Honouring, and Dishonouring. To Value a man at a high rate, is to *Honour* him; at a low rate, is to *Dishonour* him. But high, and low, in this case, is to be understood by comparison to the rate that each man setteth on himselfe.[2]

The degree of honour accorded to a man thus measures his actual value in comparison with the value he sets on himself. But the actual value is determined by what others would give for the use of his power. Honour, regarded subjectively by the recipient, is the difference between his own estimate and the market estimate of his value. But honour, regarded objectively, corresponds to the market estimate that both establishes his actual power and is established by his actual or apparent power. His actual or apparent power is made up chiefly of his power to command the services of others, and his power to command the services of others is based on the others' estimate of his present power:

> *Honourable* is whatsoever possession, action, or quality, is an argument and signe of Power. [So] Dominion, and Victory is Honourable; because acquired by Power. . . . Riches, are Honourable; for they are Power. . . . Timely Resolution, or determination of what a man is to do, is Honourable; as being the contempt of small difficulties, and dangers. . . . To be Conspicuous, that is to say, to be known, for Wealth, Office, great Actions, or any eminent Good, is Honourable; as a signe of the power for which he is conspicuous. . . . Covetousnesse of great Riches, and ambition of great Honours, are Honourable; as signes of power to obtain them. . . . Nor does it alter the case of Honour, whether an action (so it be great and difficult, and consequently a signe of much power,) be just or unjust: for Honour consisteth onely in the opinion of Power.[1]

We have here the essential characteristics of the competitive market. Every man's value, manifested by the honour given him by others, is both determined by and determines the others' opinion of his power, manifested by what they would give for the use of his power. Valuing, or honouring, is not simply a relation between one man who receives and one man who gives honour or dishonour; it is a relation between one man who receives it and all the others who give to him, i.e. all other men who have any interest, however contingent or remote, in the way he uses his power. All these other men make their estimates of his power independently. And they make their estimates of his power comparatively to the power of others, for his usefulness to them is not

[1] *Leviathan*, ch. 10, pp. 70–71.

an absolute quantity but a quantity depending on the availability of others. And everyone not only *is estimated by* all the others who have any interest in the way he uses his power, but also *estimates* all these others. Yet out of this immensely large number of independent value judgements, an objective value of each man is established. It can only be so established because every man's power is regarded as a commodity, i.e. a thing normally offered for exchange, and offered competitively. Every man is in the market for power, either as supplier or demander, for everyone either has some power to offer to others or wants to acquire the power of some others.

The same assumptions are implied in the treatment of honouring and valuing in the *Elements*. To honour a man 'is to conceive or acknowledge, that that man hath the odds or excess of power above him that contendeth or compareth himself. And HONOURABLE are those signs for which one man acknowledgeth power or excess above his concurrent in another'. So strength, victory, adventure, nobility, and the rest, are honourable; 'riches are honourable; as signs of the power that acquired them.' '... and according to the signs of honour and dishonour, so we estimate and make the value or WORTH of a man. For so much worth is every thing, as a man will give for the use of all it can do.'[1] Here, as in *Leviathan*, the objective value is established by the estimates of others, which estimates are based on the usefulness of his apparent power to them. Every man's value is established as prices are established in the market. A market determines the price only of things which are normally offered for sale and wanted by purchasers. To speak of the value or price of every man, therefore, is to assume that every man is either a seller of his power or a buyer of others' power (or both).

Hobbes's analysis of valuing and honouring, enlarging as it does on the definitions of power and descriptions of kinds of power, substantially completes his argument that the necessary behaviour of all men in society is an endless

[1] *Elements*, part i, ch. 8, sect. 5, pp. 26–27.

struggle for power over others. He has moved from the definition of power as present means to obtain future good, through a redefinition of power as the excess or eminence of one man's means in comparison with another's. The second definition is established by the postulate that the means of every man to obtain his future good is opposed to the means of every other man. Hobbes has described, and in effect defined, acquired power as power to command the services of other men. He has assumed that acquired power is so generally wanted, and that power is so generally transferable, that there is a pervasive market in power, which establishes the value of every man. In the course of his argument he has made several assumptions not contained in the original psychological analysis. The most important is the assumption that the power of every man is opposed to the power of every other man, which appears to be a social, not a physiological, postulate.

From this account of Hobbes's argument, the point at which he has added a social assumption to his physiological postulates is immediately after the neutral definition of power; the rest of his discussion of power, valuing, and honouring simply makes more explicit the theory of the motions of men in society which is already implied in the postulate that the power of every man opposes the power of every other man. That postulate, along with the physiological postulate that every man seeks to continue his own motion, is enough to produce the search of every man for power over others.

However, the postulate that the power of every man opposes the power of every other man is not offered by Hobbes as self-evident but is supported by other postulates which are logically prior. As to what the prior postulates were, two views are possible, depending on the interpretation of some of Hobbes's statements. In the view which seems to me more solidly based, Hobbes was consistent in deriving this opposition of powers from (a) the physiological postulate that some, not all, men innately desire ever more power and delight, while the rest desire only to continue at their present level, and (b) the implied postulate that society is so fluid or fragmented that the behaviour of the immoderately desirous men compels all the others to enter the contest for power over others. In the other view, Hobbes was inconsistent. While he sometimes derived the opposition of powers from the postulate that some but not all men innately desire ever more, he also sometimes derived it from the single physiological postulate that all men innately desire ever more power over others. It is not disputed, in the second view, that Hobbes did state that only some men are innately immoderate; it is only asserted that he was inconsistent in so doing.

The evidence for Hobbes's position that only some men innately desire ever more power is clear. It will be remembered that Hobbes had stated earlier[1] that not every man wants more power, riches, knowledge, or honour than he has already, either for their own sake or for the pleasure they give him, and this assertion is repeated in chapter 11 of *Leviathan*, in the immediate context of the struggle for power in society: it 'is not alwayes that a man hopes for a more intensive delight, than he has already attained to; or that he cannot be content with a moderate power: but because he cannot assure the power and means to live well, which he hath present, without the acquisition of more'.[2] Every man's innate desires are indeed incessant, but not every man's are for an increased level of satisfactions or power. All men in society (and in the hypothetical state of nature as well) do seek ever more power, but not because they all have an innate desire for it. The innately moderate man in society must seek more power simply to protect his present level. And Hobbes's conclusion that all of them must

---

[1] *Leviathan*, ch. 8, p. 56.

[2] Ibid., ch. 11, p. 75. The same distinction is made again in ch. 13, in the context of the state of nature: 'there be some, that taking pleasure in contemplating their own power in the acts of conquest, which they pursue farther than their security requires; . . . others, that otherwise would be glad to be at ease within modest bounds . . . ' (p. 95).

so act implies that the social arrangements are such as to permit every man's natural powers to be invaded by others: if there were any customary protection of individuals' livings, or customary limitation of their competitive activities, in any ranks, not all of them would have to, or not all of them would be able to, enter the contest for more power.

Thus if we take it to be Hobbes's considered position that not all men innately desire ever more power or delight, his postulate that the power of every man in society is opposed to the power of every other man requires the assumption of a model of society which permits and requires the continual invasion of every man by every other. And hence his conclusion that all men in society do strive for ever more power over others depends on the same assumption about society.[1]

The other view of Hobbes's position, which has been persuasively put forward by Strauss,[2] is that Hobbes (inconsistently) conceived the striving for limitless power to be a natural, innate appetite of man as man, that 'man desires power and ever greater power, spontaneously and continuously, in one jet of appetite . . .'.[3] Of the passages cited by Strauss in support of this contention, only one seems to me clearly to support it. This is Hobbes's statement that 'men from their very birth, and naturally, scramble for every thing they covet, and would have all the world, if they could, to fear and obey them'.[4] This, however, was a passing remark, made in a very late work, the *Decameron Physiologicum* of 1677, and made rather lightly, by way of explaining why Hobbes's old enemies, the natural philosophers, had gone in for so much charlatanry and cozening. Hobbes did not follow it up in any way; not much can be built on it.

[1] His conclusion that all men in the hypothetical state of nature would necessarily strive for ever more power over others requires, of course, only the postulate that there is no law: given that there is no law, everyone is open to invasion by anyone, and the moderate men will be invaded by those who innately seek more.

[2] Leo Strauss, *Political Philosophy of Hobbes*, pp. 8–12.

[3] Op. cit., p. 10. Richard Peters, *Hobbes* (1956), unfortunately quotes this (p. 153) as if it were a statement by Hobbes.

[4] Hobbes, *English Works*, vii. 73.

The other passages cited by Strauss seem to me not to imply necessarily any more than an innate hunger for limitless power or delight in some men and a socially acquired desire in the rest. One of the strongest passages is that in which Hobbes notices that 'as men attain to more riches, honours, or other power; so their appetite continually groweth more and more', and concludes that felicity consists 'not in having prospered, but in prospering'.[1] This passage is certainly consonant with Strauss's interpretation, but in view of Hobbes's explicit statements that not all men naturally desire more delights or power, it may as well or better be read as a statement about those who attain more because they started with the innate desire.

Strauss recognizes that Hobbes stated that not all men naturally desire more delights or power, and reconciles this with the opposite position he attributes to Hobbes by saying that there are in Hobbes two kinds of striving after power: an irrational striving, which is a natural appetite of man as such, and the rational striving of those who would be content with a moderate power but find they must strive for more power to protect what delight they have. Hobbes does indeed say that some men strive for ever more power naturally (which may well be called an irrational striving), and that some men seek more power only to protect the moderate delights and power that would satisfy them (which may well be called a rational striving); but it cannot be inferred from this that Hobbes was attributing the innate or irrational striving to all men.

Strauss points also[2] to the fact that Hobbes found the striving for honour, or precedence over others and recognition of this precedence, to be a universal characteristic of man. So he did, but he did not say this was innate in all men. Like the striving for power, the striving for honour may be fully explained as innate in some men and (therefore) copied by others. Much of Hobbes's language about

---

[1] *Elements*, part i, ch. 7, sect. 7, p. 23.
[2] Strauss, op. cit., pp. 11–12.

precedence is consonant with Strauss's interpretation. But Hobbes's most explicit statements are to the contrary.

. . . considering the great difference there is in men, from the diversity of their passions, how *some* are vainly glorious, and hope for precedency and superiority above their fellows, not only when they are equal in power, but also when they are inferior; we must needs acknowledge that it must necessarily follow, that *those men who are moderate*, and look for no more but equality of nature, shall be obnoxious to the force of others, that will attempt to subdue them. And from hence shall proceed a general diffidence in mankind, and mutual fear one of another.[1]

All men in the state of nature have a desire and will to hurt, but not proceeding from the same cause. . . . For *one man*, according to that natural equality which is among us, permits as much to others, as he assumes to himself (which is an argument of a temperate man, and one that rightly values his power). *Another*, supposing himself above others, will have a license to do what he lists, and challenges respect and honour, as due to him before others, (which is an argument of a fiery spirit). This man's will to hurt ariseth from vain glory, and the false esteem he hath of his own strength; the other's, from the necessity of defending himself, his liberty, and his goods, against this man's violence.[2]

All men desire precedence, honour, and glory, just as all men desire more power. But in both cases, some are born with the desire, some have it thrust upon them.

Indeed, the desire for honour can be reduced to the desire for power: 'Desire of Power, of Riches, of Knowledge, and of Honour [may all] be reduced to the first, that is Desire of Power. For Riches, Knowledge and Honour are but severall sorts of Power.'[3] The desire for glory is not a passion independent of the desire for power; it is a result of the desire for power, and is defined in terms of the desire for power: 'Glory, or internal gloriation or triumph of the mind, is that passion which proceedeth from the imagination or conception of our own power, above the power of him that

---

[1] *Elements*, part i, ch. 14, sect. 3, p. 54 (my italics).
[2] *Rudiments*, ch. 1, sect. 4, pp. 25–26 (my italics).
[3] *Leviathan*, ch. 8, p. 56.

contendeth with us.'[1] The universality of the desire for glory is not independent; it is a consequence of the same factors which produce the universal contention for power over others. Glory is comparative and contentious for the same reason that power is comparative and contentious: because 'the power of one man resisteth and hindereth the effects of the power of another'.[2] In view of the evidence it seems to me closer to Hobbes's intention to treat the striving for power and precedence which he finds to be characteristic of all men in society (and in the state of nature) as an innate striving in some men and an acquired behaviour in others.

However, we must notice what follows if Hobbes be taken to have meant, sometimes, that all men innately seek precedence and power over others without limit. If this is postulated of all men, then no further assumption is needed to demonstrate that all men *in the state of nature* must be in continual opposition to each other. This would follow from the physiological postulate alone. In that case, however, we should be entitled to say that what Hobbes had done was to introduce an essentially social assumption into his physiological postulates. For the innate striving of all men for unlimited power over others is not a self-evident physiological postulate in the way that the desire for continued motion is. The postulate of innate desire of all men for more power without limit is only apparently tenable about men who are already in a universally competitive society.

But we need not pursue this point. It is more important to notice that even if this is allowed as a physiological postulate, all that follows from it without a further social assumption is that all men *in the state of nature* must be in continual opposition to each other. A further assumption, however, is needed to demonstrate that all men *in society* must be in continual opposition to each other and so must strive for more power over others, which is what Hobbes does try to demonstrate in his analysis of power, valuing and honouring.

[1] *Elements*, part i, ch. 9, sect. 1, p. 28.
[2] Ibid., ch. 8, sect. 4, p. 26.

The further assumption needed is at least a model of society which permits every man's natural powers to be continually invaded by others, a society in which each can continually seek to transfer to himself some of the powers of others.

No society could permit this to be done by individual violence. If there were such continual conflict between all individuals there would be no society, certainly no civilized society. But Hobbes finds this constant striving of every man for power over others to be the actual behaviour of men in civilized society. His whole description of the market in power, and of honouring and valuing as concomitants of power, is asserted of established societies. All the many ways of honouring and dishonouring, by which a man's value and power are manifested, confirmed, or acquired, are asserted of civil societies, though some are read into a state of nature as well: some are 'naturall . . . as well within, as without Common-wealths', others are only found (and are only conceivable) in commonwealths.[1] Since Hobbes is attributing this necessary behaviour to men in society, he must be assuming some kind of society which provides peaceful, non-violent ways by which every man can constantly seek power over others without destroying the society.

Thus on either reading of Hobbes's argument from the physiological to the social motion of man, a social assumption is needed besides the physiological postulates. We have to inquire, then, what kind of society is consistent with this assumption. In Section 3 I show that only one kind of society, which I call possessive market society, does meet the requirement of Hobbes's argument, and I argue that Hobbes was more or less consciously taking that society as his model of society as such.

3. Models of Society

i. The use of models

The construction of models of society is an unusual, and may be thought an unnecessary, procedure in an analysis of

[1] *Leviathan*, ch. 10, p. 69.

political theory. What value it has must be left to the reader's judgement of its results, but its probable usefulness in analysing Hobbes's theory is suggested by Hobbes's own method. He constructed a model of man, which he built up carefully by logical connexion of postulated elements of human nature. He constructed also a notable model of relations between men, the state of nature, which he deliberately set up as a limiting case. It might be called a model of non-society, and it is so impressive as to overshadow the model of society contained in his discussion of power, honour, and value. The fact that Hobbes had, in effect, a model of society other than the state of nature is often quite overlooked. His model of society is not as explicitly constructed as his other models, but it is fully as important in his argument. We may therefore hope to make a more precise analysis of his argument than would otherwise be possible, by comparing his model with models of society more explicitly constructed. By so doing we should also be able to test the consistency of his model, and its degree of approximation to actual societies.

These purposes have determined the nature and the number of models here constructed. The problem was to construct the fewest possible models to which all known kinds of society could be assimilated and which would isolate their features in such a way as to permit comparisons with Hobbes's model. Three models appear to be sufficient. It need scarcely be said that the models used here would not be sufficient or appropriate for general sociological or historical analysis. The first model, for instance, which I call customary or status society, is drawn broadly enough to include societies as widely different as the ancient empires, feudal societies, and tribal societies. The second model, the simple market society, is drawn very narrowly; it is less a model of any historical society than an analytical convenience for isolating certain features of the more fully developed market societies of modern times. The third model, which is intended to correspond to modern market societies, I have called the possessive market society. Its essential difference from the other two models may be indicated here, before it is more fully examined, partly in order to explain why that name has been chosen.

By possessive market society I mean one in which, in contrast to a society based on custom and status, there is no authoritative allocation of work or rewards, and in which, in contrast to a society of independent producers who exchange only their products in the market, there is a market in labour as well as in products. If a single criterion of the possessive market society is wanted it is that man's labour is a commodity, i.e. that a man's energy and skill are his own, yet are regarded not as integral parts of his personality, but as possessions, the use and disposal of which he is free to hand over to others for a price. It is to emphasize this characteristic of the fully market society that I have called it the *possessive* market society. Possessive market *society* also implies that where labour has become a market commodity, market relations so shape or permeate all social relations that it may properly be called a market society, not merely a market economy.

The concept of possessive market society is neither a novel nor an arbitrary construction. It is clearly similar to the concepts of bourgeois or capitalist society used by Marx, Weber, Sombart, and others, who have made the existence of a market in labour a criterion of capitalism, and like their concepts it is intended to be a model or ideal type to which modern (i.e. post-feudal) European societies have approximated. It differs from theirs chiefly in that it does not require any particular theory of the origin or development of such society. It is not concerned about the primacy or relative importance of various factors such as Marx's primary accumulation, Weber's rational capital accounting, or Sombart's spirit of enterprise. Its use does not require acceptance of the whole of any of these contentious theories. And it may claim the positive merit of drawing attention directly to two essential features of such society, the pre-eminence of market

relations and the treatment of labour as an alienable possession.

ii. *Customary or status society*

The essential properties of a customary or status society
may be defined as follows:

(*a*) The productive and regulative work of the society is
authoritatively allocated to groups, ranks, classes, or persons.
The allocation and performance are enforced by law or
custom.

(*b*) Each group, rank, class, or person is confined to a way
of working, and is given and permitted only to have a scale
of reward, appropriate to the performance of its or his function, the appropriateness being determined by the consensus
of the community or by the ruling class.

(*c*) There is no unconditional individual property in land.
Individual use of land, if any, is conditional on performance
of functions allotted by the community or by the state, or on
the provision of services to a superior. There is hence no
market in land.

(*d*) The whole labour force is tied to the land, or to the
performance of allotted functions, or (in the case of slaves)
to masters. The members of the labour force are thus not
free to offer their labour in the market: there is no market in
labour. (There may be a market in slaves, but a market in
slaves comprises only an exchange relation between masters,
not between slave and master, and is therefore not a market
relation between all the persons concerned.)

From these properties of a status society certain characteristics follow. In the absence of markets in land and labour,
individuals (except in the upper ranks) have no means of
continually seeking to alter their place in the scale of power,
that is, of changing the amount of their natural power that is
being extracted from them or the amount that they are extracting from others. There is room in this model for men
at the upper levels of power, who want more delights, to
invade others at those levels forcibly, and so to compel

others at those levels (including any who would otherwise be content) to enter the competition for power. There is room, that is, for dynastic struggles, palace revolutions, and baronial conflicts. But this is competition between rivals for the benefits already being extracted from the subordinate population. It cannot be general throughout the society, because the existence of the society, and the continued extraction of the benefits being fought for by the rivals, require that the customary allocation and enforcement of the productive and directive work of the society be maintained. The bulk of the society must be confined to ways of working and living which are set by the contribution they are required to make to the society, and these allow them no general opportunity of invading or subduing their fellows. Since there is no free market in individuals' labour, i.e. in their natural powers, competition between individuals for acquiring some of the natural powers of others cannot permeate the whole society. There is room in the model too for those at the bottom to resist, by force, increases in the exactions demanded of them by their superiors. Such resistance will be infrequent if it is assumed that the level of exactions embodied in custom is normally as high as is safe and profitable for the ruling class. In any case, combined resistance by members of a lower class is not in itself, and does not produce, a general pattern of invasion of each individual by his fellows.

In short, the model of a customary status society, while it permits perennial forcible invasion between rivals at the top, and occasional forcible invasion between classes or sections of classes, does not permit perennial invasion, either forcible or otherwise, of individuals by individuals throughout the society. The model neither permits nor requires the constant search for power by individuals over individuals, of such extent that all individuals must seek more power in order to protect what delights they have. It is apparent that the model of a status society does not meet Hobbes's requirements. The essential shortcoming is that in the status model the natural powers, i.e. the labour, of individuals are not freely transferable. Only in a society in which every man's labour is an exchangeable commodity can the transfer of control of individuals' powers be as ubiquitous as is required by Hobbes's assumptions.

iii. *Simple market society*

The simple market society also falls short of the requirement, for we define it as a society in which the production and distribution of goods and services is regulated by the market but in which labour itself is not a market commodity. It is doubtful if a society closely approximating to this model has ever existed for very long. But the model is introduced in order to separate the features common to all market societies from those which are found only in full market societies. The separation is useful in drawing attention to features of the full market society which are not emphasized in the familiar economists' models. For purposes of economic analysis the most essential features may be those common to all market societies; for purposes of political analysis the most essential features are those peculiar to the full market society.

The simple market society has the following properties:

(*a*) There is no authoritative allocation of work: individuals are free to expend their energies, skills, and goods as they will.

(*b*) There is no authoritative provision of rewards for work: individuals are not given or guaranteed, by the state or the community, rewards appropriate to their social functions.

(*c*) There is authoritative definition and enforcement of contracts.

(*d*) All individuals seek rationally to maximize their utilities, that is, to get the most satisfaction they can for a given expenditure of energy or goods, or to get a given satisfaction for the least possible expenditure of energy or goods.

(*e*) All individuals have land or other resources on which they may get a living by their labour.

From these properties of the model certain consequences follow. In search of the means to live, individuals will deploy their energies, skills, and material resources in ways which the society (i.e. the same individuals as consumers) is willing to pay for. The productive and other functions of society will thus be performed by individuals in search of rewards that can only be had by using their energies and resources. Since individuals seek the maximum return for their work, and since division of labour is more efficient than is each doing everything for himself, individuals will exchange products of their labour and resources for goods produced by others. There will thus be a market in products. Prices will be determined by competition between sellers and between buyers, and will determine how individuals allocate their labour and resources between different kinds of production. The market is self-regulating in that prices will move so that what is offered for sale will be bought and what is wanted will be produced and offered for sale.

There is no reason in this model for the market in products to be extended to a market in labour. To rule out a market in labour absolutely a further postulate would be necessary:

(f) That the satisfaction of retaining control of one's own labour is greater than the difference between expected wages and expected returns as an independent producer.

Since in the simple market society individuals retain the control of their own energies and skills, and exchange is only between products, market exchange cannot be a means by which individuals gain by converting some of the powers of others to their use in such a way as to require the others to change their ways. It is true that everyone in this model exchanges products in the market, and may be said thus to convert indirectly some of the powers or labour of others to his use. And everyone enters the market for gain, and does gain by entering the market. But the gain each gets in this market is the greater utility he gets by producing one thing for exchange rather than everything for himself. No one's gain is at the expense of others; no one converts more of the powers of others to his use than they convert of his. If there are some men who want more than they have, who want to increase the amount of satisfactions they enjoy, they can do so by exerting more energy or skill and so producing more and getting more in exchange. But in doing so they are still not converting more of the powers of others to their use than others are converting of theirs. And their action does not require any counteraction by the others who are content with the level they have. The simple market society therefore does not meet the requirements of Hobbes's society. Individuals who are content with their existing level of satisfactions are not pulled into competition for more power in order to protect the level they have.

The model of the simple market society obviously falls far short of correspondence with modern market societies. If we dropped postulates (e) and (f) and simply added the stipulation that there is a competitive market in labour, we would have a sufficient model of a fully competitive market society. But rather than simply stipulating that there is a market in labour, it will be more useful to see what further postulates are required to bring about a market in labour. We shall therefore construct the model of a full market society by adding the postulates which are necessary and sufficient to bring about a transformation of the simple to the full market society.

iv. *Possessive market society*

The model of the simple market society is transformed into the possessive market model by retaining the first four postulates of the simple model and adding four more. We thus have the following postulates:

(a) There is no authoritative allocation of work.

(b) There is no authoritative provision of rewards for work.

(c) There is authoritative definition and enforcement of contracts.

(d) All individuals seek rationally to maximize their utilities.

(e) Each individual's capacity to labour is his own property and is alienable.

(f) Land and resources are owned by individuals and are alienable.

(g) Some individuals want a higher level of utilities or power than they have.[1]

(h) Some individuals have more energy, skill, or possessions, than others.

When the four new postulates are added to the first four postulates of the simple market society, a full market society follows. Those who want to increase their level of utilities or power, and who have either greater possessions which they can use as capital (and the skill to use them profitably), or superior energy and skill by which they can accumulate capital, will seek to employ the labour of others for a price, in the expectation of getting from the labour they employ a value greater than its cost. Individuals who have less land or resources, or less skill, than can regularly give them a subsistence by their independent production, will accept wages that will give them a subsistence.

The greater efficiency of combined labour organized by men of superior skill, energy, or resources will, in the competitive market, drive down the prices of the products, so that increasing numbers of solitary producers find it impossible, or less profitable, to continue independently, and therefore offer their labour in the market. Thus, in a society where labour is alienable, and where there are different levels of desire and of ability or possessions, a competitive market in products brings about a general competitive market. Labour, land, and capital, as well as products, become subject to the determination of the market: prices for all of them are set by competition between sellers and between buyers so that

---

[1] Since postulates (d) and (g) are superficially similar it is perhaps worth emphasizing their difference. Postulate (d) stipulates that everyone wants to get as much as possible for as little as possible, but not that anyone wants to get more than he has.

what is offered will be bought and what is wanted will be offered.

We thus have the essential features of a modern competitive market society. Without any authoritative allocation of work or rewards, the market, responding to countless individual decisions, puts a price on everything, and it is with reference to prices that the individual decisions are made. The market is the mechanism through which prices are made by, and are a determining factor in making, individual decisions about the disposal of energies and the choice of utilities.

Exchange of commodities through the price-making mechanism of the market permeates the relations between individuals, for in this market all possessions, including men's energies, are commodities. In the fundamental matter of getting a living, all individuals are essentially related to each other as possessors of marketable commodities, including their own powers. All must continually offer commodities (in the broadest sense) in the market, in competition with others.

Competition in this market, unlike that in the simple market in products, is a means by which men who want more may convert more of the powers of others to their use than others convert of theirs. For the effect of competition in this market is to compel entrepreneurs (who must have had some capital initially, with which to hire labour) to use increasing amounts of capital as a means to more efficient production. The greater the capital required in order to stay in the market, the less possible is it for men of little property to enter into, or stay in, independent production. As the greater efficiency of more highly capitalized production permits the population to increase, such production becomes indispensable for the larger society. And as the land runs out (which it does the more quickly because land has become a kind of capital), an increasing proportion of the population becomes dependent on selling its labour. Thus a class division between those with land and capital, and those without, sets in (if it was not in existence already). When land and capital are all owned by one set of people, there is a permanent change in the distribution of the whole product between persons, to the disadvantage of the persons without land and capital. Since the latter cannot resort to independent production, they cannot demand in wages an amount equal to what would be the product of their labour on land or capital of their own. Those who have the capital and land can therefore, by employing the labour of others, get a net transfer of some of the powers of others (or some of the product of those powers) to themselves.

In speaking of this process as a net transfer of some of the powers of one man to another, we are taking the powers of a man to be (following Hobbes's definition) the whole of a man's present means to obtain future apparent goods. The powers of a man therefore include not only his energy and skill, or capacity to labour, but also his access to the means (land, materials, or other capital) without which his capacity to labour cannot become active labour and so cannot produce any goods. No narrower definition of man's powers is consistent with a model of a society of *men*, at least with any society in which men must produce in order to eat. For if a man, to remain a man (i.e. to continue to exist), must produce, then he must, to remain a man, have both the capacity to labour and access to the means of labour. The powers of a *man* must therefore by definition include access to the means of labour.[1] A man's powers are therefore reduced when he has less than free access to the means of labour. If he can get no access, his powers are reduced to zero, and in a competitive society he ceases to exist. If he can get access, but not freely, his powers are reduced by the price he has to pay for access, and that price measures the amount of his power that is transferred to another.

[1] A narrower definition of a man's powers is possible only in a model of an *economy* which abstracts so far from man's human quality as to consider him not even as a system of matter in motion which must be in continual motion, but merely as the owner of a factor of production called labour.

As between the simple market model (where everyone has land or materials to work on) and the possessive market model (where some men have no land or capital of their own), what some men have lost is free access to the means of turning their capacity to labour into productive labour. Having lost this part of their powers they must continually sell the remainder of their powers to those who have the land and capital, and must accept a wage which allows part of the product to go to the owners of land and capital. This constitutes the net transfer of part of their powers to others. It is a continual transfer, since it proceeds as production takes place. Its amount is not fixed, but fluctuates in the competitive market with changes in the supply of labour and of capital.[1]

A net transfer is, of course, not unique to the full market society. For while it cannot exist in the simple market society, it does exist in all those customary and status societies where a ruling class maintains itself by tributes, rents, or slavery. What is unique about the transfer in the market society is that there it is maintained by continual competition between individuals at all levels. Everyone is a possessor of something, if only of his capacity to labour; all are drawn into the market; competition determines what they will get for what they have to offer. Their net return registers the net amount of their own powers that has been transferred to others (or whose benefit or product has been transferred to others), or the net amount of others' that they have transferred to themselves. Since this is determined by the impersonal operation of the market, in which relative prices change in response to changes in wants, changes in energy and skill expended, innovations in production, changes in the ratio of labour to capital, and other factors, everyone is potentially in movement up or down the scale of power and satisfactions.

The possessive market model requires a compulsive framework of law. At the very least, life and property must be

[1] See Note B, p. 293.

secured, contracts must be defined and enforced. The model also permits state action much beyond this minimum. The state may control land use and labour use, may interfere with the free flow of trade by embargoes and customs duties, may assist one kind of industry and discourage another, may provide free or subsidized services, may relieve the destitute, may require minimum standards of quality or of training, and may by these and other kinds of interference prevent prices (including wages) reaching the levels which an un-regulated or less regulated market would produce. What the state does thereby is to alter some of the terms of the equations each man makes when he is calculating his most profitable course of action. But this need not affect the main-spring of the system, which is that men do calculate their most profitable courses and do employ their labour, skill, and resources as that calculation dictates. Some of the data for their calculations is changed, but prices are still set by competition between the calculators. The prices are different from what they would be in a less controlled system, but as long as prices still move in response to the decisions of the individual competitors and the prices still elicit the produc-tion of goods and determine their allocation, it remains a market system. The state may, so to speak, move the hurdles to the advantage of some kinds of competitors, or may change the handicaps, without discouraging racing. The state may, of course, deliberately or otherwise, by the same sort of intervention put racing out of business. But it need not do so. One cannot infer from the fact of intervention that the intention is, or that the effect will be, to weaken the system. The possessive market model thus does not require a state policy of *laissez-faire*; a mercantilist policy is perfectly consistent with the model and may indeed be required at some stages in the development of a possessive market society.[1]

Whatever the degree of state action, the possessive market model permits individuals who want more delights than

[1] Cf. below, p. 62 and p. 96.

they have, to seek to convert the natural powers of other men to their use. They do so through the market, in which everyone is necessarily involved. Since the market is continually competitive, those who would be content with the level of satisfactions they have are compelled to fresh exertions by every attempt of the others to increase theirs. Those who would be content with the level they have cannot keep it without seeking more power, that is, without seeking to transfer more powers of others to themselves, to compensate for the increasing amount that the competitive efforts of others are transferring from them.

The possessive market society, then, does meet Hobbes's requirements. It is a society in which men who want more may, and do, continually seek to transfer to themselves some of the powers of others, in such a way as to compel everyone to compete for more power, and all this by peaceable and legal methods which do not destroy the society by open force. The possessive market society is the only one of our three models which does meet Hobbes's requirements. And it is difficult to conceive of any other model which would do so. Only in a society in which each man's capacity to labour is his own property, is alienable, and is a market commodity, could all individuals be in this continual competitive power relationship.

The fact that the possessive market model meets (and is the only model that does meet) Hobbes's requirements may of course be attributed to the fact that we put in that model (and excluded from the other models) certain postulates which Hobbes explicitly makes about his society. Certainly, postulates (g) and (h)—that some individuals want more delights than they have, and that some have more abilities than others—are explicit in Hobbes, and it might be thought that they were not really needed to produce our model. It is important to notice, therefore, that both these postulates, and indeed all the four postulates stipulated for converting the simple market model to the full market model, are needed to produce a model that corresponds in essentials with actual competitive market societies.

Postulate (e), that each individual's capacity to labour is his own property and is alienable, is self-evidently required: without it, one of the essential features of modern competitive market societies would be impossible. The same may be said of postulate (f), that land and resources are owned by individuals and are alienable. This postulate is not required for, although it is consistent with, the simple market society: the simple market in products could operate even with fixed and inalienable rights in land. But it is required for a full market society. For unless land and resources can be transferred through a market, and so be combined with labour in the most profitable way, full advantage cannot be taken of the availability of labour. Postulate (g), that some individuals want a higher level of utilities or power than they have, is equally required for a modern competitive market society. For without this postulate there would be no incentive to accumulate capital and use it to employ labour, and hence no general market in labour. This postulate, like (f), is not required for, although it is consistent with, a simple market society; but it is required for a full market society. Finally, postulate (h), that some individuals have more energy, skill, or possessions than others, is required for a modern competitive market society. For unless some individuals have more possessions than others to begin with, or have abilities to acquire more than others, there could be no accumulations of capital, without which there could be no general employment of labour.

All four of the postulates that distinguish our full market model from the simple market model are needed to produce a model that corresponds in essentials with actual competitive market societies. And it is these postulates which, by producing a market relationship in labour as a commodity, produce the essential requirement of Hobbes's society, namely, the mechanism by which those who want more power or delight than they have can engage in continual, non-violent competition for the power of others, which compels the others to enter the competition.

v. *Hobbes and the possessive model*

I have shown so far that the model of a possessive market society, and no other, does correspond in essentials to modern competitive market societies, that each of its postulates is required to produce that correspondence, and that that model and no other does meet the essential requirements of Hobbes's society. It cannot, of course, be inferred from this that Hobbes had some such market model clearly in mind. He worked with models, indeed, a mechanical model of man, a model of social relations where there was no law-enforcement, and a model of civilized society in between. But the models we have just examined are post-Hobbesian constructions, and as such are not self-evidently attributable to Hobbes. Nor can it be argued that Hobbes must have been using some such market model on the ground that the market nature of English society was too plain for so keen an observer to have missed.

There is plenty of evidence that England approximated closely to a possessive market society in the seventeenth century. Very nearly half the men were full-time wage-earners; if the cottagers are counted as part-time wage-earners, the proportion is over two-thirds.[1] And while the wage relationship was not as completely impersonal as it was to become in the following century, it was already, as Hobbes knew,[2] essentially a market relationship. The tendency for land to be exploited as capital was already well advanced, to the detriment of such paternal relations between landlord and tenant as had survived the changes of the sixteenth century.[3]

[1] See Note T, p. 301. Cf. Clapham, *Concise Economic History of Britain* (Cambridge, 1949), who finds (pp. 212–13) that life-long wage-earners were a majority well before the end of the seventeenth century.

[2] *Behemoth*, ed. Tönnies, p. 126, as quoted below, p. 66.

[3] Cf. G. Davies, *The Early Stuarts* (Oxford, 1945), who says (p. 271) of the new landlords that came into being as a result of the civil wars, that 'between them and their tenants there was no personal tie—nothing except a cash nexus'.

State policy towards the operation of the market economy was, of course, very far from *laissez-faire*. Government regulation, control, and interference with the free play of market forces, by statute and administrative decree, was omnipresent. Neither the markets in capital nor land, produce nor labour, were permitted to be entirely self-regulating. Even when allowance is made for the fact that much of the legislation and administrative action was ineffective, judging by the frequency with which it was repeated, the extent of state control and interference is impressive. But it was because possessive market relations were penetrating society so decisively that such extensive state regulation was required. Some of the regulation was designed, whether well- or ill-advisedly, to promote industry and trade; the greater part of it was designed to prevent or reduce market fluctuations, or to protect social order against the effects of fluctuations. It was largely because so many men were now dependent on employment, and their employment was dependent on the vagaries of commodity markets which produced recurrent unemployment on a scale endangering public order, that governments were compelled to interfere so strenuously and in so many ways.[1] Government regulation in the seventeenth century presupposed a possessive market society.

All the evidence, then, points to seventeenth-century English society having become essentially a possessive market society. The question remains, how far was Hobbes aware of this? There is, fortunately, some evidence bearing on this question. In the first place, Hobbes's statement that 'a mans Labour also, is a commodity exchangeable for benefit, as well as any other thing',[2] although made only

---

[1] B. E. Supple, *Commercial Crisis and Change in England 1600–1642* (Cambridge, 1959), in a masterly analysis of the instability of the market economy of that time, has shown that the incessant state interference with wages, prices, investment, and trade was a protracted attempt 'to protect England against the harsher repercussions of economic fluctuation without regressing in terms of the industrial and commercial structure', and that the main mover was 'a valid fear of unemployment and economic instability' (p. 251; and cf. ch. 10 generally).

[2] *Leviathan*, ch. 24, p. 189.

incidentally to a discussion of foreign trade, is presumptive evidence that he was taking for granted the normality of the wage relationship. More important is his treatment of commutative and distributive justice, which suggests that he was deliberately rejecting the model of a customary status society in the knowledge that it was an alternative model to his own, and that it was still generally accepted.

The received concepts of commutative and distributive justice, as Hobbes describes them, are concomitants of the model of a customary society. They suppose the validity and the enforcement of standards of reward other than those determined by the market. Commutative justice is placed 'by Writers', says Hobbes, 'in the equality of value of the things contracted for; And Distributive, in the distribution of equall benefit, to men of equall merit'.[1] Hobbes's scorn for these concepts is unconcealed. Both are dismissed in a sentence: 'As if it were Injustice to sell dearer than we buy; or to give more to a man than he merits.'[2] And what has made the old concepts an object of scorn is one of the attributes of the market model, namely, that the value of anything is simply its price as established by supply and demand. 'The value of all things contracted for, is measured by the Appetite of the Contractors: and therefore the just value, is that which they be contented to give.'[3] Since there is no measure of value except market price, every exchange of values between freely contracting persons is by definition an exchange of equal values. The old concept of commutative justice thus becomes meaningless. 'To speak properly, Commutative Justice, is the Justice of a Contractor; that is, a Performance of Covenant, in Buying, and Selling; Hiring, and Letting to Hire; Lending, and Borrowing; Exchanging, Bartering, and other acts of Contract.'[4]

Similarly with distributive justice: the distribution of equal benefit to men of equal merit becomes meaningless as an overriding principle by which to decide the justice of any actual distribution of rewards, for there is in Hobbes's

[1] Ibid., ch. 15, p. 115.   [2] Ibid.   [3] Ibid.   [4] Ibid.

model no measure of merit other than the actual market
assessment of a man's merit. There is no room in Hobbes's
model, as there is in the status model, for an assessment of
the merit of different men in terms of the contribution they
make to the purposes of the whole society or in terms of
their needs as functioning parts of a social organism. Distributive justice, therefore, becomes nothing more than 'the
Justice of an Arbitrator; that is to say, the act of defining
what is Just. Wherein . . . [the Arbitrator] is said to distri-
bute to every man his own . . .'.[1] And what is properly a
man's own is to be determined initially not by any concept
of the purposes of society, but by a standard as far removed
from that as Hobbes can conceive, a standard deliberately
emptied of all social valuation: it is to be *determined by Lot.
For . . . other means of equall distribution cannot be imagined*.[2] In treating commutative and distributive justice in
this way, Hobbes is drawing the logical conclusions from his
model of society: where all values are reduced to market
values, justice itself is reduced to a market concept. And in
demanding that a market concept of justice should replace
the customary concept, he seems both to be claiming that a
fully market society is here to stay, and to be acknowledging
that it has only recently come.

There are further indications, in the book Hobbes devoted to analysing the Long Parliament and the Civil War,
that he saw competitive market relations as an encroachment
on an earlier model of English society. One of the reasons
he found for the defection of so many from the king, and
hence for the Civil War, was that 'the people in general'
(i.e. the men of some property, for 'there were very few of
the common people that cared much for either of the causes,
but would have taken any side for pay or plunder'[3]) believed that each man was 'so much master of whatsoever he
possessed, that it could not be taken from him upon any
pretence of common safety without his own consent'.[4]

---

[1] *Leviathan*, ch. 15, p. 115.
[3] *Behemoth*, ed. Tönnies, p. 2.
[2] Ibid., p. 119.
[4] Ibid., p. 4.

Hobbes saw, accurately, that this belief was no part of the formerly prevailing feudal concept of property, and that the belief had now grown to the point where it could be held responsible for the Civil War. He observed that the same men who held this new concept of unconditional individual right to property used the old order of ranks merely to subserve their new purposes: 'King, they thought, was but a title of the highest honour, which gentleman, knight, baron, earl, duke, were but steps to ascend to, with the help of riches.'[1]

It was to the new strength of market morality and of market-made wealth that Hobbes attributed the Civil War. He treated the war as an attempt to destroy the old constitution and replace it with one more favourable to the new market interests. The king's enemies, 'that pretended the people's ease from taxes, and other specious things, had the command of the purses of the city of London, and of most cities and corporate towns in England, and of many particular persons besides'.[2] The people were seduced partly by the new religious doctrines (one of the most important of which, the Presbyterian, was well received because, among other reasons, it did not 'inveigh against the lucrative vices of men of trade or handicraft . . . which was a great ease to the generality of citizens and the inhabitants of market-towns'[3]), and partly by their new belief in unconditional property right.[4] That the people were so seduced, and that the merchants had the money to support an army, was a sufficient explanation of the war. There is a Harringtonian touch in the comment offered at this point by the interlocutor in Hobbes's dialogue: 'In such a constitution of people, methinks, the King is already ousted of his government, so as they needed not have taken arms for it. For I cannot imagine how the King should come by any means to resist them.'[5]

---

[1] Ibid.   [2] Ibid., p. 2.   [3] Ibid., p. 25.
[4] Ibid., p. 4.
[5] Ibid. Cf. Harrington, *Oceana*: 'Wherfore the dissolution of this government caus'd the war, not the war the dissolution of this government' (*Works*, 1771, p. 65).

Later in his analysis, Hobbes returns to the crucial part played by the new market wealth. The parliamentary forces were supplied by 'the city of London and other corporation towns',[1] their grievances being taxes, 'to which citizens, that is, merchants, whose profession is their private gain, are naturally mortal enemies; their only glory being to grow excessively rich by the wisdom of buying and selling'.[2] Hobbes was aware, too, that their wealth was made by buying the labour of others. He dismisses the commonplace justification of their activities, that 'they are said to be of all callings the most beneficial to the commonwealth, by setting the poorer sort of people on work', with the curt remark 'that is to say, by making poor people sell their labour to them at their own prices; so that poor people, for the most part, might get a better living by working in Bridewell, than by spinning, weaving, and other such labour as they can do; saving that by working slightly they may help themselves a little, to the disgrace of our manufacture'.[3] Hobbes has seen through the paternalistic justification of the wage relationship. He has seen that it is anachronistic to justify wage labour in terms of a paternalistic model of society which is fundamentally inconsistent with a market relationship.

The England that Hobbes describes in *Behemoth* is a fairly complete market society. Labour is a commodity, and there is such a large supply of it that its price is driven down, by the buyers, to a level of bare subsistence.[4] Wealth derived from market operations has accumulated to the point where its holders are able to challenge a state whose taxing power they regard as an encroachment on their rights. The challenge is successful because they have the money to supply an army; the challenge is possible at all only because the people have come to place a higher value on the acquisition of wealth through the market than on

---

[1] *Behemoth*, p. 110.   [2] Ibid., p. 126.   [3] Ibid.

[4] One wonders if it was from this observation that Hobbes derived the view that the value or price of a man is determined by the buyer, not the seller (*Leviathan*, ch. 10, p. 67).

traditional obligations or established ranks. It is because English society has changed in those ways that the Civil War has come about.

Hobbes's explanation of the causes of the Civil War thus implies some recognition on his part that the market society was an encroachment on an earlier society. His recognition of this was not full or clear. Had it been so, he could scarcely have treated society as such as essentially a series of market relations, as he did in *Leviathan* and the other theoretical treatises. Yet even in them there is some recognition, as in his treatment of commutative and distributive justice, that market morality was different from the traditional morality. We may conjecture that the ease with which Hobbes attributed essentially market relations to all societies was due to his having shared the view, common to men of the Renaissance, that civilized society was limited to classical Greece and Rome and post-medieval western Europe. Since the classical societies were to some extent market societies they could easily be taken to fit a model drawn primarily from the more completely market society of his own time. And once the model was established it was not difficult to apply it to the most nearly civilized section of all other societies, that is, to the active upper classes of other societies, for the relations between the men at the top in non-market societies tended to consist in a competitive struggle for power that approximated the market relation. Whether or not this was the order of Hobbes's thought, and however consciously he drew his model of society from his appreciation of the market attributes of seventeenth-century society, it is clear that his model approximates most nearly to the model of the possessive market society.

I have shown that Hobbes's argument from the physiological nature of man to the necessary attempt of all men in society to seek ever more power over others requires the proposition that every man's power resists and hinders the powers of others; that this proposition, even if supposedly deduced from a physiological postulate that all men innately desire limitless power over others, requires at least the further assumption of a model of society which permits continual peaceful invasion of each by each; and that if the proposition is taken to be deduced from the physiological postulate that only some men innately want ever more, it requires a model of society which not only permits continued invasion of each by each but also compels the moderate men to invade; that the only model which satisfies these requirements is the possessive market society, which corresponds in essentials to modern competitive market societies; that Hobbes's explicit postulates (notably, that labour is a commodity, that some men want to increase their level of delight, and that some have more natural power than others) are essentially those of a possessive market society; that the model of society which Hobbes constructed in his analysis of power, valuing, and honouring, and confirmed in his analysis of commutative and distributive justice, corresponds essentially to the possessive market model; and that although Hobbes was not fully conscious of such correspondence, there is some evidence to suggest that he was aware of the peculiar suitability of his analysis to seventeenth-century society.

vi. *The inadequacy of the state of nature*

We have reached the position, then, that Hobbes moved from his original physiological postulates to the conclusion that all men necessarily seek ever more power over others, by introducing assumptions which are valid only for possessive market societies. And it was only after he had established his conclusion that all men in society necessarily seek ever more power over others that he introduced his hypothetical state of nature, from which in turn he deduced the necessity of the sovereign state. I proposed earlier[1] that Hobbes's social assumptions were required not only for his deduction that all men in society necessarily seek more power over others, but also for his deduction of the behaviour of man in

[1] Above, pp. 19, 34.

the state of nature. It may be thought that this has not yet been established. For it has not been specifically shown that his conclusion that all men seek more power over others, or his social analysis that led to that conclusion, was required for his deduction of the behaviour in the state of nature. Could he not have deduced the behaviour of men in the state of nature directly from the physiological postulates without having shown that all men in society seek more power over others? The question is perhaps not very important, since in fact he did go to great pains to show that all men in society must seek ever more power, before he put these men in the hypothetical state of nature. However, we can easily see that he could not have deduced the behaviour of the state of nature from the physiological postulates alone.

It is true that he could have deduced the behaviour of the state of nature merely from the physiological postulate that all men seek to continue their own motion, plus the postulate that *some* men seek ever more power over others:[1] these two would, when all law is removed by hypothesis, produce the necessity of *all* men seeking more power over others, i.e. the behaviour of the state of nature. But this second postulate is got not from physical observation or analysis, but from observation and analysis of social relations. If we call it a physiological postulate, we must say that even Hobbes's physiological postulates are about the physiology of socialized men. But, not to stand on definitions, there is another reason why Hobbes could not have deduced the behaviour of the state of nature from the physiological postulates alone, even if the postulate that some men seek more power over others is taken to be a physiological one. It would not have been consonant with his method or his purpose.

For his purpose was to persuade men that they needed to acknowledge a sovereign, and his method of doing so was 'only to put men in mind of what they know already, or may

---

[1] Or, of course from the single postulate that all men innately seek limitless power over others, which as I have already argued (p. 45, above) is not strictly a physiological postulate.

know by their own experience'.[1] The whole success of his
endeavour necessarily depended on this. And to do this, he
had to show them to themselves as they were, in society.
He might, perhaps, have shown the necessity of a sovereign
without using the artificial hypothesis of the state of nature
at all, simply by deduction from the conclusion that all men
in society necessarily seek more power over others. But he
could not have hoped to show his readers the necessity of a
sovereign from a hypothetical state of nature alone, without
having shown the necessary behaviour of men in society.
It was only in so far as the behaviour of men in the hypothetical state of nature corresponded to their necessary behaviour in society that deductions made from the state of
nature could have any validity for men already in (an admittedly imperfect) society.

I conclude that Hobbes did need the social postulates in
order to move from his physiological postulates to a statement of the necessary behaviour of men in a state of nature
from which the necessity of a sovereign could validly be
deduced.

4. *Political Obligation*

i. *From motivation to obligation*

Once Hobbes has established that the general inclination
of all men is the search for ever more power over others, he
is easily able to show that if there were no power able to
overawe them all, their lives would necessarily be miserable
and insecure in the utmost degree. He has already postulated that men necessarily seek to live, and to live commodiously. It follows that rational men who fully calculate the
consequences must shun such a condition by acknowledging
a power able to overawe them all. To do so they must make,
or act as if they had made, a covenant with each other by
which they all simultaneously transfer to some man or body
of men the rights they would have to protect themselves if

[1] *Elements*, part i, ch. 1, sect. 2, p. 1.

there were no common power to protect them. It is this transfer of rights which creates their obligation to the sovereign. And since this covenant is a restraint on the appetites, it cannot be binding without a power to enforce it; hence men must transfer their natural powers at the same time as their natural rights. This gives the sovereign absolute authority, and sufficient power to wield that authority effectively. Only by acknowledging such authority can men (a) hope to avoid the constant danger of violent death and all the other evils which they would otherwise necessarily bring upon themselves because of their otherwise necessarily destructive search for power over each other; and (b) hope to ensure the conditions for the commodious living which they necessarily desire. Hence every man who understands the requirements of men's nature, and the necessary consequences of those requirements, must acknowledge obligation to a sovereign.

In this way Hobbes believes he has deduced the necessity of every man's acknowledging obligation to a sovereign, and deduced it from the facts of man's nature and the necessary consequences of those facts. He believes that the obligation thus deduced is a moral obligation; once a man has transferred rights to another 'then is he said to be OBLIGED, or BOUND, not to hinder those, to whom such Right is granted . . . from the benefit of it: and that he *Ought*, and it is his DUTY, not to make voyd that voluntary act of his own . . .'.[1] In short, Hobbes believes that he has deduced moral obligation from fact, ought from is.

Our analysis in Sections 2 and 3 has not touched on this claim. We have shown only that the facts from which Hobbes deduced political obligation included certain facts about the historically or socially acquired character of men, facts some of which could properly be postulated only of man in a possessive market society. The questions, whether Hobbes's political obligation is properly moral rather than merely prudential obligation, and whether his implied claim to have

[1] *Leviathan*, ch. 14, p. 101.

deduced moral obligation from fact can be accepted as in any sense valid, are still open and have now to be considered.

ii. *Moral or prudential obligation?*

From the very summary account just given of Hobbes's deduction from motivation to obligation, it might seem that his political obligation is prudential only. He has, it appears, demonstrated only that in a long view of their own interest men should acknowledge obligation to a sovereign. Obligation which is based entirely upon self-interest cannot, it is said, properly be called moral obligation.[1] If one finds that Hobbes did deduce his political obligation solely from self-interest, and if one accepts the definition of moral obligation as an obligation based on something other than self-interest, then of course the question is settled: Hobbes's obligation is not moral obligation. But this is too easy an answer. It simply raises a further question: is there any more reason to accept than to reject that definition, and with it the sharp distinction between prudential and moral, and the implied superiority of the moral obligation? Hobbes rejected it. Some of his critics treat it as self-evident. Is there any way of deciding between them?

The moralists' case for the distinction seems to rest on a supposedly serious difference in the probable effectiveness of the two kinds of obligations. It is said that an obligation which is based only on enlightened self-interest cannot be counted on to bind when it conflicts with short-run self-interest, whereas a properly moral obligation is not subject to this weakness because it is based on some principle beyond self-interest. But this distinction, and the superiority of moral obligation, are simply created by definition. For the distinction to be of serious practical importance it would have to be shown that a 'moral' principle of obligation was more likely to hold more firmly than a prudential principle. The weakness of prudential obligation is evident. But unless it can be shown that 'moral' obligation does not contain equal or greater weakness, the distinction is not a significant one. The ability of either kind of obligation to oblige can only be tested in practice; it rests on the ability of either kind to get itself accepted.

Hobbes saw no evidence that any principle of obligation based on something beyond self-interest was likely to be more widely and firmly accepted than one based on self-interest: more widely accepted, that is to say, on its rational merits, apart from having 'spirits invisible' enlisted on its side. A principle of obligation said to be ordained by God may hold more firmly than a principle that has to compete on its merits. But if you reject, as Hobbes rejected, such imposed principles,[1] you are left with no clear difference between a prudential obligation and any other kind of rational obligation. The effectiveness of moral philosophies in the past did not impress Hobbes: he thought the new kind of obligation he proposed was more likely to be effective, as being more strictly related to man's capacities and needs.

If the obligation he proposed was based on man's self-interest and, even less nobly, on fear, it was also based on man's reason. He thought it the best that men were capable of without fraudulently bringing in religious sanctions, and he thought it more moral that men should stand on their own reason than that they should invoke imagined and unknowable deities or essences. He thought that his rational, albeit self-interested, obligation was as moral an obligation as could be found. To say that Hobbes had as good reason to call his kind of obligation moral as other philosophers had, or have, to deny it that title, is not to claim that Hobbes's obligation is more effective than, or even as effective as, some other. It is simply to say that the burden of proof must be put as much on the others as on Hobbes. What Hobbes did, in effect, was to shift the burden of proof to the moralists, knowing that the burden was an impossible one for them to sustain. In the absence of such proof, Hobbes's obligation can still be called moral.

[1] See Note D, p. 294.

But Hobbes did not claim a victory merely by default. His confidence in his own position rested partly on a postulate which we have so far noticed only incidentally and must now examine more closely. This is the postulate of the equality of man. We have noticed it so far only as a postulate needed to show why the struggle for power in a state of nature could never end. But it is a far more important postulate than that. It is by means of this postulate that Hobbes deduces right and obligation from fact.

iii. *The postulate of equality*

Hobbes postulates two kinds of equality between men: equality of ability and equality of expectation of satisfying their wants. Each kind entails, in Hobbes's view, an equality of right. The equality of ability is stated as evident from experience and observation. Men are not absolutely equal in ability, but are so equal that the weakest can easily kill the strongest, and this implies a moral equality. The point is put in all three versions of Hobbes's theory.

And first, if we consider how little odds there is of strength or knowledge between men of mature age, and with how great facility he that is the weaker in strength or in wit, or in both, may utterly destroy the power of the stronger, since there needeth but little force to the taking away of a man's life; we may conclude that men considered in mere nature, ought to admit amongst themselves equality. . . .[1]

For if we look on men full-grown, and consider how brittle the frame of our human body is, . . . and how easy a matter it is, even for the weakest man to kill the strongest, there is no reason why any man trusting to his own strength should conceive himself made by nature above others: they are equals who can do equal things one against the other; but they who can do the greatest things, (namely, kill) can do equal things. All men therefore among themselves are by nature equal. . . .[2]

Nature hath made men so equall, in the faculties of body, and mind; as that though there bee found one man sometimes manifestly stronger in body, or of quicker mind then another; yet when all is reckoned together, the difference between man, and man, is not so considerable,

[1] *Elements*, part i, ch. 14, sect. 2, p. 54.   [2] *Rudiments*, ch. 1, sect. 3, p. 25.

as that one man can thereupon claim to himselfe any benefit, to which another may not pretend, as well as he. For . . . the weakest has strength enough to kill the strongest. . . .[1]

In each of these versions we find a principle of right or obligation derived from a statement of observed fact. From the stated equality it is held to follow that men *ought* to admit amongst themselves equality (*Elements*); that *there is no reason why any man should* conceive himself above others (*Rudiments*); that one man cannot (rightfully) *claim* any benefit above another (*Leviathan*). Hobbes takes it that an equality of fact sets up an equality of right, without bringing in any outside value judgement or moral premisses. He does not prove that fact entails right, he simply assumes that it does because there is no reason why it should not. There is no reason why any man *should* conceive himself above others; hence it is self-evident that he should not.

The second kind of equality Hobbes postulates is equality of expectation of want satisfaction. In *Leviathan* he presents this as a consequence of the first kind of equality: 'From this equality of ability, ariseth equality of hope in the attaining of our Ends.'[2] In the *Elements* and *Rudiments* the emphasis is rather on the fact that all men equally desire to preserve their lives, and in both these statements an equality of right is taken to be implied in the equality of fact.

And forasmuch as necessity of nature maketh men to will and desire *bonum sibi*, that which is good for themselves, and to avoid that which is hurtful; but most of all that terrible enemy of nature, death, from whom we expect both the loss of all power, and also the greatest of bodily pains in the losing; it is not against reason that a man doth all he can to preserve his own body and limbs, both from death and pain. And that which is not against reason, men call RIGHT, or *jus*. . . .[3]

For every man is desirous of what is good for him, and shuns what is evil, but chiefly the chiefest of natural evils, which is death; and this he doth, by a certain impulsion of nature, no less than that whereby a stone moves downward. It is therefore neither absurd, nor reprehensible, neither against the dictates of true reason, for a man to use all

[1] *Leviathan*, ch. 13, p. 94.   [2] Ibid., p. 95.
[3] *Elements*, part i, ch. 14, sect. 6, pp. 54–55.

his endeavours to preserve and defend his body and the members there-of from death and sorrows. But that which is not contrary to right reason, that all men account to be done justly, and with right. . . .[1]

It may be objected that in these passages Hobbes is smuggling a moral connotation into his 'reason' or 'right reason'. But it may equally well be said that he is simply doing here what he did in his argument from the equality of ability to equality of right, namely, taking it that those consequences of man's natural needs which are not evidently absurd or reprehensible are to be assumed to be right. The burden of proof is, so to speak, again shifted to the moralists. Hobbes has deduced rights from the fact that every man has wants which he does and must seek to satisfy.

It may still be objected that Hobbes has not deduced right from fact but has introduced beside the postulate of fact a postulate of right, namely, an equal right to life. An equal right to life is certainly being asserted, but the point is that Hobbes treats it as contained in the postulate of fact. He is able to treat it so because of his original postulate of mechanical materialism. Since men are self-moving systems of matter which equally seek to maintain their own motion, and are equally fragile, there is no reason why they should not have equal rights. These are the rights whose transfer to a sovereign establishes political obligation. Hobbes is able to treat his political obligation as a moral obligation because it is derived from a transfer of rights which he treats as moral rights. Morality enters the argument not at the late stage of the making of the social contract but at the early stage of deduction of equality of right from the stated equality of ability and need.

In thus deriving right and obligation from fact, Hobbes was taking a radically new position. He was assuming that right did not have to be brought in from outside the realm of fact, but that it was there already: that, unless the contrary could be shown, one could assume that equal right was en-tailed in equal need for continued motion.

[1] *Rudiments*, ch. 1, sect. 7, pp. 26–27.

This is a leap in political theory as radical as Galileo's formulation of the law of uniform motion was in natural science, and not unrelated to it. In each case a revolutionary change was initiated by a simple shift in assumptions. Before Galileo, it was assumed that an object at rest would stay there for ever unless some other thing moved it, and would only go on moving as long as some outside force was applied. Galileo assumed that an object in motion would stay in motion for ever unless something else stopped it, and that its motion did not require the continued application of outside force.

Hobbes's reversal of assumptions was similar. While it may be said that, from Plato on, rights and obligations had always been inferred from men's capacities and wants, the inference had always been indirect: from men's capacities and wants to some supposed purposes of Nature or will of God, and thence to human obligations and rights. Men's capacities and wants were treated as effects of the purposes of Nature or will of God; the latter, being treated as the cause of men's capacities and wants, were assumed also to be the source of moral right and obligation. Purpose or Will, brought in from outside the observed universe, was hypostatized as an outside force constantly imposing itself (by way of reason or revelation, or both) on men. Obligations and rights, on this assumption, would not exist were it not for the outside force which imposed them. What the obligations and rights were, depended on whatever purpose or will a particular philosopher ascribed to the outside force; and the philosophers generally found them to be unequal.[1]

Hobbes reversed the assumption. Instead of finding rights and obligations only in some outside force, he assumed that they were entailed in the need of each human mechanism to maintain its motion. And since each human mechanism, to do so, must assess its own requirements, there could be no question of imposing a system of values from outside or from above. Hence there could be no question of finding

[1] Cf. below, p. 89.

a hierarchy of wants or of rights or obligations. Everyone's must be assumed to be equal.

It was Hobbes's refusal to impose moral differences on men's wants, his acceptance of the equal need for continued motion as the sufficient source of rights, that constituted his revolution in moral and political theory. Hobbes was the first to deduce rights and obligations from facts without putting anything fanciful into the facts.

iv. *Morality, science, and the market*

When Hobbes's thought is seen in this way, a fundamental connexion between his political theory and his scientific materialism becomes evident. His reduction of human beings to self-moving and self-directing systems of matter, enabled (and required) him to assume that the continued motion of each was equally necessary. His acceptance of the assumption of the new science, that continuous motion did not require the application of continuous outside force, enabled him to dispense with any postulate of moral purpose imposed from outside, and to assume that moral values, rights, and obligations were entailed in the capacities and needs of equally self-moving mechanisms. Since motion is equally necessary to each mechanism, and since there is nothing else but motion, the only morality there can be must be deduced from that motion. Morality is what is most conducive to continued motion. Hence, at a primary and simple level, each has a right to its continued motion. And each, being a rational, calculating, self-correcting machine, is capable of obligating itself to those rules which can be shown to be necessary to ensure the maximum chance of continued motion. Since their motions, if not self-corrected, would bring them into continual collision, with resultant loss of motion, the correction (i.e. a moral system of obligation) is necessary as well as possible.

Thus Hobbes's deduction of right and obligation from fact, by way of the postulate of equality, seems to have been made possible by his acceptance of the materialist assumptions which he took over from the new science of the seventeenth century. In this view, Hobbes's materialism was neither an afterthought nor a window-dressing but an essential part of his political theory. His materialism was a necessary condition of his theory of political obligation.

His materialism was not, of course, a sufficient condition of his theory of obligation. For besides the materialist assumption that men are self-moving systems of matter in motion, he needed the postulate that the motion of every individual is necessarily opposed to the motion of every other. This latter postulate was not contained in his mechanical materialism but was derived, as we have seen, from his market assumption. The postulate of opposed motion was what enabled him to treat all individuals as equally insecure, and hence as equally in need of a system of political obligation.

Thus both the materialist and the market assumptions were required to enable Hobbes to deduce political obligation. The materialist assumption enabled him to say that individuals had equal need of continued motion, and to argue that, in the absence of reasons to the contrary, equal need could be taken as establishing equal moral right, and so providing the possibility of moral obligation. The market assumptions enabled him to say that men were equal in insecurity, and so to infer the necessity of moral obligation. In other words, both the materialist and the market assumptions were needed to produce the supposed facts—the two kinds of equality—from which it was conceivable for Hobbes to deduce obligation.

Since both the materialist and the market assumptions were needed, and both were used, we need not conjecture which is the more important, or which came first in Hobbes's thinking. But we may notice that the market assumptions were essential: it is only a society as fragmented as a market society that can credibly be treated as a mechanical system of self-moving individuals. Whether his vision of society as a system of market relations led Hobbes to his bold materialist hypothesis, or whether his enchantment with the new science started him casting about for a model of society which would be susceptible to treatment in mechanical terms, and so led him to discover the market model, we do not know. But we can say that it was the market assumptions that made possible Hobbes's attempt to transfer the mechanical postulates of the new science to the analysis of society.

There is one further respect in which the market assumptions contributed to Hobbes's belief that he could deduce obligation from fact. The possessive market society has the unique characteristic that in it the value or worth of every man is determined by the market. Values, entitlements, and hence actual rights, are in fact determined by a force which is neither purely subjective nor supernatural. Hobbes seized on this and concluded that no other standard of value or rights was needed: the old ideas of commutative and distributive justice, based on a standard of right that stood outside of and above any facts, were in his view entirely superseded. A standard of value was provided by the facts of the market system. He thought it could be taken as a standard of justice because it met one requirement of any moral principle, that is, it transcended each man's subjective desires. Hence it could be thought to render unnecessary any further reliance on moral principles imported from outside the facts.

To sum up, Hobbes's market assumptions provided two separate reasons for his thinking that he could deduce moral obligation and right from the facts. First, the facts of man's condition in society, as he analysed them, included an equal need for continued motion, a universal opposition of motions, and hence an equal insecurity. The equality of need and of insecurity, being on his analysis more fundamental than any inequalities, enabled him to assume equal moral rights, and hence the possibility of moral obligation, without postulating any purpose or will outside of the individuals themselves. Secondly, the facts as he analysed them included an objective but not supernatural standard of right.

Either of these two supposed attributes of the facts might well have been enough to make Hobbes presume that he could deduce obligation from the facts alone, without any inconsistency or logical fallacy. The two together, reinforcing each other, are quite enough to have led him to that presumption. Whether or not we find fault with his presumption that it could be done, or with the way he did it, we may concede that he thought it could be done. There is no warrant, therefore, for seeking any greater measure of consistency in his theory by assuming that he was doing something altogether different. If we are to understand Hobbes, and criticize him, we should follow up the relation he saw between the facts and obligation, rather than setting it aside on the ground that no consistent thinker could have made such a presumption.

v. *The presumption of obligation from fact*

We have seen so far how Hobbes's recognition of the essential attributes of market society led him to believe that the facts about society contained all that was needed for the deduction of a political obligation that would be morally binding on rational men. Before examining the merits of his particular deduction, we have to consider whether the deduction of obligation from fact is ever in principle logically possible.

It has become axiomatic in recent years that no moral principle can logically be deduced from any statements of fact; so much so that a simple reference to the axiom is generally considered enough to dispose of the question. But to dispose of the question in this way is to leave unconsidered a highly important innovation of Hobbes. I shall argue that in any sense short of strict logical entailment it is possible to deduce obligation from fact; that senses short of entailment are so important as to make it humanly necessary to attempt such deduction; that the deduction is possible, even in these senses, only when the social facts contain a significant equality of men; that Hobbes grasped this; and that his attempt to deduce obligation from fact was therefore valid in principle.

The idea that obligation cannot be deduced from fact is a comparatively recent innovation. It is commonly attributed to Hume, although it is doubtful if it goes back that far.[1] Earlier political philosophers, including those before Hobbes and some after him, had generally derived moral and political obligation and rights from the observed needs and capacities of men. But they had done so only with the aid of some postulate as to the purpose or will of Nature or God, if only the postulate that Nature makes nothing in vain. With such a postulate they could proceed to argue from men's capacities and needs to a system of obligations and rights. The argument appeared to be a deduction of right from fact, though it was not, and it was generally accepted in principle that obligation and right could be deduced from fact.

Since Hume, critics have seen that the earlier philosophers were not doing what they had thought they were doing, or what they had been thought to be doing. It was seen, that is, that they had not been logically deducing obligation from fact, but had been bringing in an extraneous postulate. This point has been seized by modern critics, most emphatically by the linguistic analysts. They, seeing the logical invalidity of treating as deductions from fact the earlier supposed deductions which had relied on an extraneous postulate, have inferred that the invalidity of the earlier systems lay in the very attempt to deduce obligation from fact, and have raised it to a first principle that obligation cannot be deduced from fact.

This inference I think is mistaken. It must be granted that on the model of formal calculi, moral utterances cannot be entailed in factual statements.[2] But there is no reason why all thought should be reduced to that model. And there is a strong reason, in the nature of human needs, why all thought should not be reduced to that model. It is not disputed that

[1] Cf. A. C. MacIntyre, 'Hume on "Is" and "Ought"', *Philosophical Review*, lxviii (1959), 451 ff.
[2] MacIntyre, op. cit., p. 462.

some kind of social order, and therefore rights, and therefore obligation, are necessary to human existence. One may, of course, deny that there is any point or value to human existence. But short of this abdication of humanity, one must proceed on the assumption that a system of rights and obligations can be derived from something.

One may, admitting this, still deny that it can be derived from men's needs and capacities alone, without bringing in some imposed will or purpose from outside. This is a perfectly tenable position, but there is no reason for making it a logical imperative. It is equally tenable that the same facts (viz. human needs and capacities) which make a system of obligation and rights necessary, also make such a system possible. It is tenable, that is to say, that the facts of human capacities and needs contain enough data for the deduction of a system of obligation and rights.

Now a system of obligation that is, or can become, morally binding on all individuals in a society, must be one which all of them are capable of accepting as binding. One of the facts that must be present (either observable or establishable by analysis) before such obligation can be deduced from the facts, is that individuals are capable of acknowledging such obligation. This condition can be met if the society is one in which individuals are capable of seeing themselves as equal in some respect more important than all the respects in which they are unequal. Only in such a society can it be said, and accepted, that there is no reason why any man should claim superior rights. For if men do not acknowledge such equality, they can claim unlimited superiority; claiming this, they cannot be morally bound by any non-supernatural system of obligation.[1] A factual equality, which men can see as overriding all their factual inequalities, is thus a prerequisite of deducing, from the facts alone, morally binding obligation.

Hobbes grasped this. It was, as we have seen, from his postulate of equality that he argued that there was no reason

[1] See Note E, p. 294.

why anyone should have more rights than others, and from this to the possibility and necessity of obligation. The supposed factual equality from which he argued directly to the necessity of political obligation was the equal ability of men to kill each other, which in the hypothetical state of nature entailed an equal insecurity of life and possessions. This supposed equality is not, however, a sufficient basis for political obligation of men *in society*. For while the brittleness of the human frame is a physiological fact as true of men in society as of men in the hypothetical state of nature, it is only in the hypothetical state of nature that it entails total, and therefore equal, insecurity of life and possessions. But Hobbes's state of nature is by definition not a political society at all. In any kind of political society there is some protection of the life of each individual against attacks by other individuals; and since there is not total insecurity there is not necessarily equal insecurity. If Hobbes is to show that individuals in society can and should acknowledge obligation he has to show that individuals *in society* are, and can see that they are, equal in some respect more important than the respects in which they are unequal. The artificial equality of the hypothetical state of nature is not enough.[1] We are therefore thrown back to Hobbes's model of society. Is there, in his model, such an equality? If so, his deduction of obligation is valid in principle. And is such equality as is found in his model consistent with the other attributes of his model? If so, his deduction should be valid for the possessive market society, since the other attributes of his model are the attributes of possessive market society.

In Hobbes's model of society, as it can be collected from his analyses of power, honour, value, and justice, there may be said to be two kinds of equality: equal insecurity and equal subordination to the market. Everyone is necessarily pulled into the competition for power over others. Everyone seeks to acquire more power than he naturally has, and can do so only by converting to his own use some of the powers

[1] Cf. above, sect. 3, vi.

of others. Hence everyone is liable to incessant invasion of his powers by others. Hobbes treated this as an equality of insecurity. He saw this equality of insecurity as so close to the surface of men's lives that any rational man could see it and acknowledge its necessary consequences as soon as it was pointed out. But, as we have seen, the only society in which there can be this incessant invasion of every man's power by others is the possessive market society. We have therefore to ask whether the insecurity of every man in possessive market society can accurately be treated as equal insecurity.

It is immediately apparent that while every individual in that society is insecure, they are far from equal in insecurity. For the possessive market society requires a substantial inequality of command over resources. There must be a class of men with sufficient resources to employ the labour of others, and a class of men with so little resources as to offer themselves for employment. While the members of each class are insecure, i.e. open to invasion of their powers through the market, the insecurity of the two classes is quite unequal. They cannot therefore be expected to perceive themselves so equal in insecurity as to acknowledge, on that ground alone, a binding obligation to a common authority. Thus Hobbes failed to allow in his model for the inequality of insecurity which the other attributes of his model necessarily imply. If Hobbes had relied solely on the supposed equality of insecurity in his model of society, we should have to say that he had failed to make his case for all men in society acknowledging a common political obligation.

However, there is in his model of society another feature which may be considered a kind of equality: the equal subordination of every individual to the laws of the market. In Hobbes's model, which in this respect coincides with the model of possessive market society, everyone is subject to the determination of the competitive market for powers. Hobbes saw, accurately, that in a possessive market society all values and entitlements are in fact established by the operation of the market, and all morality tends to be the morality of the market. The possessive market society *does* establish rights by facts: every man's entitlements are determined by the actual competitive relationship between the powers of individuals. If the determination of values and rights by the market is accepted as justice by all members of the society, there is a sufficient basis for rational obligation, binding on all men, to an authority which could maintain and enforce the market system. Hobbes thought that this condition was met: he thought that the market concept of justice was the only one that could be entertained by a rational individual who realized his true position as a mere unit in a market society.[1] In this he was at least partly mistaken. It is also possible for rational men to resist or reject the whole market system.

Yet it must be allowed that in assuming the inevitable dominance of possessive market values Hobbes had the facts on his side. He was perhaps a little ahead of his time, for there were still substantial numbers in English society who rejected the claims of market morality. The Civil War, on Hobbes's own interpretation of it, was a contest between those who supported traditional values and those who aligned themselves with the morality of the market. And however one interprets the Restoration and the Whig Revolution it cannot be said that support for traditional values had become entirely insignificant by the end of the century, or even later. Locke tried to combine traditional and market morality; so did Burke, in a more fundamental and more desperate way, a century later. But by that time the morality of the market had come to prevail, and it was not seriously challenged again until well on in the nineteenth century. Hobbes, then, was substantially right after all, at least for as far ahead as he could see, which turned out to be about two centuries, in assuming that the market system once established was so powerful that no individual in it could escape from it, and hence that all rational men in it had to accept the market concept of justice as the only possible one.

[1] Cf. above, pp. 63–64.

So Hobbes appears to have found a basis for a rational obligation for all members of a possessive market society. For if there is no alternative to the market society, or if the only alternative is anarchy, every man in it who sees his true position has no rational alternative but to support a political authority which can maintain that society as a regular orderly system. In other words, every individual in it can and must in his own interest acknowledge obligation to a political authority with enough power to enforce the rules of a competitive society. And this obligation may as well be called moral as prudential; it is the highest morality of which market men are capable. When Hobbes's theory is thus seen as a statement of what kind of political obligation is possible and necessary in a possessive market society, his deduction of obligation from fact may be allowed to be valid.

5. *Penetration and Limits of Hobbes's Political Theory*

i. *Historical prerequisites of the deduction*

I have argued that the difference between moral and prudential obligation becomes insignificant as soon as reliance on some transcendental will or purpose is rejected; that when it is rejected the significant question is whether any obligation that can be expected to be binding on rational individuals is possible; that such obligation is possible if men see themselves, or can be expected to come to see themselves, as equal in some respect more vital than all their inequalities; that Hobbes grasped this; and that the equal subservience of all men to the determination of the market which he put in his model of society, and which is an attribute of possessive market societies, is a sufficient basis for the deduction of obligation binding on all rational men in that society, so long as possessive market relations prevail and are thought inevitable.

This is a greater measure of validity than is usually allowed Hobbes's system, though it would not have satisfied

Hobbes, who thought he had deduced from eternal facts of man's nature the one kind of political obligation that would always be necessary and possible. But if his own claims for his theory were too high, his achievements are still remarkable. He opened a new way in political theory. And he penetrated closer to the nature of modern society than any of his contemporaries and many of his successors. Each of these achievements deserves our notice.

Hobbes's most valid claim is perhaps his most arrogant one: 'Civil Philosophy [is] no older . . . than my own book *De Cive*.'[1] Hobbes was the first political thinker to have seen the possibility of deducing obligation directly from the mundane facts of men's actual relations with each other, including the equality inhering in those relations; having seen this possibility, he was the first to be able to dispense with assumptions of outside purpose or will. The Stoic and Christian natural law traditions had of course asserted the equality of all men, but this was an assertion less of fact than of an aspiration that men should think of themselves as equal by reflecting on their common rationality or common creation. Common rationality is a tenuous and imprecise quality in comparison with the insecurity and subservience to the market which Hobbes found just beneath the surface of everyday life. Perhaps because rationality was so tenuous, divine purpose and will had early been brought in to the natural law tradition to support the postulate of common rationality, and with their introduction the question of getting obligation from the mundane facts no longer arose.

It is not surprising that Hobbes was the first political thinker to break away from the traditional reliance on a supposed will or purpose infusing the universe, and base himself on a supposed mundane equality.[2] Before Hobbes, everything had conspired to make political thinkers rely on

---

[1] *English Works*, i, p. ix.

[2] The distinction of being the first to have broken away might be claimed for Grotius, who did detach natural law from divine will and purpose. But Grotius relied on a supposed factual quality of sociability which was almost as tenuous as the earlier rationality.

standards of value and entitlement imported from outside the observed facts. For one thing, market relations had no-where penetrated all social relations sufficiently to make it conceivable that values could be established by the operation of objective but not supernatural forces. For another, most political thinkers before Hobbes had worked in markedly class-divided societies in which hierarchical order appeared to be the only alternative to political and moral anarchy. In hierarchical societies the danger of slave or peasant revolts or popular equalitarian movements is never entirely absent. As long as such movements are thought to be anarchical, thinkers who are constructing theories of political obligation must assume some functional or moral inequality between classes of men, for hierarchical society requires unequal rights and obligations. And since the merits of hierarchy and an inequalitarian moral code could not be expected to be made rationally evident to a class which might consider itself oppressed, there was an additional reason to deduce a code of obligation from some divine or transcendent order rather than directly from the capacities and needs of men.

Hobbes also lived in a class-divided society. But he did not find it necessary to impute significantly unequal capaci-ties or needs to different classes of men. For on his reading of the facts of seventeenth-century society, social order was no longer dependent on the maintenance of hierarchy. He thought that the objective market had replaced, or could replace, the inequality of ranks, and had at the same time established an equality of insecurity. He did not, of course, rely on the market alone to provide order. A political sove-reign was necessary to guarantee order, by enforcing rules which would prevent the peaceful competition of the market turning into, or being supplemented by, open force. But the authority of the sovereign could now be made to rest on a rational transfer of rights agreed upon by men who were equal in a double sense: their value and entitlements were equally governed by the market, and in the face of the market they appeared to be equally insecure. Hobbes, unlike his predecessors, did not need to impose a hierarchy of unequal values on his data, because he did not see any need to read unequal values out again, into his moral and political rules, as unequal rights and obligations. And for the same reason he was able, unlike his predecessors, to dispense with supposed divine or natural purposes: because he did not need to impute inequality, he did not need to assume an unobservable purpose or will into which inequality of value and entitlement could be inserted.

In short, the development of a market society had, by Hobbes's time, provided two necessary conditions for a deduction of political obligation from mundane facts, neither of which conditions had been present earlier. First, it had created, or was visibly creating, an equality before the law of the market, sufficiently compelling to be made the basis of an obligation binding on rational men who saw their real position. The presence of this equality, as I have argued, made the deduction of obligation from fact logically unobjectionable. Secondly, the development of a market society had replaced or was visibly replacing hierarchical order by the objective order of the market, which did not require unequal rights for different ranks. The decline of hierarchical order thus provided, for the first time, at least one of the conditions which would make the deduction of obligation from fact politically unobjectionable. To say that the social conditions which made Hobbes's deduction logically and politically possible were not present before his time is not to belittle his achievement. It is rather to recognize the insight with which he penetrated to the essential relations of his own society, and the skill with which he built on them.

ii. *The self-perpetuating sovereign*

This assessment of Hobbes's achievement seems strikingly at variance with the actual reception of his doctrine in his own day. If, as I have argued, he grasped the essential relations of his own society and built logically on them, his conclusions should surely have been acceptable at least to the new men of the mid-seventeenth century and later, to those who welcomed the incursion of market relations in English society. Yet we know that Hobbes's doctrine was not accepted by any significant group or movement in England in his own century. Neither royalists nor parliamentarians, neither traditionalists nor radical republicans, neither Whigs nor Tories, could stomach it. Many of his critics, including the most vocal, rejected both his premisses and his conclusions.[1] But even those who substantially accepted Hobbes's analysis of human nature and shared his view of society as a market, among whom we may include Harrington[2] and even Locke,[3] rejected his full conclusions. When we notice what of Hobbes's conclusions they rejected and what they accepted, we shall see more clearly what part of his doctrine is in principle acceptable, and what part unacceptable, in a market society.

Neither Harrington nor Locke objected to sovereign power. Both held that there must be somewhere in any civil society a political power to which every individual must be understood to have resigned all his rights and powers, and which must be unlimited by any conjoint or superior human power. Harrington was perfectly explicit: 'Where the soverain power is not as entire and absolute as in monarchy itself, there can be no government at all.'[4] Locke put sovereign power in the civil society, i.e. in the majority: since they were assumed to will nothing but the public good they could safely have sovereign power, and somebody had to have it.[5] The man or assembly to whom the civil society then entrusted legislative and executive power was, of course, not sovereign; but where this power was given to an elective

---

[1] Cf. John Bowle, *Hobbes and his Critics* (1951).

[2] Harrington endorsed Hobbes's 'treatises of human nature, and of liberty and necessity' as 'the greatest of new lights, and those which I have follow'd, and shall follow' (*Prerogative of Popular Government, Works*, 1771, p. 241). For Harrington's appreciation of society as a market, see below, ch. iv, sect. 2.

[3] See below, ch. v, sect. 4, esp. pp. 239–41, 245.

[4] *Art of Lawgiving*, Book III, Preface (*Works*, 1771, p. 404).

[5] *Second Treatise*, sects. 89, 95–99.

assembly rather than to a self-perpetuating assembly or a monarch, Locke allowed it to exercise virtually sovereign power.[1] What both Harrington and Locke thought unnecessary, and inconsistent with the only purposes for which individuals could conceivably authorize sovereign power, was that the sovereign power should be put irrevocably in the hands of a person or body of persons with authority to appoint his or their own successors. They objected not to perpetual sovereign power but to a self-perpetuating sovereign person or body.

Yet Hobbes had insisted that the person or persons who held the sovereign power at any given moment should be self-perpetuating. This of course put the holders of sovereign power always beyond the control of the people or of any section of the people; and this, however unfortunate, was in Hobbes's view unavoidable. He considered self-perpetuating power an essential attribute of sovereignty. 'There is no perfect forme of Government, where the disposing of the Succession is not in the present Soveraign.'[2] A sovereign assembly must have the right to fill vacancies in its membership; a sovereign monarch must have the right to appoint his successor. No one after Hobbes, however much they agreed with Hobbes's estimate of men as self-interested calculating machines and however much they accepted the values of a market society, could agree that this required men to acknowledge the sovereign authority of a self-perpetuating body. Practice also contraverted Hobbes's conclusion. England was governed successfully, at least from 1689 on, by a body, the king in parliament, which was sovereign except in the one power of self-perpetuation: the king could not appoint his successor, nor could the members of a given parliament appoint theirs.

The fact that English society soon came to be adequately governed by a sovereign body without self-perpetuating power shows that Hobbes's full prescription was not neces-

---

[1] *Second Treatise*, sects. 138, 142. Cf. below, ch. v, pp. 256-61.
[2] *Leviathan*, ch. 19, p. 149.

sary for the maintenance of a stable society. It shows also that, in the measure that English society was then a possessive market society, Hobbes's prescription was not necessary for a possessive market society. Yet Hobbes's prescription was a deduction from the necessary behaviour of men in his model of society, which we have seen to be substantially the same as the model of the possessive market society. Where, then, was the error?

The source of the error was in the one significant shortcoming of Hobbes's model already noticed. His model failed to correspond to the possessive market model in that he did not allow for the existence of politically significant unequal classes. He saw society as so necessarily fragmented by the struggle of each for power over others that all were equal in insecurity. He failed to see that the very same characteristic of a society which makes it an incessant competition of each for power over others, makes it also an unequal class-divided society. The characteristic is the all-pervasive market relationship. Only where all men's powers are marketable commodities can there be an incessant competition of each for power over others; and where all men's powers are commodities there is necessarily a division of society into unequal classes.[1]

It was Hobbes's failure to see this that led him to see society as so completely fragmented. And it was from his view of society as so completely fragmented that he deduced the need for a self-perpetuating sovereign person or body. He argued[2] that if the person or persons who hold sovereign power were not acknowledged to have the right to appoint their successors, then whenever any successors had to be chosen, the real power would be thrown back to the fragmented and opposed powers of all the separate members of the society, thus negating the whole purpose for which they had authorized sovereign power.

What Hobbes missed, then, was the possibility of class cohesion offsetting the fragmenting forces in market society.

[1] See above, pp. 55-56.   [2] Leviathan, ch. 19, p. 149.

If one assumes no class cohesion, as Hobbes did, there is no way to provide the necessary political power except for all individuals to hand everything over to a self-perpetuating sovereign body. But if there is a cohesive class, its sense of common interest may be strong enough to make its members capable of upholding a sovereign government and of holding it ultimately responsible to themselves by retaining the right of appointing or electing to the sovereign body. Hobbes was not so blind as to have missed the fact that there was a class division in England, as is evident from his remarks in *Behemoth*.[1] He saw, too, that the growth of the market relation had undermined the old values, and that the new men of mercantile wealth had enough cohesion to foment a civil war. But he was apparently more impressed with the divisive effects of the loss of old values, and with the contests for power between different groups on the parliamentary side which broke out as soon as the monarchy had been thrown over, than by the cohesion that had enabled the opponents of the old structure to overthrow it. At any rate, he did not put class division into his model. There, the universality of the competitive struggle between individuals is assumed to have dissolved all class inequalities and all class cohesiveness. Hobbes's model failed to correspond, in this one essential, to the model of possessive market society as well as to the actual English society.

This shortcoming in Hobbes's model of society was what misled him to conclude that a self-perpetuating sovereign body was necessary. It made his conclusions inapplicable to the possessive market society, and unacceptable to the proponents of market society in seventeenth-century England. Since he left class division and class cohesion out of his model, there was no place in his conclusions for a sovereign body tied to one class. Yet that is the kind of government most agreeable to the model of a possessive market society. Those who possess substantial property need a sovereign state to sanction the right of possession.[2] They must there-

---

[1] See above, pp. 64–66.   [2] See below, pp. 95–96.

fore authorize a sovereign body to do whatever is necessary to maintain the right of possession, and the sovereign body must have the right to decide what is necessary. But the men of property need not give up their right or power to choose the persons who shall from time to time be the members of the sovereign body. And since they need not do so, they cannot, as rational men, do so. They need not do so because, as possessors of substantial property, they are capable of enough cohesion for the recurrent choice of members of the sovereign body to be left to them without all authority being dispersed among myriad conflicting wills every time a choice of members has to be made. The argument on which Hobbes rested the necessity of a self-perpetuating sovereign body is thus without basis in a class-divided society with a cohesive possessing class; and the very fact that a society is so divided tends to give a sufficient degree of cohesion to the possessing class.

iii. *Congruence of sovereignty and market society*

Although Hobbes was in error in concluding that the men of his society needed or could sustain a self-perpetuating sovereign body, he was right in concluding that they needed and could sustain an irresistible sovereign power. The argument on which he based the need and possibility of every man acknowledging an obligation to a sovereign power remains valid for a possessive market society, even when its class division is taken into account. For even a cohesive possessing class still needs a sovereign power. A sovereign is needed to hold everyone within the limits of peaceful competition. The more nearly the society approximates a possessive market society, subject to the centrifugal forces of opposed competitive self-interests, the more necessary a single centralized sovereign power becomes. In a customary society a network of conditional property rights may be maintained without a single central sovereign. But in a market society, where property becomes an unconditional right to use, to exclude others absolutely from the use of,[1] and to transfer or alienate,[2] land and other goods, a sovereign is necessary to establish and maintain individual property rights. Without a sovereign power, Hobbes said, there can be no property,[3] and he was right about the kind of property characteristic of a possessive market society.

A sovereign is also needed 'to appoint in what manner, all kinds of contract between Subjects, (as buying, selling, exchanging, borrowing, lending, letting, and taking to hire,) are to bee made; and by what words, and signes they shall be understood for valid'.[4] Hobbes presented this as a need in any society. It is not so in every society, but it is so in a market society. And it is an especially pressing need, requiring a strong sovereign power, when a possessive market society is replacing a customary society, for then customary rights have to be extinguished in favour of contractual rights. A sovereign power is necessary also, especially when market society is not yet firmly established, to instil the motivations or behaviour required in the formative stages of market society. Luxurious consumption must be discouraged, thrift and industry encouraged, the able-bodied 'are to be forced to work; and to avoyd the excuse of not finding employment, there ought to be such Lawes, as may encourage all manner of Arts; as Navigation, Agriculture, Fishing, and all manner of Manifacture that requires labour'.[5]

The need for a sovereign power in a possessive market society, and especially in an emerging one, is thus evident. And it was evident to Hobbes. He held, indeed, that a sovereign power was needed for these purposes in any society. He reached this conclusion because he had put into his model of society as such the essential relations of the possessive market society. If he was at fault in the breadth of his generalization, he was far ahead of any contemporary political thinker in the depth of his insight.

---

[1] Rudiments, ch. 14, sect. 7, p. 160; Leviathan, ch. 24, pp. 190–1.
[2] Ibid., pp. 192–3; Elements, part ii, ch. 3, sect. 5, pp. 100–1.
[3] Leviathan, ch. 24, pp. 189–90.　　　　　　　　　　　[4] Ibid., p. 193.
[5] Ibid., ch. 30, p. 267; cf. Rudiments, ch. 13, sect. 14, pp. 150–1.

But it is not enough to establish the need for a sovereign power unless at the same time and from the same postulates one can establish the *possibility* of a sovereign power. Can the kind of society which especially needs sovereign power sustain sovereign power? Can the individuals in such a fragmented and competitive society possibly support a political power fully and steadily enough to render it a sovereign power? Here we must distinguish between individuals of the possessing and the non-possessing classes.

The rational man who, in such a society, possesses substantial property, or hopes to acquire it and hold it, is capable of acknowledging obligation to such a sovereign. He is used to long-term contracts, he sees the point of the rule that contracts must be performed. He conducts his affairs by rational calculation of long-run advantage; he does what his rational calculation tells him he should do. He is precisely the kind of man who can see the net advantage of the kind of contractual order which a sovereign power can provide. He is, of course, not a perfect calculator. If he and his fellows were all perfect calculators, steadily seeing the net advantage of staying within the rules of a contractual society, no sovereign would be needed to regulate relations among them (though one might still be needed to regulate relations between them and the non-possessors). Market men are good enough calculators to see the net advantage of everybody sticking to the rules, but each of them cannot be relied on to keep this long-run advantage steadily in his mind alongside the short-run advantage he may see from time to time in breaking the rules. But each is capable of seeing the net advantage to himself of having a sovereign to enforce the rules on everybody. For it is easier to comply with rules so institutionalized; it leaves each man freer to make the day-to-day decisions of net advantage if he does not have to calculate, every time, the probable effect of his breaking the rules on other people's conformity to the rules, or even worse, the probability of others independently breaking the rules and acting in unpredictable ways. Only where there is a sovereign to enforce the rules, is the number of variables in each man's calculation reduced to manageable proportions.

On these grounds, individuals of the possessing class in a market society may well be thought capable of acknowledging obligation to a sovereign who can enforce the rules necessary for the operation of that kind of society. Here again we must credit Hobbes with the essential insight. True, he generalized too widely in attributing this capacity to men in every kind of society. But he got to the heart of the matter. The rational capacity on which he based the need and possibility of men acknowledging a sovereign is precisely the kind and degree of rational calculation that can be expected of the rational man who is making his way in a possessive market society.

What of the man without substantial property or hope of acquiring it? Is the lifelong wage-earner, living at bare subsistence level, capable of acknowledging obligation to a sovereign whose main function is to make and enforce the rules of contract and property, rules which the wage-earner may feel are what have put him and keep him in this precarious position? Yes, so long as he can see no alternative to the possessive market society. If he can see no alternative, he has no rational choice but to acknowledge obligation to a sovereign power which can at least protect his life. Perhaps that is why Hobbes was not at all worried by the objection he foresaw would be made to his doctrine, namely, that 'Common people are not of capacity enough to be made to understand' the principles on which their obligation rests.[1] He thought them perfectly capable of it, more so than 'the Rich, and Potent Subjects of a Kingdome, or those that are accounted the most Learned'. The common people, he said, have no interest contrary to their acknowledging a sovereign; a sovereign power does not bridle or diminish them as it does the Potent and the Learned. Rather, 'the Common-peoples minds, unlesse they be tainted with dependance on the Potent, or scribbled over with the opinions of their Doctors,

---

[1] *Leviathan*, ch. 30, p. 260.

are like clean paper, fit to receive whatsoever by Publique Authority shall be imprinted in them'. Since they can be brought to acquiesce in religious doctrines which are above reason and against reason, they are capable of accepting this doctrine of obligation to the sovereign 'which is so consonant to Reason'.[1] All that is necessary is that the common people be instructed in it, which Hobbes thought might be done by 'setting a part from their ordinary labour, some certain times, in which they may attend those that are appointed to instruct them'.[2]

In dealing thus with the common people Hobbes shows some awareness of their characteristics as a separate class. He does not say they are capable of this obligation because they see their position is inevitable, but he assumes that in so far as they are made aware of their true position they will see that it is inevitable. In this assumption Hobbes was not far from the mark. The common people, the men of no property, had no alternative to the acceptance of the possessive market society.

I have argued that the society about which Hobbes wrote with such prescience, needed and could support a sovereign power. I have found only two faults with his doctrine. The first is that he mistakenly attributed the characteristics of market society to all societies, and so claimed a wider validity for his conclusions than they can have; this, however, is a fault that does not affect the validity of his conclusions for possessive market societies. The second is that he failed to see, or to give sufficient weight to, the class division which a possessive market society necessarily generates, and so concluded mistakenly that the sovereign power must and could be in a self-perpetuating person or assembly. When his theory is reduced to historical measure, when it is treated as a theory about possessive market society, only this second fault is, on our analysis, to be alleged against it. This second fault is indeed a serious one, enough by itself to make his full theory untenable for such societies.

[1] Ibid.   [2] Ibid., p. 262.

But it is still worth while to insist that, apart from this one error, Hobbes's analysis and conclusions are substantially valid for possessive market societies. When his theory is read as a theory about possessive market societies, he makes his case that individuals need, and are capable of acknowledging steady obligation to, an all-powerful sovereign body (though not a self-perpetuating one). That is as much as should be claimed for Hobbes. When no more is claimed, some of the main objections that are generally taken to his theory lose much of their force.

iv. *Some objections reconsidered*

The most serious and persistent difficulty in Hobbes's theory, when it is taken as a theory about man and society as such, is that men who are moved, as Hobbes has them moved, by unlimited competitive appetites, seem incapable of acknowledging a binding obligation which limits their motion. If all men are so moved that they are necessarily engaged in an incessant competitive struggle for power, how can they admit an obligation which overrides this? If men are necessarily so impelled to invade each other that they need a sovereign, how can they be capable of supporting a sovereign? No very satisfactory answer can be given to these questions when they are posed so generally. But when the questions are asked about men in possessive market societies they can be answered. Such individuals both need a sovereign and can support a sovereign. For in such societies they can incessantly invade each other without destroying each other. They need a sovereign to keep their invasions within non-destructive bounds, and they are capable of sustaining such a sovereign because they can go on invading under the sovereign's rules. They support a sovereign in order to permit themselves to go on invading each other. It is only in possessive market society that all men must invade each other, and only there that all can do so within the rules of the society. They can, therefore, support those rules, and the power necessary to enforce them, without stultifying themselves. One of the central difficulties in Hobbes's theory of obligation thus disappears when the theory is treated as a theory of and for possessive market societies.

Another logical difficulty is also easier to deal with when the whole theory is regarded in this way. Hobbes claimed to have shown from a scientific analysis of men's nature that men ought to acknowledge a steadier obligation to a sovereign than they do now acknowledge. That is to say that men must act in a way they do not now act, if they are to be consistent with their own nature. This seems to be a flat contradiction. Yet it is what Hobbes gets by his application of Galileo's resolutive-compositive method. As Watkins has well pointed out, that method operates differently in political science from the way in which it operates in mechanics or geometry.

When one applies [the resolutive-compositive method] to a physical effect or a geometrical figure the recomposed whole, which one now understands, is still the whole with which one had previously only been acquainted. But when this method is applied to society the recomposed whole may very well differ from the original. An actual society may be inconsistent, at war with itself. But when a system of political authority is rationally reconstructed by deduction from the nature of the system's elements it will obviously be consistent with them. To apply the resolutive-compositive method to society is to discover what men *are* and what the State *ought to be* to be consistent with their nature.[1]

This very perceptive account of what happens when the resolutive-compositive method is applied to politics seems to me to be rather a statement than a resolution of the difficulty. If men's natures, as discovered by scientific resolution, are such as to render them at war with each other (or society at war with itself), men are consistent with their nature in so acting. Hobbes's composition of the elements of men's nature is different from the arrangement of those elements which actually prevails. How can it be called more consistent with their natures than the arrangement which actually exists in their present composite natures?

[1] J. W. N. Watkins, 'Philosophy and Politics in Hobbes', *Philosophical Quarterly*, vol. v, no. 19 (1955), 133.

There is no mystery about what Hobbes thought. He thought that men now calculate or weigh means and ends less efficiently than they could do; and that they could learn to do it (under Hobbes's tutelage) more efficiently. Men could learn to build better than they do.[1] Educability is one of the assumed elements of human nature. But even if educability is granted, what expectation can there be, except from the accident of Hobbes's publishing his doctrine, that men can now do what they have not yet done? Hobbes relied on a general tendency, supported by historical observation, that when men see some new knowledge to be to their advantage they will use it.

Time, and Industry, produce every day new knowledge. And as the art of well building, is derived from Principles of Reason, observed by industrious men, that had long studied the nature of materials, and the divers effects of figure, and proportion, long after mankind began (though poorly) to build: So, long time after men have begun to constitute Commonwealths, imperfect, and apt to relapse into disorder, there may, Principles of Reason be found out, by industrious meditation, to make their constitution (excepting by externall violence) everlasting. And such are those which I have in this discourse set forth. . . .[2]

If it be granted as a law of human nature that men always use new knowledge which they see to be to their advantage, their failure to have acknowledged steady obligation to a sovereign hitherto must be due to one of two reasons: either they had not discovered that it was advantageous, or it had not in fact been as advantageous to them earlier as it was now. Hobbes was satisfied with the first of these reasons. When challenged on the ground that the principles would have been discovered already if they were really so advantageous, he was able to point to the record in the physical sciences, where new principles were being discovered in his century which he thought might as well have been, but which in fact had not been, discovered earlier. The parallel, however, is not exact. For on Hobbes's own analysis of the elements of human nature, the urgency of political science

[1] *Leviathan*, ch. 20, p. 160.   [2] Ibid., ch. 30, pp. 259–60.

was, and always had been, greater than the urgency of the natural sciences. Natural philosophy produces commodious living, lack of natural philosophy withholds these pleasant commodities; but lack of civil philosophy produces calamity:

the utility of moral and civil philosophy is to be estimated, not so much by the commodities we have by knowing these sciences, as by the calamities we receive from not knowing them. Now, all such calamities as may be avoided by human industry, arise from war, but chiefly from civil war; for from this proceed slaughter, solitude, and the want of all things.[1]

And the cause of civil war was that men had not learned the rules of civil life sufficiently, the knowledge of which rules was moral philosophy. This being so, and avoidance of violent death being (and always having been) man's greatest need, the slow rate of discovery in natural philosophy can scarcely account for the slow rate in moral and civil philosophy. If men's need for moral and civil philosophy had always been so great, they could reasonably be expected to have made Hobbes's discovery earlier.

It is not a sufficient reply to say that the reason men have not embraced true principles of civil philosophy is that those principles cross their own interests. Hobbes sometimes suggested this, as in his comparison of mathematical and dogmatical learning:

The former is free from controversies and dispute, because it consisteth in comparing figures and motion only; in which things truth and the interest of men oppose not each other. But in the later there is nothing not disputable, because it compareth men, and meddleth with their right and profit; in which, as oft as reason is against a man, so oft will a man be against reason.[2]

But if true principles of civil philosophy crossed men's interests before, and if men's interests have not changed, the principles must still cross their interests to the same extent. One might conclude from this, as some critics of Hobbes have done, that Hobbes's analysis of human nature was simply incorrect: the reason men had not made and used

---

[1] *English Works*, i. 8.   [2] *Elements*, Ep. Ded., p. xvii.

Hobbes's discovery earlier is that men's nature does not contain the balance of interests or balance of motives that Hobbes said it did. If Hobbes was simply wrong about man's nature, there is no problem about why men have not acted in the way Hobbes said they should act to be consistent with their nature. And if Hobbes was simply wrong about man's nature, the fully rational man need not act in the way Hobbes said he should: Hobbes's whole case collapses.

But it is not necessary to go so far. The reason why men had not hitherto made and used Hobbes's discovery may be neither that he was simply wrong about human nature, nor (as Hobbes alleged) that men hitherto had failed through lack of application or logic to make this advantageous discovery earlier, but that the principle of obligation which Hobbes had discovered had not been as advantageous to men in earlier societies as it now was to men in possessive market society. It may be, in other words, that Hobbes's principle of obligation did cross men's interests (and their capacities) before the arrival of the possessive market society, and does not cross them in that society. A market society needs peace and order to a degree which others do not. War, plunder, and rapine are ordinary and honourable in many non-market societies, but they are inconsistent with market society. They cannot, in possessive market society, be allowed as between citizens of one national community (and it was only the internal relations that Hobbes was dealing with[1]) nor are they needed in a possessive market society to give thrusting men room for their appetitive behaviour. And not only does a market society need internal peace; equally important, men who accept and promote market society can be expected, unlike men in other societies, to see the advantages of it and therefore the advantages of

---

[1] Hobbes did not hope to make a commonwealth immune from external violence. He thought that international hostilities were less of an evil than internal warfare. Because sovereigns, by international hostility, 'uphold thereby, the Industry of their Subjects; there does not follow from it, that misery, which accompanies the Liberty of particular men' (*Leviathan*, ch. 13, p. 98).

Hobbes's discovery. They need only be shown the logic of their (new) situation; that is all that is needed to render men in the new market society capable, as men were not capable before, of seeing and using Hobbes's doctrine. True, it is only the enterprising men of property who can be expected to see it. But that is enough: the common people need not see it for themselves but can be taught it by authority.

Market men, then, are peculiarly apt learners of Hobbes's doctrine. So if his theory is taken only as a theory of and for possessive market society he is saved in some measure from the reproach of being contradictory about men's capacities. More accurately, he is saved from that reproach if his theory is taken as a theory of and for a possessive market society which is relatively new. So understood, his theory is an attempt to persuade present men, by showing them their actual nature, to behave differently from the way in which men have hitherto behaved, and in which they are now still behaving simply for lack of realizing what is demanded of and permitted to men in possessive market society. Hobbes was addressing men who did not yet think and behave entirely as market men, whose calculation of the kind of political obligation they should acknowledge was still based on less than a full appreciation of what was most to their own interest, most consistent with their true nature as competitive men. He was asking those men to bring their thinking into line with their real needs and capacities as market men. He was so intent on doing this that he presented their real needs and capacities not as new needs and capacities (which they were) but as the needs and capacities of men of all times and places. In so doing he involved himself in the inconsistency of saying that men's nature requires them to do something they have not been doing. But his fault is less grave than his accusers make it. He could have cleared himself entirely had he claimed less than universal validity for his analysis.

Finally we may notice that when his theory is treated as a theory of and for possessive market society, the main moral objection to his doctrine turns out to be not so much an objection to his doctrine as to the morality of that society. If the real basis of Hobbes's political obligation is, as I have argued, the rational perception of men in possessive market society that they are all irretrievably subject to the determination of the market, then the somewhat inhuman flavour of Hobbes's political obligation is at once explained and justified. The compulsions of the market society do somewhat demean the free rational individual who is usually put at the centre of ethical theory. The morality of the market is not entirely acceptable to the humanist. A theory of obligation built on a recognition and acceptance of the compulsions and morality of the market must seem perverse to the humanist who does not fully accept the values of the possessive market society as the highest, or a sufficient, morality.

Yet Hobbes, in building on the compulsions and morality of the market, penetrated to the heart of the problem of obligation in modern possessive societies. The paradox of Hobbes's individualism, which starts with equal rational individuals and demonstrates that they must submit themselves wholly to a power outside themselves, is a paradox not of his construction but of the market society. The market makes men free; it requires for its effective operation that all men be free and rational; yet the independent rational decisions of each man produce at every moment a configuration of forces which confronts each man compulsively. All men's choices determine, and each man's choice is determined by, the market. Hobbes caught both the freedom and the compulsion of possessive market society.

The English possessing class, however, did not need Hobbes's full prescription. And they had some reason to be displeased with his portrait of themselves: no reader, except the fashionably flippant, could relish such an exposure of himself and his fellows, especially when it was presented as science. Before the end of the century, the men of property had come to terms with the more ambiguous, and more agreeable, doctrine of Locke.

III

THE LEVELLERS: FRANCHISE AND FREEDOM

1. *The Problem of the Franchise*

Ever since an unfortunate footnote of Firth's when he first published the text of the Putney debates,[1] it has been generally asserted with little or no qualification that the Levellers were advocates of manhood suffrage. Many Leveller statements apparently to that effect may of course be cited,[2] and the famous debate on the franchise at Putney began in a way that makes it easy to read it, as Gardiner did,[3] as a debate on manhood suffrage. Yet in fact from the first time the specific extent of the proposed franchise is mentioned in the Putney debate, through to the final manifesto of the Leveller movement, the Levellers consistently excluded from their franchise proposals two substantial categories of men, namely, servants or wage-earners,[4] and those in receipt of alms or beggars. The general misunderstanding of the Levellers' actual position on the franchise has somewhat obscured their concept of freedom and has let some fundamentals of their political thinking go unnoticed. Our first problem, then, is to elicit the Levellers' full position on the franchise; our second, to consider what revision of the prevailing interpretation of their political theory is then possible. If the space devoted to the first problem seems dispropor-

[1] C. H. Firth (ed.), *The Clarke Papers*, vol. i (Camden Society Publications, N.S. 49, 1891), p. 299, n.: 'The supporters of the Agreement, as the debate shows, advocated manhood suffrage.' Cf. p. xlix: 'the first article [of the First *Agreement*] claimed manhood suffrage'.

[2] The leading statements generally cited are examined below, pp. 122–6, 129–36.

[3] S. R. Gardiner, *History of the Great Civil War 1642–1649*, vol. iii, 1891, p. 225. Gardiner also refers (op. cit., p. 215) to *The Case of the Army truly stated* as proposing manhood suffrage (except for delinquents). On this, see below, p. 130.

[4] In seventeenth-century usage servants meant wage-earners, anyone who worked for an employer for wages. See Appendix, pp. 282–3.

tionate, it is no more than is needed to clarify an unusual degree of confusion.

The facts have so often been imperfectly or incorrectly stated that it will be well to set out at once the explicit Leveller statements of the exclusion. In the famous debate (29 October 1647) on the franchise clause of the First *Agreement of the People* at Putney, Petty, a Leveller spokesman, in reply to a question from Cromwell, gave 'the reason why we would exclude apprentices, or servants, or those that take alms';[1] the fact that the Levellers *would* exclude them was taken for granted by both sides. Two subsequent Leveller statements about their position in the Putney debate may be noticed. *A Letter sent from several Agitators of the Army to their respective Regiments*, of 11 November 1647, reports that after long debate on the franchise proposal at Putney 'it was concluded by vote in the affirmative: *viz., That all soldiers and others, if they be not servants or beggars, ought to have voices in electing those which shall represent them in Parliament, although they have not forty shillings per annum in freehold land.* And there were but three voices against this your native freedom'.[2] The franchise excluding servants and beggars is claimed as a victory for 'native freedom'. John Harris, in *The Grand Designe* (8 December 1647), makes it clear that in the franchise clause of the *Agreement* the Levellers were demanding the franchise for 'all men that are not servants or Beggers'.[3]

The Leveller manifestoes of the next two years are even more explicit. The *Petition* of January 1648 demands the

---

[1] A. S. P. Woodhouse, *Puritanism and Liberty* (1938), p. 83. This is the first specific mention of the extent of the intended Leveller franchise in the debates. Its relation to other mentions of the franchise in the debates is examined below, pp. 122–9.

[2] Woodhouse, op. cit., p. 452. Whether this vote was in fact taken or whether it was only a propaganda claim, is irrelevant here. Doubt has been raised by D. M. Wolfe (*Leveller Manifestoes of the Puritan Revolution*, 1944, p. 61, n. 10) whether the vote, which he confusingly describes as a vote on manhood suffrage, did actually take place. The ground of his doubt is that Clarke did not report it in the record of that day's proceedings at Putney. But there is a confusion of dates. The vote alleged in the *Letter* was probably not on 30 Oct. (as Wolfe assumed) but on 4 Nov., which is one of the days of which Clarke has no record, so there need be no question of Clarke's deliberate omission of the vote from his record of the day's proceedings.

[3] B.M., E. 419 (15), fol. 7 verso.

franchise for all English men 'which are not, or shal not be legally disfranchised for some criminal cause, or are not under 21 years of age, or servants, or beggers'.[1] The Second *Agreement*, of 15 December 1648, narrows the franchise a little further: persons receiving alms, and servants or wage-earners, are again excluded, but so are all men who are not 'assessed ordinarily towards the relief of the poor'.[2] The Third *Agreement*, of 1 May 1649, reverts to the position of the *Petition* of January 1648, excluding only servants and those receiving alms.[3]

Thus in the Putney debate on the First *Agreement*, in the *Petition* of January 1648, and in the Second and Third *Agreements*, which appear to be all the authoritative Leveller documents throughout that period that state the extent of the proposed franchise,[4] the Leveller exclusion of servants and alms-takers is quite explicit.

Most authorities since Firth have either neglected this exclusion or, while noticing some instances of it, have continued to refer to the Levellers as advocates of manhood suffrage and have seen no problem of inconsistency.[5] It was, perhaps, these scholars' very familiarity with the Leveller idiom and assumptions that led them to see no such problem. They may have concluded both that the Levellers did identify manhood franchise with franchise excluding servants and beggars, and that the postulates that enabled the Levellers to do so were too obvious to require comment. But if that is what they meant, they have not said so. In any case, the result has been unfortunate.

Where no notice is taken of any Leveller exclusion, the student may easily infer that they did demand unqualified manhood suffrage, which was not the case. Where notice is taken of some instances of Leveller exclusion of servants and alms-takers, but no problem is seen, the student who is not

---

[1] Wolfe, *Leveller Manifestoes*, p. 269.

[2] Woodhouse, op. cit., p. 357; Wolfe, op. cit., p. 297.

[3] Wolfe, op. cit., p. 403. Both the Second and Third *Agreements* also exclude for some years those who had supported the king in the Civil Wars.

[4] See p. 118, n. 1.   [5] See Note F, pp. 294–5.

content to dismiss the whole matter as trivial is apt to conclude that the excluded classes were numerically insignificant, which was not the case. Or, if he accepts the implication that the Levellers did, without any thought of inconsistency, equate manhood franchise with franchise excluding servants and alms-takers, he is still left without any insight into the theoretical basis which allowed the Levellers to take that position.

Nor is the modern student much aided by those few scholars who, going beyond those cited above, have re-marked that there was, strictly speaking, some inconsistency in the Leveller position on the franchise, and have offered explanations, for their explanations are not entirely satisfy-ing.[1] Nor are matters much improved by the analyses of still other scholars who have remarked on the temporary change in the Leveller position in 1648 (embodied in the Second *Agreement*) but have wrongly identified the change as one *to* a ratepayer franchise (which it was) *from* a manhood franchise (which it was not).[2]

The student who consults the standard literature may be forgiven for thinking that some clarification of the Levellers' position on the franchise would be useful. Once the record is set straight, the problem of their consistency appears formid-able. But the very process of disentangling the record brings to light some postulates and concepts which suggest an underlying consistency in the Levellers' franchise ideas. These concepts and postulates, which have to do with the nature of freedom, in turn suggest a new interpretation of the Levellers' individualism, and hence of their contribution to the liberal, rather than the radical democratic tradition of English political thought. In short, the solution of the prob-lem of apparent inconsistency about the franchise leads, it will be argued, to a deeper understanding of the Levellers' whole political thought, and thereby throws some new light on the sources of the liberal-democratic tradition.

In what follows, the record is examined (in Section 3) in sufficient detail to establish the extent of the apparent

[1] See Note G, p. 295.   [2] See Note H, pp. 295–6.

inconsistency in the Leveller position on the franchise, and to dispose of the possibility that they might have changed their position from manhood franchise to a franchise excluding servants and alms-takers. It is argued that the Levellers always intended not a manhood franchise in the ordinary modern sense of the term, but a franchise excluding servants and alms-takers; and that they saw no inconsistency between this exclusion and their assertion of the natural right of every man to a vote, because of certain assumptions they made about the nature of freedom.

The examination of their statements about franchise and freedom is preceded (Section 2) by an attempt to clarify the differences between the various franchise proposals that were in dispute between the Levellers and the army leaders and parliamentary Independents. For unless we are clear about what classes were included and excluded in each of the four kinds of franchise that were apparently in dispute at the time (the freeholder property franchise, the ratepayer franchise, the non-servant franchise, and manhood franchise), and have some notion of their numerical extent, we shall not understand the intensity of the dispute between the freeholder and the non-servant positions, nor the degree of compromise involved in moving from either of those to the ratepayer franchise.

The quantitative estimates of the franchise classes are only incidental to our main argument, but since they may be of some value to the understanding of seventeenth-century thought, and since they may be thought to require some justification, they are set out in an Appendix.

Finally, in Section 4, the implications of the Leveller postulates about freedom are discussed more generally.

2. *Types of Franchise*

Four different franchises were actually or apparently under discussion by the Levellers and their parliamentary and army opponents. The four may be distinguished as follows:

(A) The franchise limited to owners of freehold land of a value of 40 shillings a year and freemen of trading corporations. This was the franchise consistently advocated by Cromwell and Ireton[1] and consistently attacked by the Levellers. I shall refer to it as the *freeholder franchise*. It excluded the copyhold and leasehold farmers. It excluded all the non-freehold artisans, tradesmen, and dealers who were not freemen of trading corporations. It excluded also all servants and those in receipt of alms.

This was the franchise that had been in force since the statute of 8 Henry VI, c. 7. The assertion that it excluded copyholders and leaseholders is open to two objections, which must be noticed here. First, as to copyholders, while it is certain that copyholders who held at the will of the lord were never regarded as freeholders, it is possible that another kind of copyholders, namely, those who held not at the will of the lord but according to the custom of the manor, and whose tenure was described as 'customary freehold' or 'free copyhold' or 'copyhold of frank tenure', were, in seventeenth-century law and electoral practice, regarded as freeholders. Coke[2] leaves the matter in doubt. Blackstone[3] argued, after the question had been raised in the Oxfordshire election of 1754, that they were not freeholders and had never been intended to have the vote, but whether they had ever in fact exercised the franchise is not known. It seems probable, however, that Cromwell was assuming that no copyholders had the vote under existing law. For he speaks of the possible admission of some 'copyholders by inheritance' as a change from the existing franchise.[4] Since he would consider admitting them only because their tenure was comparable in security to a freehold tenure, he must have been thinking of customary copyholders, not copyholder

---

[1] Except that at one point in the Putney debate Cromwell was prepared to admit some of the copyholders by inheritance (Woodhouse, op. cit., p. 73), and except for the qualified concession in the Committee on 30 Oct. 1647 (see below, Note **K**, p. 297) and the temporary concession of the Second *Agreement* (see below, pp. 115–17).

[2] Coke, *The Compleate Copyholder*, 1644, sects. 15–17.

[3] Blackstone, *Considerations on Copyholders*, 1758.   [4] Woodhouse, p. 73.

at will. It follows that he took the customary copyholders to be excluded from the existing franchise. I conclude that the freeholder franchise that was in dispute at Putney was assumed to exclude all copyholders.

Secondly, as to the exclusion of leasehold farmers, it must be noticed that there was no simple distinction in law between freeholders and leaseholders. Both were tenants. The distinction was in the determinateness of the tenure. Roughly, tenants for life or lives were freeholders; tenants for years, and tenants for years or lives, were not. More precisely, tenants whose leases were for a fixed period (e.g. five years, ninety-nine years, even a thousand years) and tenants whose leases were for a fixed maximum but indeterminate minimum period (e.g. leases for 'ninety-nine years or three lives', whichever was the less) were in law not freeholders, no matter how long the term of the lease. Those whose tenure of land was for an indeterminate period, and who held on free (i.e. not base or servile) tenure, were freeholders, whether the tenure was to a man and his heirs for ever, or for the term of his own life or for the term of another's life.[1] This had been the law ever since Bracton. I am assuming that this was the distinction in ordinary usage as well. The few references to leaseholders in the text of the Putney debates do no more than indicate that tenants for years were excluded.[2] In the absence of any more definite evidence in the text of the debates, we may assume that both sides in the debate were following the well-established legal distinction between freehold and non-freehold tenants. Our category 'leasehold farmers', understood as comprising leaseholders for years and for years or lives, is thus assumed

[1] G. Jacob, *A New Law-Dictionary*, 1750, s.v. 'Freehold'; Wm. Cruise, *A Digest of the Laws of England Respecting Real Property*, 4th ed. 1835, vol. i, pp. 47–48 (Title I, nos. 10–12).

[2] Cromwell says that 'an inhabitant upon a rack rent for a year, for two years, or twenty years' cannot be thought to have a fixed or permanent interest (Woodhouse, p. 62). Petty's incomplete sentence, 'A man may have a lease for one hundred pounds a year, a man may have a lease for three lives' (ibid., p. 61), does not clarify his position; if the sentence were completed as Woodhouse proposes, without any qualification, it would seem to be a misstatement of fact, for the tenant whose lease was for three lives had in law a freehold.

to be excluded from the freeholder franchise in dispute at Putney.

The freeholder franchise in the 1640's would comprise about 212,000 men.[1]

(B) The franchise for all male householders assessed ordinarily towards the relief of the poor, and excluding servants and alms-takers. This franchise, while on a different basis from the freeholder franchise, may be taken to have included virtually the whole of the freeholders and freemen of corporations, for it may be assumed that few of them would escape being assessed for the poor-rates. It would include also, for the same reason, the bulk of the copyhold and leasehold farmers. It would include, finally, some, probably most, of the traders, shopkeepers, tradesmen, and artisans who were neither freemen of corporations nor freeholders; of this whole group, only those who were so poor as not to be assessed for the poor-rates would be excluded. This was the franchise proposed in the Second *Agreement*. It was retained in the Officers' *Agreement* of 20 January, 1649.[2] I shall refer to this as the *ratepayer franchise*. It would comprise about 375,000 men.[3]

(C) The franchise for all men except servants and alms-takers. This was the franchise demanded by the Levellers in the Putney debate and in all their subsequent franchise proposals (except the Second *Agreement*) with minor variations.[4] I shall refer to it as the *non-servant franchise*. It would comprise about 417,000 men.[5]

It will be noticed that there was relatively little difference, either qualitative or quantitative, between the ratepayer franchise and the non-servant franchise. Both excluded the wage-earners and alms-takers. Both included the freeholders, freemen of corporations, copyholders, and other tenants, at least all of these who were not so poor as to

---

[1] See Appendix, esp. pp. 288, 291.   [2] Wolfe, op. cit., p. 342.   [3] See Appendix.
[4] e.g. at Putney apprentices were specifically bracketed with servants; in the *Petition* of Jan. 1648 criminals were excluded; those who had assisted the king in the Civil War were excluded for some years by the Second and Third *Agreements*.
[5] See Appendix.

escape assessment for the poor-rates. Only two categories are included in the non-servant and excluded from the ratepayer franchise. These are, first, the traders, shopkeepers, tradesmen, and artisans who were neither freeholders nor freemen of trading corporations and who were not ratepaying householders. I have estimated their number at about 19,000, assuming that only half of these independent men were non-ratepayers. But even if the proportion were much higher, the difference between the ratepayer franchise and the non-servant franchise would still not be nearly as great as that between the freeholder franchise and the ratepayer franchise.[1] The second category to be included in the non-servant and excluded from the ratepayer franchise is those soldiers in the parliamentary army whose civilian status had been wage-earners or alms-takers. The Levellers assumed that such men had earned their franchise by taking active part in the Civil War.[2] These are estimated to be about 22,000 men.[3] So the whole difference between the ratepayer franchise and the non-servant franchise is only about 41,000.

(D) The franchise for all men, or for all except criminals and delinquents. This may be properly described as *manhood franchise*, and is apparently demanded in various Leveller statements before and during the Putney debate. Manhood franchise would comprise about 1,170,000 men,[4] less any allowance for criminals and delinquents.

The Leveller position on the franchise may now be summarized in terms of these four franchise proposals. They were always opposed to the freeholder franchise. In some of their writings before Putney and some of their statements at Putney they appeared to be speaking for manhood franchise. At Putney and in all their proposals after Putney they stipulated the non-servant franchise, except for the Second *Agreement* which proposed the slightly narrower ratepayer franchise.

We can dispose at once of the complication of the Second

---

[1] See Appendix, pp. 289–90. The figure of 21,400 given there for this category is the figure before converting from 1688 to 1648 population; the conversion brings it to 19,300 (Appendix, p. 291).   [2] See Note K, p. 297.

[3] See Appendix, pp. 291–2.   [4] See Appendix.

Agreement. That document was a compromise drawn up by a committee representing the Levellers, the army leadership, the Independents, and a parliamentary group. It is, however, generally regarded as a Leveller document, since the Levellers were at that moment in the strong position of holding virtually a balance of power between the army leadership and parliament and so were able to carry most of their demands. The ratepayer franchise proposed in the Second *Agreement* was, as we have just seen, only slightly narrower than the non-servant franchise which the Levellers had been consistently advocating for more than a year previously. At most, the franchise of the Second *Agreement* would exclude, in comparison with the non-servant franchise, only two groups: the small independent men who escaped paying rates, and those former wage-earners who were in the army. These together amounted to some 41,000 men, less than one-tenth of the whole number included in the non-servant franchise. I say this number *at most* would be excluded. But the number understood by the Levellers to be excluded may well have been only the 19,000 independent non-ratepayers. For it is quite possible that the Levellers, in proposing or accepting the franchise clause of the Second *Agreement*, thought that the army leaders were implicitly including anyone who had fought for the parliamentary cause in the Civil War, since it had been agreed by the Army Council Committee at Putney on 30 October 1647, that those who had fought for parliament should have the franchise although they were 'not in other respects within the qualifications' that were still to be determined.[1] If this was the understanding in the Second *Agreement*, the proposed franchise of that document was very little smaller in numbers than, and could scarcely be said to involve any departure in principle from, the Levellers' previous non-servant franchise. Even if this was not the understanding in the Second *Agreement*, the franchise proposed in it was, in numbers at least, much less a compromise on the part of the

1 See Note K, p. 297.

Levellers than on the part of the army leadership. For the latter, it involved a very substantial compromise. It meant extending the franchise from 212,000 to 375,000 by letting in all the non-freehold farmers and most of the non-corporate tradesmen and dealers. For the army leadership, however, it was an expedient compromise which they probably never intended to adhere to; at any rate they soon shelved the whole *Agreement* by referring it to a parliament which they had purged. The franchise clause of the Second *Agreement* has been the subject of some confusion in modern treatments of the Levellers where it has been treated as an expedient compromise by the Levellers. If it was so at all, the analysis just made suggests it was so only to a slight extent. I shall therefore in the rest of the analysis disregard the difference between the ratepayer franchise of the Second *Agreement* and the non-servant franchise of all the other documents from Putney to the Third *Agreement*.

But while the difference between the ratepayer and non-servant franchises was slight, the difference between the non-servant and freeholder franchises was very substantial indeed. We need not wonder, therefore, that the controversy, from Putney on, between the Levellers' non-servant franchise and the army leaders' and Independents' freeholder franchise, was strenuous. If our estimates are at all trustworthy, the Levellers were demanding a franchise almost twice the size of the freeholder franchise.

The intensity of the franchise dispute between Levellers and their opponents, then, is quite explicable when the Leveller demand is taken never to have been more extensive than the non-servant franchise. But we have still to examine the inconsistency between their apparent manhood franchise statements and their non-servant franchise demands.

3. *The Record*

i. *The chronology*

Since the problem is one of apparently inconsistent statements, we have first to examine whether the Levellers ever changed their position from advocacy of manhood franchise to advocacy of the non-servant franchise. If that were so, it might sufficiently explain the inconsistencies. It must be noticed that the question here is of a change from full manhood franchise to a non-servant franchise, and that this is an entirely different matter from the temporary and relatively insignificant change from the non-servant franchise to the ratepayer franchise which has just been discussed.

If we were to look only at the chronology of the Leveller statements on the franchise we might think that there had been a change from manhood to non-servant franchise. For all[1] of the Levellers' unqualified, or apparently unqualified, assertions of the right of every inhabitant, or of every man born in England, to have a vote, occur before or during the Putney debate, and in all the (rather few) references to the franchise before Putney no explicit exclusion of servants or alms-takers is stated. *Per contra*, all the statements which explicitly exclude servants and alms-takers occur during or after the Putney debate, and all the specific franchise demands after Putney do contain that exclusion.[2] From the chronology alone, then, it might appear that the Levellers had changed their position on the franchise during the course of the Putney debate, that they had receded from an

---

[1] 'All', in this paragraph, means all that are to be found in what might be called the standard Leveller documents; namely, those printed in Woodhouse, in Wolfe, in Haller and Davies, *The Leveller Tracts 1647–1653* (1944), and in Haller, *Tracts on Liberty in the Puritan Revolution 1638–1647* (1934), and, in addition, those cited or quoted with reference to the franchise by any of the authorities mentioned in Notes F, G, and H.

[2] In the dying days of the Leveller movement one proposal, for an extraordinary general election, did include servants. *A Charge of High Treason exhibited against Oliver Cromwell, Esq., for several Treasons by him committed*, of Sept. (or August) 14, 1653 (B.M., 669. f. 17 (52), and in part in *Somers Tracts*, VI, 302) proposed a spontaneous election: 'it is desired, that upon the 16th of October 1653 . . . all the people of *England* would as one man, as well Masters, Sons, as Servants, repair unto every County-Town, or some other convenient place within *England*, and *Wales*, and appear Armed with such weapons of war as with conveniencie they can, then and there to Elect, and Chuse such and so many persons as the people of the respective Counties, Cities, and Boroughs wont to chuse for to represent them in Parliament.' This handbill, a last desperate throw, is the only Leveller piece of any kind I have found which proposes admitting servants; its intemperateness is quite unlike the measured franchise proposals in the official Levellers manifestoes.

earlier manhood suffrage position when faced with the
powerful opposition of Cromwell and Ireton, who wanted
the traditional freeholder property qualification. It is plausible that the Levellers might, even though unconvinced by
the opposition arguments, have relinquished their previous
stand in the hope of saving something. Nevertheless, the
evidence does not support such a view.

In examining the record we shall start with the Putney
debates, for it is here that the extent of the proposed franchise
is first made explicit. It is in the Putney debates also, and in
some of the post-Putney documents referring to the debates,
that we find both the non-servant franchise and, apparently,
the manhood franchise being advocated sometimes simultaneously. Since none of the pre-Putney mentions of the
franchise are at all specific, one can only proceed by putting
a construction on the evidence of the debate (and of later
documents), and then considering the earlier statements in
the light of that construction.

It may be said at once, however, that the fact that none
of the pre-Putney documents states a specific exclusion is
not very significant, for the Levellers were in that period
too much concerned with other matters to give much attention to the franchise, let alone to formulate a position on it.
Before the Putney debate there are few references of any
kind to the extent of the franchise; it is scarcely discussed,
and never clearly defined, in the Leveller manifestoes down
to and including the First *Agreement* (20/28 October 1647).[1]
It was only during the Putney debates that the franchise
became a pre-eminent issue. This is readily understandable.
For only at Putney had the Levellers attained a strong
enough position, in relation to the army leaders and various
parliamentary groups, both to think as far ahead as the
question of the extent of the franchise, and to make an issue
of it. Before that, the Levellers were fully occupied with
matters still more important: struggle against the arbitrary

[1] The First *Agreement* was written before 28 Oct., when it was first mentioned in
the General Council of the Army, and probably after 20 Oct. See Wolfe, p. 224.

proceedings of parliament and its committees, which violated the civil liberties established by the Petition of Right and the common law; struggle for religious toleration, against a Presbyterian parliament; insistence that parliament must be made responsible to the people, by annual elections without the necessity of writs, and by redistribution of seats; demands for constitutional guarantees against the Commons' tyranny and for the abolition of the negative voice of king and Lords; denunciation of the continuing oppression of tithes, monopolies, unequal taxation, imprisonment for debt, and exorbitant legal fees and delays.

From the beginning of the Leveller movement through most of the year 1647, these matters had priority, and most of them remained important even after the franchise issue was added to them. The first, and continuing, concern of the Levellers was to win recognition for two principles: that parliament's power was a trust from the people, and that even that power should not be used to abridge certain civil, economic, and religious liberties of the individual. Only by Putney was it important as well to establish a definition of 'the people'. So it cannot be said that the absence of specific exclusions in the pre-Putney references to the right to vote, which were general and imprecise, gives any indication of the extent of franchise the Levellers may then have had in mind.

ii. *Putney and after*

It is necessary first, in assessing the Putney debate, to try to make clear what the franchise issue was. It is often misread as a clear issue between a property franchise and manhood franchise. Cromwell and Ireton clearly were advocating a property franchise, i.e. one confined to owners of freehold land and freemen of corporations (which we refer to as the freeholder franchise). The Levellers opposed any property qualification, and opposed it strenuously. But it cannot be inferred from this that the Levellers were demanding the franchise for all non-property-owners, including servants and alms-takers. All that can be inferred is that the Levellers were demanding that the franchise be extended to a substantial class of men who would be excluded by Ireton and Cromwell.

That there was a substantial class of such men we have already seen: the copyholders and tenant farmers, and those independent craftsmen, dealers, and traders who neither had freehold land nor were members of trading corporations. Many of these entrepreneurs operated on a small scale.[1] No one doubts that it was their burdens, or rather, the burdens they shared with the yeomen freeholders, that the Leveller programme was designed to remove. Excise and customs, tithes, conscription, the insolence of office, the law's delays and privileges, and all the rest that the Leveller manifestoes inveighed against, fell heavily upon these men. *Prima facie*, when it came to the matter of the franchise, the Levellers would be their spokesmen.[2]

Without pre-judging the Leveller position on servants and alms-takers we may notice that the small independent enterprisers were, in the Levellers' eyes, in a wholly different class from servants and alms-takers. Assertion of the rights of the former in no way necessarily involved an assertion of the rights of the latter. Cromwell and Ireton, indeed, paid little attention to the difference; during most of the debate they impatiently lumped the two classes together, for in their view the all-important distinction was between freeholders (including freemen of corporations) and all the non-freeholders. Much of the confusion in interpreting the position of the two sides in the debate has been due to neglecting this difference of viewpoint.[3]

The debate on the franchise was opened[4] by Ireton immediately after the reading of the first article of the

[1] e.g. Baxter's 'poor husbandmen' (Unwin, *Studies in Economic History*, p. 347).

[2] The Levellers' close affiliation with this class is generally recognized, but we may notice particularly how frequently they speak in the Putney debate for those who had lost their previous freehold because of their service in the army; e.g. Rainborough, pp. 56, 67, 71, and Sexby, pp. 69, 74, in Woodhouse, op. cit.

[3] See below, pp. 126–8.

[4] 29 Oct. 1647. Text in Woodhouse, op. cit., pp. 52 ff.

Leveller (First) *Agreement*. That article was not precise: it declared that the people of England, for the election of their deputies in parliament, 'ought to be more indifferently proportioned [as between counties, cities and boroughs], according to the number of the inhabitants'.[1] Ireton began by demanding to know whether this was meant to give the vote only to those who had formerly had it, that is, those who had the property qualification, or whether it meant that every inhabitant was to have an equal voice in the election; if it meant the latter, he would have something to say against it. The issue as stated by Ireton was property franchise *v.* (apparently) universal suffrage.

But this was not precisely the issue which the Levellers took up. The immediate Leveller reply was made by Petty: 'We judge that all inhabitants that have not lost their birthright should have an equal voice in elections.'[2] Thus in the very first Leveller statement on the franchise during the debates, one category of inhabitants was excluded. The question is, what was meant by those who had 'lost their birthright'? If this meant only criminals and delinquents,[3] we should perhaps be justified, by common usage, in referring to the franchise as manhood franchise. But the only consistent construction of the debate as a whole suggests that the Levellers (and their opponents) assumed that servants and alms-takers, as well as criminals and delinquents, had lost their birthright.

For when the debate next came down to particulars— and it did not do so until after a protracted argument on the fundamental, but general, issue of freeholder franchise *v.* some broader franchise—it appears that the Levellers had been assuming the exclusion of 'servants' all along, and that this was understood by the Levellers' opponents as well. The passage is worth attention:

---

[1] Woodhouse, pp. 443–4; Wolfe, p. 226.   [2] Woodhouse, p. 53.

[3] 'Delinquents' was generally used to mean those who had supported the king in the Civil War; occasionally the term was used more broadly, as when the anti-Leveller *Declaration of Some Proceedings* uses it to refer to 'seditious incendiaries', i.e. in this case the Levellers (Haller and Davies, *The Leveller Tracts 1647–1653*, 1944, p. 121).

Cromwell: If we should go about to alter these things, I do not think that we are bound to fight for every particular proposition. Servants, while servants, are not included. Then you agree that he that receives alms is to be excluded?

Lt.-Col. (Thomas) Reade: I suppose it's concluded by all, that the choosing of representatives is a privilege; now I see no reason why any man that is a native ought to be excluded that privilege, unless from voluntary servitude.

Petty: I conceive the reason why we would exclude apprentices, or servants, or those that take alms, is because they depend upon the will of other men and should be afraid to displease (them). For servants and apprentices, they are included in their masters, and so for those that receive alms from door to door. . . .[1]

It is to be noticed that Cromwell started here from what he took to be an agreed point, that servants were not included in the proposed Leveller franchise, and went on to ask the Leveller position on alms-takers. Reade, who was not a Leveller,[2] though his position here is somewhat to the left of Cromwell's, assumes that voluntary servitude is ground for exclusion from franchise. Petty, the Leveller, far from rejecting either the exclusion of servants or the ground offered for it, states the Levellers' reasons for that exclusion and also for the exclusion of alms-takers. Both are excluded because they depend on the will of others, and are 'included in their masters'.

Can we properly infer that the servants and alms-takers who are now specifically mentioned as excluded on the ground that they are not free, are the categories that the same Leveller spokesman, Petty, had initially mentioned as excluded, namely those who had 'lost their birthright'? To sustain this inference we must show that the Levellers did think of the birthright to a voice in elections as something that could be lost or forfeited, and forfeited by becoming a servant or dependent on alms. The evidence on this is clear.

In the first place, there is ample evidence, apart from Petty's statement just quoted, that in the Levellers' minds

[1] Woodhouse, pp. 82–83.
[2] Firth and Davies, *Regimental History of Cromwell's Army*, 1940, pp. 563–5.

the birthright or native freedom of freeborn men could be
forfeited. Delinquency was frequently asserted to be an
offence depriving men of their birthright.[1] Secondly, and
more specifically, that the Levellers assumed that the birthright to a voice in elections was forfeited by servants and
beggars is clearly indicated in the franchise clause (section
11) of the *Petition* of January 1648:

> Whereas it hath been the Ancient Liberty of this Nation, that all
> the Free-born people have freely elected their Representers in Parlia-
> ment, and their Sheriffs and Iustices of the Peace, &c. and that they
> were abridged of that their native Liberty, by a Statute of the 8.H.6.7.
> That therefore, that Birth-right of all English men, be forthwith re-
> stored to all which are not, or shal not be legally disfranchised for some
> criminal cause, or are not under 21 years of age, or servants, or
> beggers. . . .[2]

Here the Levellers equate the right of 'all the Free-born
people' with the 'birthright of all English men', and see
nothing incongruous in denying it to servants and beggars,
any more than to minors and criminals. The birthright, we
may presume, was not only forfeitable for acts against society,
but was also forfeited, or not even entered upon, by those
whose age or whose status as servants or beggars was deemed
inconsistent with the free exercise of rational will. In any case,
there could scarcely be a clearer indication that the Levellers
assumed that those who became servants or beggars thereby
forfeited their birthright to a voice in elections.

It may properly be inferred, then, that the first Leveller
statement about the franchise in the debate, excluding those
who had 'lost their birthright', was intended to exclude servants and beggars from the franchise. Presumably this is
what Cromwell took the Levellers' meaning to be when he
brought the argument down to particulars in the passage
quoted above.[3] Certainly it is what the Leveller John Harris
took the franchise clause of the First *Agreement* to mean. In
his pamphlet *The Grand Designe*, December 1647, he quotes

---

[1] e.g. *Case of the Army truly stated* (15 Oct. 1647), in Wolfe, op. cit., p. 212.
[2] Ibid., p. 269.   [3] Woodhouse, p. 82.

the first article of the *Agreement* and explains that its demand is that

> from henceforth their might be persons chosen for Representatives for every County, proportio[n]able to the number of Inhabitants in each County, and that not by freeholdolders (*sic*) only, but by the voluntary assent of all men that are not servants or Beggers, it being pure equity, that as all persons are bound to yeild obedience to the decrees of the Representative or Parliament, so they should have a voyce in the electing their Representatives, or Members of Parliament.[1]

Whatever may be thought of this as a statement of the Levellers' meaning in October, it must be given some weight as another indication that there was no difference in the Leveller mind, in the context of the franchise, between all persons and all men who were not servants or beggars.

It may be added that in the franchise clause of the Third *Agreement* 'natural right' was given as the ground for demanding the franchise excluding servants and beggars: 'in the choice of [Representatives] (according to naturall right) all men of the age of one and twenty yeers and upwards (not being servants, or receiving alms, or having served the late King in Arms or voluntary Contributions) shall have their voices'.[2]

If it is allowed that the Levellers assumed the exclusion of servants and beggars to be understood from the beginning of the franchise debate, how are we to understand the dozen or so passages from then until the explicit mention of the exclusion[3] in which either the Leveller spokesman apparently demanded unqualified manhood franchise, or the opposition seemed to attribute that demand to the Levellers without contradiction?

There is no great difficulty in this when we recall the terms in which the debate was being conducted. The wholly unqualified phrases used by Levellers, 'every inhabitant',

---

[1] *The Grand Designe* by Sirrahniho (John Harris), 1647, fol. 7, r. and v. The Thomason date is 8 Dec. (B.M., E. 419 (15)). Wolfe cites this (*Leveller Manifestoes*, p. 65), but does not quote it or notice its significance.

[2] Wolfe, op. cit., pp. 402–3.

[3] i.e. between p. 52 and p. 82 of the text in Woodhouse.

'every person in England',[1] may quite as well have been understood to exclude servants as they undoubtedly were understood to exclude women.[2] The other broad terms used by Levellers range from Rainborough's 'the poorest man in England' and 'every man born in England', and Rainborough's and Audley's 'free-born men', to Rainborough's and Clarke's 'every man'.[3] In their contexts, these terms may equally be assumed to have been understood as 'all free-born men who have not lost their birthright'. Only in that sense, indeed, are those terms consistent with the clear earlier and later exclusion of those who had lost their birthright or were in dependence on the will of others. Thus all the Leveller assertions in the debate, however apparently unqualified, may be assumed to have been understood to have excluded servants.

What of the opposition statements? They present even less difficulty. Ireton kept insisting that the question was whether the franchise should be given only to freeholders (those who have a fixed and permanent interest) or to 'all persons', 'any man that hath a breath and being', 'all inhabitants'.[4] Cromwell, arguing that the Leveller franchise proposals 'must end in anarchy', refers to 'men that have no interest but the interest of breathing'.[5] The opposition, in these passages, seems to impute to the Levellers the position of asking for manhood franchise. It is equally possible that these phrases are hyperbole, induced by Ireton's and Cromwell's desire to sharpen the issue as they saw it. For we find that even after Cromwell had explicitly recognized that the Levellers' proposal excluded servants and alms-takers, he still spoke of it as tending to anarchy because it would give a vote to 'all those who are in the kingdom'.[6] This might have been deliberate misrepresentation, but it is more likely to have been the result of Cromwell's being carried away,

---

[1] Petty, on p. 61; Wildman, on p. 66.   [2] See Note I, p. 296.
[3] Woodhouse, pp. 53, 56 (cf. 55), 67, 81, 53, 80.
[4] Ibid., pp. 57, 70, 63 (cf. 72), 77.   [5] Ibid., p. 59.
[6] Ibid., p. 454. This is Cromwell's only subsequent recorded reference to the Leveller franchise in the Putney debates.

here as earlier, by the urgency of his own view that anything wider than freeholder franchise would be ruinous.

We cannot tell whether these phrases as used by Cromwell and Ireton in the earlier part of the Putney debate were hyperbole or not, nor whether they were so taken by the succeeding Leveller spokesmen. The latter, if they did see any imputation of manhood franchise, did not trouble to contradict it. But there was no reason why they should do so. They were more concerned to refute the much more dangerous charge, which was the crucial point that Cromwell and Ireton were pressing in these passages, namely, that to extend the franchise at all beyond the freeholders and freemen of corporations would necessarily destroy all property right.

The Leveller replies sought in various ways to disprove this (with no success). It would not have helped their case at all to have pointed out here (as they did shortly afterwards) that they were not proposing to give the vote to servants and beggars; what they had to answer was Ireton's argument[1] that the principle of natural right by which the Levellers could justify any franchise wider than the freeholder one, would necessarily destroy all property right. The Leveller replies were (a) that the right to property was established by divine law (Rainborough), or by natural law (Clarke), and (b) that to give 'every Englishman' a vote was, on the contrary, 'the only means to preserve all property', since 'every man is naturally free' and all must therefore have 'agreed to come into some form of government that they might preserve property' (Petty).[2] Petty must be presumed to have excluded here, as he had done earlier and was to do later in the debate, those who had 'lost their birthright'[3] or had come to 'depend upon the will of other men';[4] they were no longer free and would have no necessary interest in preserving property; but there was no reason for Petty to have made this explicit.

---

[1] Ibid., pp. 53–55, 57–58, 62–63.
[2] Ibid., Rainborough at p. 59, Clarke at pp. 75, 80, Petty at pp. 61–62.
[3] Ibid., p. 53. [4] Ibid., p. 83.

In only one place does an opponent refer specifically to a supposed Leveller intention to include servants; and then he is contradicted. Colonel Rich shows the dire consequences to be expected 'if the master and servant shall be equal electors:'[1] 'the poor' might, as in Rome, set up a dictator. Rainborough rejects this 'fine gilded pill', says he would prefer to retain the present property qualification rather than risk that 'the poor' should out-vote 'the people', and tries to direct the argument back to the question why a distinction should be made between some freeborn Englishmen and others.[2] This is a fairly clear[3] rejection of Rich's imputation that the Levellers would include servants, and an insistence that the argument be brought back to the question of franchise for freeborn men (which in the context may be taken as non-servants) v. property franchise.

The evidence so far reviewed suggests that, in the whole course of the debate prior to the explicit statement that servants and alms-takers were excluded, neither the Levellers' unqualified statements nor their opponents' general unqualified imputations were intended or were taken to include servants and alms-takers. Rather it appears that the Levellers had been assuming all along that only 'free' men, men whose living was not directly dependent on the will of others, were entitled to the franchise. In this assumption they were at one with Cromwell and Ireton. The Levellers had no quarrel with Ireton's principle: 'If there be anything at all that is a foundation of liberty it is this, that those who shall choose the law-makers shall be men freed from dependence upon others.'[4] Where they differed was in their beliefs as to the minimum basis of such non-dependence. Cromwell and Ireton were very clear on this. The freeholder and the freeman of a trading corporation has a permanent interest 'upon which he may live, and live a freeman without dependence'.[5] Each of them is therefore entitled to the franchise. But the

---

[1] Woodhouse, p. 63. [2] Ibid., p. 64.
[3] The text is not entirely clear, but it is difficult to see what other construction could be put on it.
[4] Ibid., p. 82. [5] Ibid., p. 58; cf. p. 62.

tenant on rack rent, for one, two, or twenty years, has no such interest upon which he may live as a freeman.[1] Neither has the copyhold tenant, though at one point in the debate Cromwell allowed that 'perhaps there are a very considerable part of copyholders by inheritance that ought to have a voice'.[2] Further than that Cromwell and Ireton will not go: even when he is most conciliatory, Ireton insists on preserving 'the equitable part of that constitution' giving a voice only to those 'who are like to be free men, men not given up to the wills of others'.[3]

In short, Cromwell and Ireton held that only freeholders and freemen of corporations, and possibly those whose property was of an almost indistinguishable sort, such as some of the copyholders by inheritance, had the property basis upon which they could live as free men without dependence. The Levellers thought that all men except servants and alms-takers were free men. For both Levellers and army leaders franchise was properly dependent on freedom, and freedom meant individual economic independence. But the two groups, with different class roots, had different views of the property basis of economic independence.

We may say, then, that throughout the Putney debates, as in the post-Putney documents, the Levellers were demanding the franchise for all freeborn men who had not lost their birthright, that is, for all men except those who had become servants or alms-takers. There was no inconsistency between their limited franchise demand and their assertion of equal natural rights: the equal natural right was forfeited when a man was in one of those relations of dependence on the will of others.

iii. *Before Putney*

When we turn to the few Leveller mentions of the franchise before Putney we find nothing in conflict with our interpretation of the Leveller position at Putney. The

---

[1] Ibid., pp. 62–63.   [2] Ibid., p. 73.   [3] Ibid., p. 78.

pre-Putney mentions of the franchise were, as I have said, generally less precise than the statements at Putney and later, and most scholars have recognized that their meaning can only be made out by inference. An examination of all the pre-Putney writings which have been taken by some modern scholars as being Leveller claims for manhood franchise, shows, I shall argue, that they are much more probably only claims for the non-servant franchise.

We may notice first *The Case of the Army truly stated*[1] (15 October 1647), which does specifically include a franchise clause in its programme. That clause has often been taken as a demand for manhood suffrage. But the demand was 'that all the freeborn at the age of 21 yeares and upwards, be the electors, excepting those that have or shall deprive themselves of that their freedome, either for some yeares, or wholly by delinquency'.[2] In view of what we have just seen of the Levellers' assumption that servants and alms-takers, while such, have deprived themselves of their native freedom, it is not improbable that it was servants and alms-takers whom they had in mind here, in their reference to 'those that have or shall deprive themselves of that their freedom ... for some years'. Apprentices, indeed, fit this definition more closely than any other group. But as they were mainly under 21, and so excluded by the age clause, the 'freedom for some years' clause can scarcely have been intended for them. The harsh tone of *The Case of the Army* towards delinquents is consistent with the implication of this reading, namely, that the Levellers at this time regarded delinquency as a permanent disqualification. The inference that the Levellers had servants and alms-takers in mind in *The Case of the Army* is strengthened by the fact that it was one of the documents debated at Putney, where, as we have seen, the Levellers assumed the exclusion of those groups from the

---

[1] Printed in Haller and Davies, pp. 64–87; Wolfe, pp. 196–212; and in part in Woodhouse, pp. 429–36.

[2] Haller and Davies, p. 78; Wolfe, p. 212. Woodhouse's version, with modernized spelling and punctuation, reads 'either for some years or wholly, by delinquency' (p. 433).

franchise on the same grounds.[1] The inference is not certain, but it is sufficiently probable to cast considerable doubt on the more usual interpretation of *The Case of the Army*.

Of the other pre-Putney Leveller writings very few, as we have already noticed, were concerned at all with the franchise. Lilburne's *Englands Birth-Right Justified* (October 1645) addressed 'to all the Free-borne People of England' is more concerned with the frequency of elections than with the extent of the franchise, but one passage is sometimes cited as being a demand for manhood franchise: 'ought not the Free-men of *England*, who have laboured in these destroying times, both to preserve the Parliament, and their owne native Freedoms and Birth-rights, not only to chuse new Members, where they are wanting once every yeere, but also to renue and inquire once a yeere, after the behaviour and carriage of those they have chosen'.[2] The claim made here is on behalf of 'the freemen of England', which can scarcely be taken to include servants or others who have deprived themselves of their 'native freedoms and birth-rights'.

The *Remonstrance of Many Thousand Citizens, and other Free-born People of England* (7 July 1646), although it has been taken as suggesting a belief in the right of all Englishmen to a voice in choosing their representatives,[3] suggests if anything the opposite. It requests that the Commons order a meeting for choosing parliament-men 'to be expresly upon one certaine day in *November* yeerly throughout the Land in the Places accustomed, and to be by you expressed, there to make choice of whom they think good, according to *Law*, and all men that have a Right to be there, not to faile upon

---

[1] It might also be mentioned that the Levellers regarded the First *Agreement* as a restatement of the principles set out in *The Case of the Army*. The postscript of the *Agreement* refers to it as 'extracting some principles of common freedome, out of those many things proposed to you in the Case truly stated, and drawing them up into the forme of an Agreement' (Wolfe, p. 233).

[2] p. 33, in Haller, *Tracts on Liberty in the Puritan Revolution*, vol. iii, p. 291. Cited by Gibb, *John Lilburne, the Leveller*, p. 139, and Frank, *The Levellers*, p. 63, n. 46.

[3] Frank, *The Levellers*, p. 82.

a great penaltie but no summons to be expected'.[1] The proposal is for compulsory voting by 'all men that have a Right', not for all men to be given the right to vote.

Lilburne's *Londons Liberty in Chains discovered* (October 1646) shows some direct concern with the franchise. Dealing first with the government of the city of London, Lilburne argues that the governments of all free cities should, by natural right and by original constitution, be elected by 'the free people of each city' or by every 'free citizen and Baron'.[2] The claim so far is only for restoration of the franchise to the freemen of the corporation, which had been virtually abolished in some of the recent elections of lord mayors. This claim, of course, falls far short of manhood franchise. Later in the pamphlet Lilburne returns to the virtual disfranchisement of the poorer freemen of London, arguing that they should not pay any taxes (but leave the aldermen and livery men to bear the whole of the charges laid upon the city) 'till you be actually put in possession, and injoy your equall share in the lawes, liberties, and freedoms thereof; as by the law of nature, reason, God and the land, yea, and your own antient and originall Charters, the meanest of you ought to do, as fully and largely in every particular, as the greatest of them'.[3] The claim is still for the franchise only for freemen of the city, for the meanest as well as the greatest of the freemen.

Lilburne goes on to attack the existing parliamentary franchise in the counties as well as the boroughs. He complains of (*a*) rotten boroughs, (*b*) the disfranchising of 'thousands of people, that by name are free-men of *England*, and divers of them men of great estates in money and stock; which also also [*sic*] are disfranchised, and *undenezed*, by the fore-mentioned *unrighteous Statute* [8 Henry VI, c. 7]; because they have not in land 40s. *per annum*', and (*c*) the disproportion of seats to counties. As remedy, he suggests that

[1] Wolfe, p. 129; Haller, *Tracts*, iii. 370.
[2] *Londons Liberty*, pp. 2, 11. Cf. Gibb, *John Lilburne*, pp. 158–9.
[3] *Londons Liberty*, pp. 52–53, quoted in Frank, *The Levellers*, pp. 93–94.

the number of seats should be fixed at, say, 500 or 600; that the seats should be distributed among counties in proportion to each county's rated assessment 'towards the defraying of the Publique charge of the Kingdome';

and then each County equally and proportionable by the common consent of the People thereof to divide it selfe into *Divisions*, *Hundreds*, or *Wapentakes*, and every Division of and within themselves, *to chuse one or more Commissioners to sit in Parliament*, suitable to the proportion that comes to their share: which would put an end and period to all those inconveniences that rarely happen, which are mentioned in the foresaid Statute of 8.H.6,7 and restore every free-man of *England*, to his *native*, and legall rights and freedomes. . . .[1]

This can scarcely be considered a claim for manhood franchise. It is a proposal to do away with the 40 shilling freehold qualification, so as to enfranchise the 'thousands of people that by name are free-men of England'. There is no reason to think that this included those who had lost their freedom by being servants; it is entirely understandable as a plea for the tenant farmers and the non-corporate traders and craftsmen. No inference about the desired breadth of the franchise can be drawn from the fact that the proposed re-distribution of seats among counties is in proportion to the rates rather than to population.[2]

Two months later Lilburne produced *The Charters of London; or, The Second Part of Londons Liberty in Chaines discovered* (18 December 1646). Addressed to the citizens of London, it was designed to prove 'that the Lord Major is no legall Lord Major'. His *'third reason to prove the proposition is this*; because the only and sole legislative Law-making power, *is originally inherent in the people, and derivatively in their Commissions chosen by themselves by common consent, and no other*. In which the poorest that lives, hath as true a right to give a vote, as well as the richest and greatest. . . .'[3] In

---

[1] *Londons Liberty*, p. 54. This is cited by Frank, *The Levellers* (Cambridge, Mass., 1955), p. 94, as a demand for the free and equal franchise for all men.

[2] See Note J, pp. 296–7.

[3] *Charters of London*, pp. 3–4. Quoted in part by Wolfe, p. 14, as a justification of manhood franchise.

judging how wide a franchise was here being justified, we may set aside any inference from the context alone. It is true that the argument was addressed to the citizens of London, and was designed to show that only the councillors elected by the citizens had any legislative authority; nevertheless, the principle that the people, equally the poorest as the richest, have the right to elect, is stated with complete generality.

It is not surprising, then, that this passage has been taken as asserting the principle of manhood franchise. Yet it cannot easily be so accepted, in view of the position we have seen the Levellers to have taken in the Putney debate. There, statements of principle just as broad as this (Rainborough's 'the poorest he' and 'the poorest man in England' for instance) were being made with the implicit proviso that servants and beggars, being unfree, were excluded from the franchise. The probable inference is that here, as in the Putney debate, 'the poorest that lives' meant the poorest free man.

We must emphasize that poverty was not identical with unfreedom. The Levellers were indeed opposed to any exclusion from the franchise because of poverty. There were in fact in England plenty of poor husbandmen (some, according to Baxter's famous statement,[1] poorer than their own servants), and plenty of poor independent craftsmen and traders. For all of these the Levellers demanded the franchise. But such men, though not freeholders or freemen of corporations, were free in the Levellers' sense: they were not dependent on the will of employers or of dispensers of poor relief. The line the Levellers drew was not between poverty and wealth, but between dependence and independence, and the two lines did not coincide.

In *Rash Oaths Unwarrantable* (31 May 1647) Lilburne took up again the argument about parliamentary franchise. He repeats almost verbatim the franchise argument of

---

[1] Richard Baxter, *The Poor Husbandman's Advocate to Rich Racking Landlords*, ed. F. J. Powicke, 1926.

Londons Liberty (to which he refers the reader), rephrasing the essential part (as we quoted it above) as follows:

and then each County equally and proportionably, by the common consent of the people thereof, to divide it selfe into Divisions, Hundreds, or Weapontacks, that so all the people (without confusion or tumult) *may meet together in their severall divisions, and every free man of England,* as well poore as rich, whose life, estate, &c. is to be taken away by law, *may have a Vote in chusing those that are to make the law, it being a maxim in nature, that no man justly can be bound without his own consent. . . .*[1]

This can no more be considered an endorsement of a manhood franchise principle than can the version in *Londons Liberty*. Here it is specifically only the 'free men of England' who are entitled to vote; the poor as well as the rich, but only the free. As to the 'maxim of nature' that no man can justly be bound without his own consent, that does not apply in Leveller thinking to those who enter voluntary servitude, for they have thereby consented to be 'included in their masters'.[2]

Finally, in *Ionah's Cry out of the Whales belly* (16 July 1647), Lilburne produces an argument that might be taken as an assertion of the manhood suffrage principle. Appealing to the soldiers over the heads of their leaders, he argues that the army, having defied parliament, is no longer a constituted body but is 'dissolved into the originall law of Nature'. The soldiers consequently are now justified in acting

according to the principles of Safety, flowing from Nature, Reason and Justice, agreed on by common consent and mutual agreement amongst themselves; in which every individuall private souldier, whether, Horse or Foot, ought freely to have their vote, to chuse the transactors of their affaires, or else in the sight of God, and all rational men, are discharged from obeying, stooping, or submitting to what is done by them.[3]

This assertion of the right of every soldier to a vote is not,

---

[1] *Rash Oaths*, p. 50; quoted in part by Frank, *The Levellers*, p. 123.

[2] See also Note L, pp. 297–8.

[3] *Ionah's Cry*, p. 13. This is paraphrased by Wolfe, p. 33, in such a way as to make it apply to every man rather than to every soldier.

of course, an assertion of a manhood franchise principle, for in the Levellers' eyes the soldiers, who had fought for England's freedom, were as such free men.[1] Civilians in a dependent status would not be touched by the principle here asserted.

iv. *Summing-up*

The foregoing examination of the record, covering the Leveller mentions of and statements about the franchise from Lilburne's earliest pamphlets through to the final manifesto of the Leveller movement has, it is submitted, established the following. It has established as facts (a) that the Levellers, from the first specific mention of the extent of the franchise in the Putney debate to the final manifesto, explicitly excluded servants and alms-takers from the franchise; (b) that, during the same period, they based their demand for that franchise on grounds of birthright or equal natural right of every Englishman; and (c) that, at least from the close of the Putney debate, they assumed that the birthright to a voice in elections was not entered into, or was forfeited, by servants and alms-takers.

It has shown by inference (d) that it was because the Levellers made this assumption that they saw no inconsistency between their explicit exclusion of servants and alms-takers from the franchise, and their assertion of equal natural rights. It has further shown by inference (e) that forfeiture of birthright by servants and alms-takers had probably been continuously assumed by the Levellers during and before the Putney debate; (f) that their demands, during and before Putney, for apparently unqualified manhood franchise were probably intended to be qualified by that assumption; and (g) that because of that assumption their position was in their own minds probably just as consistent during and before Putney as it undoubtedly was after Putney.

[1] See Note K, p. 297.

4. *Theoretical Implications*

i. *The property in one's person*

It remains to examine the fundamental quality of the Levellers' individualism. Their postulate of equal natural rights and their ideas of freedom, which we have seen so far only in the context of the franchise, were based ultimately on a concept of the nature of man and society which we must try to elucidate. We can best approach it by way of their concept of property.

We may start by giving further attention to a matter we have so far noticed only incidentally: namely that while the Levellers were consistently opposed to property qualifications for the franchise, at the same time they vigorously asserted an individual right to property. Their opposition to property qualifications for the franchise was based, of course, on their assertion that every free-born man has an equal natural right to live his own life. It was quite evident to them that a parliament elected by a fixed-property franchise could not be trusted to treat those who owned no fixed property with equal consideration.

Yet the Levellers were no opponents of property. The record bears out their insistence, in 1648, that 'they have been the truest and constantest asserters of liberty and propriety (which are quite opposite to communitie and levelling) that have been in the whole land'.[1] Lilburne's concern for property right was evident as early as 1645: 'Yea, take away the declared, unrepealed Law, and then where is *Meum* & *Tuum*, and Libertie, and Propertie?' and was more specific in, for instance, his listing in 1646 as basic rights 'Liberty of conscience in matters of Faith, and Divine worship; Liberty of the Person, and liberty of Estate: which consists properly in the propriety of their goods, and a disposing power of their possessions.'[2] Overton, too, understood the right to

---

[1] Lilburne, *A Whip for the Present House of Lords*, quoted in Petergorsky, p. 110.
[2] *Englands Birth-right Justified* (Oct. 1645), in Haller, *Tracts*, iii. 261; *Vox Plebis* (19 Nov. 1646), quoted in Wolfe, p. 13.

property to be a 'propriety . . . people have in their goods to doe with them as they list'.[1] Leveller manifestoes from 1648 were explicit that parliament should bind itself, or be constitutionally bound, not to 'levell mens Estates, destroy Propriety, or make all things common'.[2]

It was, as we have seen, at Putney that the Leveller concept of property right was sharpened in the clash with the army leaders. Ireton and Cromwell were arguing that an equal natural right to life, if it went beyond the right to breathe and move, logically entailed an equal right to any goods and land, not just an equal right to bare necessities of life but a right to take anything that anyone wanted; hence, they said, the Levellers' equal natural right would destroy all property.[3]

It was in answer to this repeated argument that the Levellers brought in the natural right to property. They insisted that their principle of equal right to life could not destroy property because property itself was an individual right, established by the law of God ('Thou shalt not steal') and the law of Nature (which gives a principle for every man 'to have a property of what he has, or may have, which is not another man's, [which] property is the ground of *meum* and *tuum*').[4] Individual property in goods was a sacred natural right; it invalidated the indiscriminate right of any man to any thing which would otherwise follow from the equal right to life. (The assumption on both sides was that every man had a natural right to bare subsistence[5] but that this would not destroy property for it was already part of the fabric of society, as charity or as state poor relief.)

The Leveller position on property in goods is more fully

[1] *Appeale*, in Wolfe, p. 176.
[2] *Second Agreement*, in Wolfe, p. 301; cf. *Petition* of 11 Sept. 1648, in Wolfe, p. 288.
[3] Woodhouse, pp. 53–55, 58, 60, 63
[4] Ibid., pp. 59, 75. Cf. p. 80.
[5] Ireton (ibid., p. 60) urges that the Leveller principle of equal right to life would mean that any man could claim by the Law of Nature any goods at all 'though it be not a thing of necessity to him for the sustenance of nature'. Ireton (ibid., p. 73) states directly: 'By the right of nature I am to have sustenance rather than perish.' Cf. Locke's position, below, p. 212, n. 1.

seen in Petty's further argument that giving everyone a vote is 'the only means to preserve all property'.[1] The argument is that since every man is naturally free, therefore the reason men agreed to come into some form of government was that they might preserve property. It was taken for granted that a man's natural freedom included a property in things. The Levellers' insistence that property was prior to government —'really properties are the foundation of constitutions'[2]— drove Ireton and Cromwell to deny that property was a natural right at all. We have the curious spectacle of Ireton, who had accurately defined his own position in the debate in saying 'All the main thing that I speak for, is because I would have an eye to property',[3] denying that property is a natural right; 'The Law of God doth not give me property, nor the Law of Nature, but property is of human constitution. . . . Constitution founds property.'[4]

The Levellers' insistence, in the debate, that individual property in goods was a natural right, prior to government, was not an extemporized argument to counter Ireton's damaging attack. They had conceived of property as a natural right before, and quite independently of, the franchise debate. Indeed, it was on a concept of natural property right much wider than has yet been noticed that they based their case not only for property as a natural right (and hence for a wide range of actual property rights) but also for government by consent, and for civil and religious liberties. The fundamental postulate was that every man is naturally the proprietor of his own person.

This is most strikingly stated in some of Overton's tracts. In his *An Arrow against all Tyrants* (12 October 1646), which develops more fully the position taken by Lilburne a few months earlier,[5] and again in his *Appeale* (July 1647), Overton sets out a far-reaching doctrine of natural right. Civil and political rights are derived from natural right;

---

[1] Ibid., pp. 61–62. [2] Clarke, in Putney debate: ibid., p. 75.
[3] Ibid., p. 57. [4] Ibid., p. 69.
[5] Lilburne, *Free-man's Freedom Vindicated*, June 1646, the Postscript, in Wood-house, pp. 317–18.

natural right is derived from natural property in one's own person; property in one's own person is derived from the created instinctive nature of man.

The two opening paragraphs of the *Arrow* deserve quotation in full:

> To every Individuall in nature is given an individual property by nature, not to be invaded or usurped by any: for every one as he is himselfe, so he hath a selfe propriety, else could he not be himselfe, and on this no second may presume to deprive any of, without manifest violation and affront to the very principles of nature, and of the Rules of equity and justice between man and man; mine and thine cannot be, except this be; No man hath power over my rights and liberties, and I over no mans; I may be but an Individuall, enjoy my selfe, and my selfe propriety, and may write my selfe no more then my selfe, or presume any further; if I doe, I am an encroacher & an invader upon an other mans Right, to which I have no Right. For by naturall birth, all men are equally and alike borne to like propriety, liberty, and freedome, and as we are delivered of God by the hand of nature into this world, every one with a naturall, innate freedome and propriety (as it were writ in the table of every mans heart, never to be obliterated) even so are we to live, every one equally and alike to enjoy his Birth-right and priviledge; even all whereof God by nature hath made him free.
>
> And this by nature every one desires aimes at, and requires for no man naturally would be befooled of his liberty by his neighbours craft, or inslaved by his neighbours might, for it is natures instinct to preserve it selfe, from all things hurtfull and obnoctious, and this in nature is granted of all to be most reasonable, equall and just, not to be rooted out of the kind, even of equall duration with the creature: And from this fountain or root, all just humain powers take their original; not immediatly from God (as Kings usually plead their prerogative) but mediatly by the hand of nature, as from the represented to the representors; for originally, God hath implanted them in the creature, and from the creature those powers immediatly proceed; and no further: and no more may be communicated then stands for the better being weale, or safety thereof: and this is mans prerogative and no further, so much and no more may be given or received thereof: even so much as is conducent to a better being, more safety and freedome, and no more; he that gives more sins against his owne flesh; and he that takes more, is a Thiefe and Robber to his kind: Every man by nature being

a King, Priest and Prophet in his owne naturall circuite and compasse, whereof no second may partake, but by deputation, commission, and free consent from him, whose naturall right and freedome it is.[1]

Overton repeated the first part of this in his *Appeale*, where it was followed by a restatement of Lilburne's point that no man can hand over more power than he has and that no man by nature 'may abuse, beat, torment or afflict himself'.[2] The *Appeale* also has a more positive assertion of the necessity of natural right:

it is a firme Law and radicall principle in Nature engraven in the tables of the heart by the finger of God in creation for every living moving thing, wherein there is a breath of life to defend, preserve, award, and deliver it selfe from all things hurtfull, destructive and obnoctious thereto to the utmost of its power: Therefore from hence is conveyed to all men in generall, and to every man in particular, an undoubted principle of reason, by all rationall an iust wayes and meanes possibly he may, to save, defend and deliver himselfe from all oppression, violence and cruelty whatsoever, and (in duty to his own safety and being) to leave no iust expedient unattempted for his delivery therefrom: and this is rationall and iust; to deny it is to overture the law of nature, yea, and of Religion too; for the contrary lets in nothing but selfe murther, violence and cruelty.[3]

One is struck by the Hobbesian tone of Overton's postulate as much as by the Lockean argument that is built on it. Here is Hobbes's 'right of nature', deduced from the instinctive need to defend oneself from everything harmful or destructive; and this right becomes an 'undoubted principle of reason' and a part of the law of nature, creating a 'duty to [one's] own safety and being'. Here at the same time is the argument Locke was to make central in his doctrine: that all rightful political authority is by delegation from individuals, that no individual has a right to harm himself and

[1] Overton, *An Arrow against all Tyrants*, pp. 3–4. Parts of these paragraphs are quoted in Pease, *The Leveller Movement*, pp. 141–2; in Zagorin, *History of Political Thought in the English Revolution*, p. 22; and in Frank, *The Levellers*, p. 96.

[2] Overton, *An Appeale from the Degenerate Representative Body of the Commons ...*, in Wolfe, pp. 162–3.

[3] *Appeale*, in Ibid., pp. 159–60.

therefore cannot transfer such a right to any other, but only, in Overton's words, 'so much as is conducent to a better being, more safety and freedome, and no more; he that gives more sins against his owne flesh'.

But what we have chiefly to notice here is a still more fundamental similarity with Locke, that is, the proprietorial quality of the Levellers' individualism. It seems, at first sight, even more extreme than Locke's.[1] Not only has the individual a property in his own person and capacities, a property in the sense of a right to enjoy and use them and to exclude others from them; what is more, it is this property, this exclusion of others, that makes a man human: 'every one as he is himselfe, so he hath a self propriety, else he could not be himselfe'. What makes a man human is his freedom from other men. Man's essence is freedom. Freedom is proprietorship of one's own person and capacities.

This proprietorship, it should be noticed, was not thought of as passive enjoyment. The Levellers demanded this manifold property in one's own person as a prerequisite of active use and enjoyment of one's capacities. Men were created to improve, and enjoy by improving, their capacities. Their property in themselves excluded all others, but did not exclude their duty to their creator and to themselves.

ii. *The deduction of rights and the grounds for exclusion*

It was on this concept of man's essence as freedom, and freedom as the active proprietorship of one's person and capacities, that the Levellers grounded all their claims for specific rights, civil, religious, economic, and political. The deductions were obvious.

As to civil and religious liberty, it was plain, first, that property in one's own person required a guaranteed freedom from arbitrary arrest, trial, and imprisonment, and the right to due process of law. It was equally plain that property in one's own mental and spiritual person required freedom of speech, publication, and religion. All these civil and religious rights were demanded for every one, however dependent by reason of sex or employment. Women were created human beings. Wage-earners, although they had alienated their disposal of their own energies, had not entirely alienated their humanity. They were not slaves.

The Levellers had also a strong practical reason for demanding civil liberties for everyone, a reason nowhere better put than in Lilburne's superb statement of the case against arbitrary arrest, imprisonment, and judicial procedures:

. . . for what is done to any one, may be done to every one: besides, being all members of one body, that is, of the English Commonwealth, one man should not suffer wrongfully, but all should be sensible, and endeavour his preservation; otherwise they give way to an inlet of the sea of will and power, upon all their laws and liberties, which are the boundaries to keep out tyrany and oppression. . . .[1]

Civil and religious liberties must be for all, or they may be for nobody.

The economic rights the Levellers wanted were likewise deductions from the property in one's own person and capacities. The basic economic right was of course the right to individual property in goods and estate, which included the right not only to own but to acquire by the free exercise of a man's own energies and capacities. The particular economic rights the Levellers demanded—freedom to buy, sell, produce, and trade, without licence, monopoly, arbitrary regulation, or arbitrary taxation—were evident corollaries. Sometimes the Levellers referred to the individual right to trade as a natural right, a birthright, or a native liberty.[2] Whether so described or not, the right to trade was clearly an important kind of property on the Levellers' assumptions.[3]

[1] *The Just Defence of John Lilburne*, in Haller and Davies, p. 455.

[2] e.g. Lilburne, *Englands Birth-right Justified*, in Haller, *Tracts*, iii, 261–2; Overton, *Remonstrance of Many Thousand Citizens* (7 July 1646), in Wolfe, p. 124. Cf. the writers quoted by Petegorsky, p. 81.

[3] It was of course quite usual in the seventeenth century to speak of a right or a liberty as a property. Property (or propriety, for the terms were used interchangeably) had then its earlier sense of a right to or in something. The Levellers spoke of having a property *in* a thing, meaning a right to use, enjoy, exclude others from, or dispose of, that thing. Thus they could speak of a property in land, in estate, in right to trade, in the franchise, or in one's own person.

It made up in large part the small man's right to manage his own productive energies and life; without it he did not effectively have that property in his own person and capacities which was the fundamental right of the free-born man. These economic rights, like the civil and religious rights, were demanded for everyone. In practice, of course, the rights to produce, trade, &c., could be enjoyed only by those who had the disposal of their own labour. Servants, while servants, were incapable of using them. Yet the rights had to be established with complete generality in order to assure them to those who could enjoy them. Once admit monopoly or arbitrary regulation or taxation into any branch of industry or trade, and the damage was done: the area of enterprise was narrowed for enterprisers in general. Economic rights, like civil rights, had to be claimed for everyone in order to be assured to anyone.

The political right of a voice in choosing representatives was different. It was, like the others, grounded on the concept of man's essence as freedom, and of freedom as the active proprietorship of one's person and capacities, but it did not have to be claimed for everyone. Although the Levellers spoke sometimes of every man having an equal right to a voice in setting up a form of government,[1] they claimed a voice in choosing the legislature only for those who were not dependent on the will of other men. Servants had alienated the use and direction of their capacities (i.e. of their labour) by entering a wage-contract. Alms-takers had forfeited theirs by becoming dependent on poor-relief or charity. Both had thereby lost a crucial part of their native freedom or property, namely the property in their own capacities or labour. But the primary function of government was to secure precisely that property, that is, to make and enforce the rules within which men could make the most of their own energies and capacities. The protection of property in goods and estate was a derived or secondary function: without '*meum* and *tuum*' there would be no liberty to make the most of one's own capacities.

[1] See Note L, pp. 297-8.

Servants and alms-takers, having lost the property in their own labour, could be assumed to have no property in land or capital. They therefore had no interest in either the primary or the equally necessary secondary function of government.

True, they were still entitled to civil and religious liberties, and even possibly to economic liberties, for they had alienated only a part, not the whole, of their native human freedom or property in their own persons. But they did not need the franchise to protect these. For the civil, the religious, and some of the economic rights were to be guaranteed by constitutional limits on the power of parliament; these were the rights which the *Agreements* proposed should be reserved to the people or put beyond the competence of any parliament to abridge. Since these rights would thus be guaranteed for everyone, it was not necessary for everyone to have a vote in order to safeguard them. The economic rights which were not constitutionally guaranteed but were left to the good sense of future parliaments, could in any case be best secured by those who had a direct interest in them, namely, those who had not alienated the use or direction of their own energies and capacities by becoming wage-earners or recipients of alms.

Thus, on the Leveller concept of freedom as proprietorship of one's own person and capacities, there was no inconsistency in demanding civil, religious, and economic rights for everyone, and the franchise only for those above the level of dependence. The former rights inhered in everyone; they were inalienable, for no one could alienate the core of his human freedom, no one could divest himself of his entire property in his person.[1] But the right to a voice in elections did not inhere in everyone, for not everyone had retained that part of his human freedom which consisted in his property in his own labour. The franchise was needed and could be claimed only by those who had retained that

---

[1] For Locke's similar distinction between inalienable and alienable property in one's person see below, ch. V, pp. 219, 231.

property, and whose economic life was consequently one of active enterprise; the civil and religious rights were needed by all whose physical, mental, and spiritual life was one of active enterprise, which was, or ought to be, everyone.

When we see that the Levellers thought of freedom as a function of property in one's person, and made full freedom a function of retention of the property in one's labour, we can clear up a puzzling feature of the Leveller position in the Putney debate. It will be recalled that Petty had stated two grounds for the exclusion of servants and alms-takers: first, that they were dependent on the will of other men and would be afraid to displease them, and second, that they were included in their masters. The first ground might of course be considered merely a realistic recognition of the probability of intimidation in a system of open voting. That servants and alms-takers, if given the franchise, would be afraid of displeasing those on whom they were dependent was a plain enough inference from the facts of social life. Whether the Levellers would have excluded half the men of England on such an expedient ground, had they seen any conflict in principle with equal natural right, is very doubtful. But in our view the question does not arise, for they saw no conflict in principle. Since servants and alms-takers had already forfeited their birthright, the wrongful relation of fear was transmuted into a just relation of dependence. The just relation is expressed in the notion of inclusion in their masters. In the case of servants at least, the forfeiture of the birthright is tantamount to inclusion in the master. For the forfeiture of birthright goes with the alienation of the right in one's labour, and that alienation is not an abandonment but a transfer of right to the master. The servant's labour is thenceforth included in the master's labour; accordingly, in respect of the right to a voice in elections, the servant is included in the master.

In the case of alms-takers and beggars the forfeiture of birthright cannot be quite so clearly equated with the notion of inclusion in masters. Alms-takers and beggars have no masters in the precise sense. Yet even in their case, the notion of inclusion is not so far-fetched. We must distinguish between the impotent poor, the partially dependent poor, and the sturdy vagrant beggars. There is no difficulty about the impotent poor, whether receiving alms from door to door or on parish relief or in an endowed almshouse. They were by definition incapable of useful labour. They had no labour either to alienate or to retain. They were hence thrown upon the community, which then stood in the relation of master or guardian to them.

The partially dependent poor, those who were able to work but who could not maintain themselves and their families either by self-employment or by the sale of their labour, were similarly thrown upon the parish, which then stood in similar relation to them. It is doubtful, indeed, whether the Levellers would have thought of including in this category those honest people, mentioned frequently and piteously in Leveller petitions, who had been reduced to beggary by the Civil War and (in the Levellers' view) by the policies of parliament. These men, ordinarily self-reliant, were more likely to have been considered as only temporarily displaced; the Levellers counted on their being reabsorbed into the useful labour force following the changes in parliamentary policy which the Levellers were demanding.

The sturdy vagrant beggars, finally, may be assumed to have been left out of the Levellers' calculations entirely. They were commonly thought to have put themselves outside society by their refusal to labour usefully. It is true that they had neither lost the capacity to labour, nor transferred the rights in their labour to any other person. This was precisely the complaint against them; it was this that put them outside society. They were masterless men, and Puritan society had no place for them.

In short, for the alms-takers and beggars, as for the servants, the forfeiture of birthright, where it was not a result of rebellion against useful labour and thus against society, could be regarded as inclusion in their masters. It was by the same loss—the loss of the right in their own labour—that both groups, alms-takers and beggars, and servants, forfeited their birthright to a voice in elections, and that loss necessarily included them in someone else.

iii. *Levellers' and Independents' individualism*

We may now see a little more fully into the quality of the Levellers' individualism, by comparing their concept of freedom with that of the Independents. Both equated freedom with proprietorship. For both, the opposite of freedom or proprietorship was dependence on the will of other men. Where they differed was in their view of the kind of property that distinguished freedom from dependence. For Cromwell and Ireton, only property in freehold land or chartered trading rights made a man free. For the Levellers, property in his own labour made a man free.

At first sight the difference between these two kinds of property is more fundamental than anything they have in common. In the Levellers' minds labour was a human attribute, different in kind from land or capital. Yet their use of the term property to cover both the right to one's labour and the right to material possessions was not simply a figure of speech; the two forms of property had something fundamental in common. What they had in common may be seen in two ways. First, while in the Levellers' view labour was a human attribute it was also a commodity. It could be alienated by its natural owner, and then its price, like that of any other commodity, was determined by the market. The Levellers had no objection to this; it seemed natural to them that wages should be so determined; when they objected, as they sometimes did, to oppressively low wages, they attributed them to the operation of merchant monopolists or the excise, and saw the remedy in freer trade. In the case of labour, as in the case of land or any other commodity, what could be sold was precisely that exclusive right to its use, benefit, and product which comprised the property in it. Thus, to the extent that the Levellers conceived of labour as a commodity, they conceived of it as a property of the same kind as property in material things.

In the second place we must notice that in fact, and in the Levellers' own experience, a prerequisite of retaining the control of one's own labour was the possession of at least some working capital. To set oneself up as an independent producer, whether on the land or in a trade, and to stay independent, that is, to retain the ability to make decisions about the use of one's labour, one needed some capital.

No one would question that this was true of the farmer. Whether or not he had to buy a lease, he had to have implements and stock and enough working capital to carry him over from seed-time to harvest. Further down the scale, the domestic weaver, whether or not he owned his loom, needed, to have any independence, enough working capital to finance the purchase of his materials; failing that he must be in continual debt to the clothier, in which position he had no more control over his own labour than a wage-earner. And in those trades that could be pursued without being a freeman of a corporation, possession of some working capital was equally a prerequisite of retaining the control of one's own labour. The cobbler or the chimney-sweep did not need much capital equipment, but even he needed to have something laid by if he was not to go on the poor-rates or become a servant whenever trade was slack.

Wherever one looked, independence, or effective retention of the property in one's labour, required at least the possession of some working capital. This did not mean, of course, that poverty and dependence could be equated. You could be poor but free. The independent rack-rent farmer, though he had a substantial capital investment, might have a poorer living than the servant in husbandry; the cobbler might have a poorer living than many journeymen. Poverty, measured by standard of living, was not necessarily the same as dependence on the will of other men.

Nevertheless, lack of any working capital did mean dependence on the will of other men, that is, did mean effective loss of freedom to direct one's own energies. The Levellers, who must have known this very well from experience, did not make an explicit point of it. Intent as they were on asserting human rights rather than property rights, or rather, on basing all rights on the property in one's person rather than on property in things, and claiming full rights for all who had not given up property in their labour, they could not be expected to have emphasized that property in one's own labour did not give you independence unless you had some material property as well. Only rarely in the Leveller writings is there an implication that they are thinking in terms of proprietorship of things as well as of one's labour, as in Rainborough's statement at Putney that he would grant something of Ireton's case for basing the franchise on property but would have the question stated 'whether this be a just propriety, the propriety [that] says that forty shillings a year enables a man to elect'.[1] But whether explicitly stated or not, the Leveller criterion of freedom as proprietorship of one's own labour did necessarily carry with it a proprietorship of some material things.

I do not suggest that the Leveller criterion of freedom can thus be reduced to possession of material goods, nor that the difference between the Leveller and Independent criteria can be reduced to a quantitative difference in material possessions. There can be no doubt that the Levellers saw labour not only as a commodity but also as a human attribute, and that they were perfectly honest in emphasizing the contrast between property in one's person and property in things. What I suggest is that the Levellers had reached their concept of freedom by generalizing from the data of their own experience, that is, by generalizing from the compound phenomenon of freedom as they had known it—the freedom of the independent producer, who was free of the will of other men to the extent that he had energy and working capital. That it was the control over one's energies they emphasized is not surprising. That they called it property is not accidental.

[1] Woodhouse, p. 79.

The Leveller concept of freedom, then, differed from the Independent concept not in making freedom a function of property—both concepts did that—but in making freedom a function of a kind of property (property in one's labour) whose definition was necessarily ambiguous. Property in one's labour was both a human attribute, a part of human personality, and an alienable commodity. But the only condition on which it could be retained as a part of one's personality, rather than alienated as a commodity, was the possession of some material property along with it. It was either a property in the full sense of an alienable commodity or a property which required material property to make it effective.

Thus the Levellers' concept of freedom as proprietorship had more in common with their opponents' concept than appears on the surface, and more, probably, than they were steadily conscious of.

We may have, incidentally, in this analysis an explanation of another puzzling feature of the Putney debate. The Levellers, it has often been noticed, could not refute, even to their own satisfaction, the Cromwell-Ireton case for the fixed-property franchise. The reason for their failure, it may now be suggested, was that the Levellers were themselves thinking in terms of proprietorship, and a proprietorship not so very different in kind from their opponents'.

When the difference in kind is discounted, the difference in amount remains significant. It is true that the Independents made the criterion of freedom not the amount of material property but its fixed local character. Ireton was indeed obsessed with the importance of the permanent local interest. He went so far as to put on exactly the same footing the Englishman who has no freehold land or trading rights in a local corporation and the foreigner who lives in England and has the protection of English laws. The latter is rightfully subject to a law to which he did not give his consent; if he is unsatisfied to be subject to it, 'he may go into another kingdom. And so the same reason doth extend, in my understanding, [to] that man that hath no permanent interest in the kingdom. If he hath money, his money is as good in another place as here; he hath nothing that doth locally fix him to this kingdom.'[1] The Independents were thinking in the traditional categories of the gentry mind: domination of land was a clear title to power, domination of money was somewhat suspect.

But while it is true that the Independents emphasized fixity rather than amount of wealth, the Levellers thought that the Independent criterion would effectively come down to the amount of wealth. Rainborough identified the freeholders with the rich, and saw them making hewers of wood and drawers of water of the other five-sixths of the people;[2] the fixed property franchise gave 'power to 'men of riches, men of estates' and made the non-freeholder 'a perpetual slave'.[3] Petty saw the issue as simply whether 'the rich should conclude the poor'.[4] And within a few months after Putney the Levellers were putting out a remarkably class-conscious theory of the state, in which the Independent leaders were seen as part of a conspiracy of the rich and powerful to keep down the poorer and more industrious people.[5]

Whether the Levellers were right or wrong in seeing the freeholder franchise as essentially a means of keeping power in the hands of the rich, whether they were unduly influenced by their urban background, in which there was a visible correlation between fixity of property (i.e. membership in a trading corporation) and amount of wealth, it is clear that they took the effective substance of the Independents' fixed-property criterion to be amount rather than kind of material property.

The Levellers were, therefore, in their debate with the Independents, contrasting two criteria of freedom and franchise, one of doubtful accuracy and one of doubtful clarity.

---

[1] Woodhouse, p. 67. Cf. Locke's position, below, ch. V, p. 250.
[2] Woodhouse, p. 67.   [3] Ibid., p. 71.   [4] Ibid., p. 78.
[5] See quotations below, pp. 154-5.

Of doubtful accuracy was their interpretation of their opponents' criterion as being possession of a substantial amount of material property. Of doubtful clarity was their own ambiguous criterion of property in one's labour, a criterion they reached, I have suggested, by generalizing from their own experience, in which the property in one's labour either was an alienable commodity (and so was essentially the same as a material property) or was dependent on the possession of material property. It is no wonder that the Levellers were unable to grasp clearly the precise difference between their own position and that of their opponents.

I have argued that the fundamental quality of the Levellers' individualism is found in their concept of freedom as a function of proprietorship. The essential humanity of the individual consisted in his freedom from the will of other persons, freedom to enjoy his own person and to develop his own capacities. One's person was property not metaphorically but essentially: the property one had in it was the right to exclude others from its use and enjoyment. Property in one's labour, even more precisely than the broader property in one's person, was property in the material sense, for it was an alienable commodity. The criterion of full freedom was the retention of the property in one's labour, and the condition for its retention was the possession of material property as well.

The analysis here made of the Levellers' individualism may be thought both to be too complex and to involve concepts more sharply defined than are to be found in their writings. It would indeed be a mistake to attribute to the Levellers any considerable degree of close and steady reasoning in clear concepts. But I do suggest that these are the concepts implicit in their theory, and that much of the unsatisfactoriness of their theory is to be attributed to the fact that they did not see all the implications of their concepts. In an age when labour could be seen both as a commodity and as an essential human attribute, and would be so regarded especially by the small independent producer who felt his independence to be precarious, it is not surprising that they should start from such concepts and should fail to see their full implications.

iv. *Limits and direction of the Levellers' individualism*

We must not, however, overrate the proprietorial quality of the Levellers' individualism. If it differed from the Independents' less than is usually thought, yet when it is compared with the more sophisticated possessive theory developed by Locke, a substantial difference appears. I suggested earlier that the Levellers' postulate of a manifold natural property in one's own person as the essence of freedom and hence of humanity makes their theory appear as proprietorial as Locke's. The Levellers did indeed see the individual as the natural proprietor of his own capacities, owing nothing to society for them, and did consider life and liberty as possessions rather than as social rights with correlative duties. Yet they did not accept the full postulates of possessive individualism.

In the first place, the Levellers' right to acquire property in goods and estate was not, as Locke's was, a right to unlimited acquisition by any individual.[1] If the Levellers did not specifically denounce unlimited acquisition, they were plainly opposed to its implication, namely, the concentration of wealth and the consequent practical inequality of the right to acquire. The Levellers did not subscribe to Hobbes's dicta: 'Covetousnesse of great Riches, and ambition of great Honours, are Honourable; as signes of power to obtain them;' 'Riches, are Honourable; for they are Power'.[2] They did indeed see riches and power as concomitant, and they denounced both. The rich were using the power of the state to enrich themselves still further at the expense of the small men, both in gross (as by the excise, which 'lies heavy only upon the Poorer, and most ingenious industrious People, to their intolerable oppression; [while] all persons of large Revenues in Lands, and vast estates at usury, bear not the

---

[1] See below, ch. V, Sect. 2.   [2] *Leviathan*, ch. 10, pp. 71, 70.

least proportionable weight of that burthen'[1]) and by retail (as in the use of political office to line their pockets). Both ways, 'our Flesh is that whereupon you Rich men live, and wherewith you deck and adorn your selves'.[2] The rich and the great were even accused of keeping up faction and 'civil broyles' for their own benefit:

What else but your Ambition and Faction continue our Distractions and Oppressions? Is not all the Controversie whose Slaves the poor shall be? Whether they shall be the Kings Vassals, or the Presbyterians, or the Independent Factions? And is not the Contention nourished, that you whose Houses are full of the spoils of your Contrey, might be secure from Accounts, while there is nothing but Distraction? and that by the tumultuousnesse of the people under prodigious oppression, you might have fair pretences to keep up an Army, and garrisons? and that under pretence of necessity, you may uphold your arbitrary Government by Committees, &c.[3]

Walwyn saw the same class conspiracy, and put it even more sharply:

your great ones, whether the King, Lords, Parliament men, rich Citizens, &c. feel not the miserable effects [of civil war], and so cannot be sensible; but you and your poor friends that depend on Farmes, Trades, and small pay, have many an aking heart when these live in all pleasure and deliciousness: The accursed thing is accepted by them, wealth and honor, and both comes by the bleeding miserable distractions of the Common-wealth, and they fear an end of trouble would put an end to their glory and greatness. . . . The King, Parliament, great men in the City and Army, have made you but the stairs by which they have mounted to Honor, Wealth and Power. The only Quarrel that hath been, and at present is but this, namely, whose slaves the people shall be. . . .[4]

Wealth and honour is 'the accursed thing'. Great property is feeding on small property. But if the Levellers were

---

[1] *Petition* of Jan. 1648, article 14 (Haller and Davies, p. 113; Wolfe, p. 270). Cf. articles 6 and 7.

[2] *The Mournfull Cryes of many thousand poor Tradesmen* (Haller and Davies, p. 127; Wolfe, p. 276).

[3] *Mournfull Cryes*, Haller and Davies, p. 127; Wolfe, p. 276.

[4] *The Bloody Project* (28 Aug. 1648), Haller and Davies, pp. 144-5.

class-conscious, they were also property-conscious. The power of accumulation by privilege, as they saw most clearly in the case of monopolies, destroys 'not only Liberty but property'.[1] They demanded the restoration of liberty and property, liberty for the small man to acquire property. The next step towards freedom was therefore destruction of the privileges—tithes, excise, monopolies, and the rest—that stood in the way of the small men's right. In their determination to open to everyone the rights then effectively confined to the men of great substance they at once accepted the proprietorial postulate which equated possession with freedom and humanity, and rejected its final implication. Their thinking was possessive, but not as fully possessive as Locke's.

When we go beyond their concept of property right and consider, finally, their concept of society, we find again a difference from full possessive individualism. We noticed earlier the Hobbesian tone of Overton's natural rights theory. Rights and duties were deduced from the instinct of self-preservation. But even here, in this most extreme individualist presentation, there is a belief in the positive value of society which is quite unlike Hobbes. Self-preservation is not the ultimate postulate, but is grounded on something more fundamental, namely, the duty to preserve human society: 'humane society, cohabitation or being, . . . above all earthly things must be maintained, as the earthly soveraigne good of mankind, let what or who will perish, or be confounded, for mankind must be preserved upon the earth . . .'.[2]

This vision of human society as the ultimate good, and of the ultimate value of living together, is scattered through the Leveller writings. Lilburne, for instance, arguing that all just authority is from mutual agreement or consent, takes it as self-evident not only that such agreement cannot be made 'for the mischief, hurt, or damage of any' but also that it can

---

[1] *Petition* of Jan. 1648, article 9. Haller and Davies, p. 111; Wolfe, p. 268.
[2] *Appeale*, in Wolfe, p. 178.

be made only 'for the good benefit and comfort each of
other',[1] or, 'each to other, for their better being'.[2] Three
years later, Walwyn, summarizing the Leveller theoretical
position, opens with the self-evident proposition: 'Since no
man is born for himself only, but obliged by the Laws of
Nature (which reaches all) of Christianity (which ingages us
as Christians) and of Publick Societie and Government, to
employ our endeavours for the advancement of a communitive Happinesse, of equall concernment to others as our
selves. . . .'[3]

The Levellers' sense of community may appear to go
oddly with their possessive individual rights. Yet they saw
no incongruity. They wanted a community of enterprisers,
in the broadest sense—not only economic but spiritual and
intellectual enterprisers. If we can see now that a community
of fully competing economic enterprisers is a contradiction
in terms, we cannot expect them to have seen it then. The
only way towards a fuller life for more people that they could
see was to throw down the barriers that frustrated the small
enterpriser; and that *was* a way, perhaps the only way that
would be feasible in the next two centuries. The Levellers
did not share Winstanley's utopian insight that freedom lay
in free common access to the land. For Winstanley that was
the key to freedom, for that was the only way to assure
freedom from exploitation of man by man. The only natural
right of the individual that Winstanley recognized was the
natural right of men to labour together and live together,
governing themselves according to a natural law of social
preservation.[4]

The Levellers at times came close to this, in their glimpses
of the ultimate value of living together. Their own lives as
political organizers, creating a movement where before there
had been only individuals, and relying heavily on each other's

---

[1] *Free-man's Freedom Vindicated*, in Woodhouse, p. 317.
[2] *Londons Liberty*, p. 17.
[3] *A Manifestation* (Apr. 1649), in Wolfe, p. 388.
[4] Winstanley, *The Law of Freedom*, chs. i and iii (*Works*, ed. Sabine, pp. 519, 536).

help, in and out of prison, no doubt contributed to their sense of community. But if community could only be had by levelling of property, they would not have it. Freedom from exploitation they did want, for all enterprisers, but that did not require community of property.

The Levellers' thinking was too deeply embedded in the assumptions of their class to allow them to retreat far from the concept of freedom as the right to be separate and un-attached. They could not entertain the idea of freedom as a concomitant of social living in an unacquisitive society. That idea may have been utopian in the seventeenth century, but it is not enough to say simply that the Levellers were more realistic than the Diggers, for in practice they failed equally; it was the doctrine of full possessive individualism that triumphed.

The Levellers have generally been regarded as radical democrats, the first democrats in English political theory. We may now suggest that they ought rather to be considered radical liberals than radical democrats. For they put freedom first, and made freedom a function of proprietorship. The Levellers ought to be remembered as much for their assertion of a natural right to property in goods and estate as for any-thing else. They can claim the distinction of being the first political theorists to assert a natural right to property for which the individual owes nothing to society and which en-tails none of those duties entailed in the earlier doctrine of stewardship. The Levellers paved the way, unwittingly, for Locke and the Whig tradition, for their whole doctrine of natural rights as property, and natural right to property, could be converted as readily to Locke's purposes as to any more radical ends.

That was in fact the fate of their doctrine in seventeenth-century England. And if the Leveller ideas gave strength and comfort to radicals in America and to later democratic movements in England, their influence worked the other way as well. By putting an ill-defined but strongly asserted natural property right at the centre of their advocacy of the people's cause, they made it easy for Locke to confuse, in the general estimation, the equal right to property with the right to unlimited property, and thus to harness democratic sentiments to the Whig cause. The confusion was not repaired for two centuries.

IV

HARRINGTON:
THE OPPORTUNITY STATE

1. *Unexamined Ambiguities*

UNTIL a few years ago Harrington's place in the history of
political theory seemed secure. He had discovered a relation
between property distribution and political power that had
only been glimpsed by earlier writers, had formulated it
systematically, and used it successfully to explain political
change. He had shown not only that the relation did prevail
in history, but also that it was a necessary relation; and that,
in the measure that its necessity was understood, a permanently satisfactory frame of government could be fitted to any
nation.

Harrington thought of himself as a scientist of politics
rather than a philosopher, and the philosophers have generally left him alone. It has been the historians, not least the
economic historians, who have given him his reputation. His
handsome niche in the modern temple of fame was cemented
and elegantly decorated by Professor Tawney's Raleigh
Lecture of 1941: Harrington was 'the first English thinker
to find the cause of political upheaval in antecedent social
change'; his originality 'consisted primarily in his analysis of
the constitutional consequences of English economic development in the century and a half preceding the Civil War'.[1]
But in calling Harrington as a witness for what was to
become a highly controversial interpretation of the economic
changes of that period, Professor Tawney put him in an
unexpectedly exposed position, and Harrington now seems
in some danger of being left a casualty of the battle over 'the
rise of the gentry'. Mr. Hill's valuable but too brief essay,[2]

[1] 'Harrington's Interpretation of his Age', *Proc. Brit. Academy*, xxvii. 200.
[2] Christopher Hill, *Puritanism and Revolution* (1958), ch. 10.

putting Harrington in longer historical perspective and emphasizing the place of the people in his theory, has done much to restore his position. But something remains to be done.

With all the attention Harrington has had in the last ten years, two central ambiguities in his theory have remained unexamined. First, in a theory which hinges almost entirely on the balance of property between the few and the many, the nobility and the people, Harrington is ambiguous as to whether the gentry are included in the former or in the latter. At different stages of his analysis he puts them now in one category, now in the other. Second, the central concept of the balance, or overbalance, is itself ambiguous to the point of apparent contradiction. In the statements of the general principle of the balance, and in the demonstration that England is ready for a commonwealth, it is the overbalance of property in the few or the many (i.e. possession of more than half the land by the few or the many) that determines the system of government, and a commonwealth is consistent only with the overbalance being in the many. But once Harrington's commonwealth is set up, a law which would enable one per cent. of the citizens to acquire all the land is said to prevent them overbalancing the rest of the people, and this law is relied upon to secure the property basis of the commonwealth. The principle of the balance, used to establish the commonwealth, appears to be abrogated by the establishment of the commonwealth.

The two ambiguities do not cancel each other. But both are understandable on certain assumptions about the nature of seventeenth-century English society which Harrington can be shown, on other evidence, to have entertained. When the ambiguities are examined, Harrington's theory appears less systematic but perhaps more realistic than it has sometimes been made out to be. Harrington emerges neither as the illogical proponent of a declining gentry nor as the historian whose insight into English society, while novel, was limited to the effects of the disappearance of military tenure.

I shall argue that Harrington thought that the gentry in 1656 had less than half the land, and based his case for a gentry-led commonwealth on that assumption; that he saw far enough into the bourgeois nature of English seventeenth-century society to assume that the gentry did, and always would, accept and support the bourgeois social order which then existed and which the rest of the people wanted; and that this assumption was essential to his whole political thought.

The term 'bourgeois', having become one of the least precise in political and historical writing, requires definition. By bourgeois society I mean essentially the possessive market society as defined in Chapter II.[1] Bourgeois society, then, I take to be a society in which the relations between men are dominated by the market; in which, that is to say, land and labour, as well as movable wealth and goods made for consumption, are treated as commodities to be bought and sold and contracted for with a view to profit and accumulation, and where men's relations to others are set largely by their ownership of these commodities and the success with which they utilize that ownership to their own profit.

2. *The Balance and the Gentry*

Harrington's principle of the balance seems quite straightforward. The location of political power, as between the rule ('empire') of one man, the few or the many, must, except for short-run periods of disequilibrium, correspond to the distribution of property (in most countries, of land) between the one, the few, and the many. Thus

. . . such (except it be in a city that has little or no land, and whose revenue is in trade) as is the proportion or balance of dominion or property in land, such is the nature of the empire.

If one man be sole landlord of a territory, or overbalance the people, for example three parts in four, . . . his empire is absolute monarchy.

If the few or a nobility, or a nobility with the clergy be landlords, or overbalance the people to the like proportion, it makes the *Gothic* balance . . . and the empire is mix'd monarchy. . . .

And if the whole people be landlords, or hold the lands so divided among them, that no one man, or number of men, within the compass of the *few* or *aristocracy*, overbalance them, the empire (without the interposition of force) is a commonwealth.[1]

The necessary correspondence of the form of government with the distribution of property is presented as a deduction from self-evident propositions. Whichever of the one, the few, or the many has the power to dominate the others will do so. Since men must eat, whoever can feed them has their support. Whoever has the most land can feed and therefore command the largest army. Men depend upon riches 'not of choice . . . but of necessity and by the teeth: for as much as he who wants bread, is his servant that will feed him; if a man thus feeds a whole people, they are under his empire'.[2] Thus the distribution of property determines the distribution of political power. Disalignment between the two distributions may arise either through a group without the requisite proportion of property seizing political power, or through a change in the distribution of property not accompanied by the appropriate change in political power. In both cases, however, it follows from the postulates that an equilibrium (either the old or a new one) will be re-established. Harrington was mainly interested in the second of these kinds of change. Here he saw only one possible outcome: the old ruling class, without sufficient resources to maintain its rule, must sooner or later be overthrown by those who had the bulk of the property.

Hence, in order to have stable government, the balance of power must correspond to the balance of property. It was necessary also, for stable government, that the balance of property be decisively in the one or the few or the many.

---

[1] *Oceana*, p. 37; cf. *Prerogative of Popular Government*, pp. 227, 270; *Art of Lawgiving*, p. 363; *System of Politics*, p. 467 (where the proportion is given as two-thirds). Page references throughout this chapter are to the 1771 edition of *Oceana and Other Works*.

[2] *Oceana*, p. 37.

They must have substantially more than half the property, for if one party has only about half and the rest have the other half 'the government becoms a very shambles', each constantly attempting to subdue the other.[1] And since the balance of property could shift from various causes unforeseen by human providence,[2] it was necessary, in order to perpetuate a stable government of any type, to impose some law which would prevent a decisive shift in the balance of property.

This is the substance of the famous theory of the balance. Although the principle is stated with complete generality ('such as is the proportion or balance of . . . property in land, such is the nature of the empire') the only application Harrington makes of it is as between one man, the few or a nobility, and the whole people. It is here that the first ambiguity enters. The few or the nobility is used sometimes to include, sometimes to exclude, the gentry.

In the statement of the general principle of the balance quoted above, while there is no definition of 'the few or a nobility', the small feudal nobility is presumably meant, for the overbalance of property in their hands is made to correspond to the Gothic balance, which is Harrington's term for the feudal order.

In the historical account of the change in the English balance of property from Henry VII to the Civil War it is quite clear that the nobility is limited to the feudal peerage at the beginning and the Stuart peerage at the end, never numbering more than two or three hundred men. Down to the reign of Henry VII, we are told, the balance of land was in the nobility, the great feudal lords who, having the military services of their tenants at their disposal, 'got the trick of . . . setting up and pulling down their kings according to their various interests . . .'.[3] Henry VII abated the power of the nobility by his statutes of population, of retainers, and of alienations. The first, by requiring the

---

[1] *Oceana*, p. 38; cf. *System*, p. 466.
[2] *Prerogative*, p. 270; *Art of L.*, p. 364.   [3] *Oceana*, p. 64.

maintenance of houses of husbandry, did in effect 'amortize a great part of the lands to the hold and possession of the yeomanry or middle people', men 'of som substance, that might keep hinds and servants, and set the plow a going'; these men 'were much unlink'd from dependence upon their lords', who thus in effect lost their infantry.[1] The statute of retainers cut off their cavalry. The statute of alienations encouraged them to sell lands in order to keep up their positions, now rather as courtiers than as country nobility. The rest of the shift in the balance Harrington describes in two sentences: Henry VIII,

dissolving the abbys, brought with the declining state of the nobility so vast a prey to the industry of the people, that the balance of the commonwealth was too apparently in the popular party, to be unseen by the wise council of queen Parthenia [Elizabeth], who converting her reign thro the perpetual lovetricks that past between her and her people into a kind of romance, wholly neglected the nobility. And by these degrees came the house of commons to raise that head, which since has bin so high and formidable to their princes, that they have look'd pale upon those assemblys.[2]

The balance of property had moved from the nobility to the people by the time of Elizabeth. The only class named as beneficiary of the shift is the yeomanry, but the reference to the House of Commons as the institutional beneficiary makes it clear that Harrington was including in 'the people' the gentry as well as the yeomanry.

The same analysis of the shift, with a few more strokes of detail, is given in *The Art of Lawgiving*: the growth of the city of London is linked with 'the declining of the balance to popularity'; parliaments were, by the time of James I, 'mere popular councils, and running to popularity of government like a bowl down a hill', and neither the new peerage which he created in abundance, nor the old, availed him anything against them; 'in our days . . . the lands in possession of the people overbalance those held by the nobility, at least, nine in ten'.[3] In neither of these accounts of the shift in the

[1] Ibid.   [2] Ibid., p. 65.   [3] *Art of L.*, pp. 364–6.

English balance is there any mention of the gentry. But there can be no doubt that here, as in the account in *Oceana*, the gentry were included in 'the people', as witness the description of James's parliaments as popular, and the estimate of the present holdings of the nobility as only one-tenth of the land.[1]

When we go beyond the historical accounts of the shift in the English balance we do find explicit mention of the gentry. But whenever Harrington discusses them, whether in connexion with his law of the balance, or with the application of that law to framing a system of government for contemporary England, he equates the gentry with the nobility and contrasts them with the people.

Thus in the first part of the Preliminaries of *Oceana*, where he is discussing government in general and the law of the balance, he follows Machiavelli in using gentry as synonymous with nobility—those who have lands, castles, and treasures, whereby the rest are brought to dependence on them—while he corrects Machiavelli by saying that a nobility or gentry is destructive of popular government only if it has an overbalance of property.[2] A little farther on in the Preliminaries he argues that the gentry (still used synonymously with the nobility) and the people are as indispensable to each other in a commonwealth as are officers and soldiers in an army: the making, governing, and military leadership of a commonwealth require 'the genius of a gentleman', 'where there is not a nobility to hearten the people, they are slothful, regardless of the world, and of the public interest of liberty, as even those of *Rome* had bin without their gentry . . .'.[3] Gentry and people are separate classes,

---

[1] Even if we could not assume that Harrington knew that gentry and nobility between them had much more than one-tenth, we have evidence that he thought the two or three hundred largest landowners alone held something like one-tenth. The whole land of England he estimated as worth £10 million a year. There were, he said, at most 300 men who now had more than £2,000 a year in lands (*Oceana*, pp. 99–100). So the top 300 or so would alone account for something like £600,000 a year, and more probably, since the £2,000 is not an average but a minimum, for something like £1 million a year, i.e. one-tenth of the land.

[2] *Oceana*, pp. 39–40.   [3] Ibid., p. 53.

different in their nature and function, though necessary to
each other.

When finally Harrington comes to fit a political super-
structure to the existing balance of property in England, he
again uses gentry as synonymous with nobility and distinct
from the people. A 'nobility or gentry' is essential to a commonwealth, for politics cannot be mastered without study,
and the people cannot have leisure to study; lawyers and
divines, he adds, because of 'their incurable running upon
their own narrow biass', are of no more use for this than are
'so many other tradesmen'. Since 'neither the people, nor
divines, and lawyers, can be the aristocracy of a nation, there
remains only the nobility; in which stile, to avoid farther
repetition, I shall understand the gentry also, as the *French*
do by the word *noblesse*'.[1]

A nobility which holds an overbalance of property to the
whole people, as did the feudal nobility, is incompatible with
popular government. But a nobility which holds an underbalance to the people is 'not only safe, but necessary to the
natural mixture of a well-order'd commonwealth'; nobility
being here defined, again after Machiavelli, though now
more broadly, as *such as live upon their own revenues in
plenty, without ingagement either to the tilling of their lands,
or other work for their livelihood*'.[2] It is in this context that
England is said to be blessed in having exactly the right
ingredients for a popular government: the balance of property is in the people, and at the same time there is an
excellent 'nobility or gentry', well studied and well versed in
military leadership, combining ancient riches with ancient
virtue, ideally fitted to provide political leadership in the
senate and offices of Oceana.[3]

In short, it is because the English 'nobility or gentry' do
not possess an overbalance of property that they can safely
be allowed the leadership in the proposed English republic.
Harrington makes his whole case for the erection of a gentry-
led commonwealth in England in 1656 rest on this. It is

[1] Ibid., p. 124.   [2] Ibid., p. 125.   [3] Ibid., pp. 123–5.

only, he insists, when a nobility or gentry have an underbalance of land that they can safely be permitted in a commonwealth; the English nobility or gentry, he insists equally,
now are safe and necessary to the commonwealth.

Harrington is saying, then, that the nobility and gentry
together held in 1656 less than half the land,[1] substantially
less than half, for their underbalance is of such degree as to
permit a stable commonwealth to be constructed on it, whereas whenever the balance between nobility and people is nearly
equal there can be no stability.[2] And since he has said that
the peers have not more than 10 per cent. of the land, the
distribution he believes to exist in 1656 is: peers, 10 per
cent. or less; gentry, substantially less than 40 per cent.;
yeomanry and townsmen, substantially more than 50 per
cent.

How, then, it may be asked, could Harrington have
written his account of the shift in the English balance in such
a way as to leave the impression that the balance had shifted
to the gentry? That he did leave this impression on some of
his contemporaries and on some later scholars is evident in
Professor Trevor-Roper's account, to which we shall turn
in a moment. A sufficient reason for this impression is not
difficult to see. The chief evidence Harrington offered for
the shift away from the nobility to the people was the shift of
power in the country and in parliament from the nobility to
the independent commoners. The balance was so much in
'the popular party' by Elizabeth's time that she reigned by
courting the people and neglecting the nobility, so that the
House of Commons came to be dominant; James I's parliaments were 'mere popular councils'. Since it was obvious,
then as now, that the Commons under Elizabeth and James
were gentry rather than any lower rank, it was natural to
conclude that Harrington meant that the balance of land was
in the gentry. But the conclusion does not follow. For

---

[1] This follows only if Harrington is here using underbalance in the sense required
by his statements of the principle of the balance, not in the peculiar sense in which
he later uses it. The ambiguity is examined below, p. 189.

[2] *Oceana*, p. 38.

Harrington believed that the ordinary people, if not injured by 'the better sort', naturally defer to them,[1] and naturally elect as many of the better sort as they can,[2] so much so that he thought a special constitutional provision necessary to ensure that in the new commonwealth the main representative body would contain some of the lower sort.[3] All that follows from the description of Elizabethan and Jacobean parliaments as popular is that the balance of land was in the gentry and people together.

With this much elucidation of Harrington's own view of the gentry we may look briefly at the treatment he has had in the gentry controversy. We must look at it, for while the interpretation of Harrington is only marginal to the controversy, the controversy has become crucial to the interpretation of Harrington, and in a dangerously misleading way. Tawney, in using Harrington as a witness for the rise of the gentry, accurately described the shift that Harrington had seen as a shift from the nobility to the gentry and yeomanry, not to the gentry alone;[4] Harrington's statement was evidence for the rise of the gentry only when taken together with the evidence of other observers as to the decline in the position of the yeomanry towards 1600 when long leases fell in.[5]

Trevor-Roper,[6] attacking Tawney's thesis, gives Harrington short shrift, first seeking to discredit him as a witness, then presenting his theory as the doctrine—demonstrably false—of the declining gentry in their hopeless struggle to restore their position. Both arguments depend on lumping together Harrington and several 'Harringtonians' who echoed or supported or used his theory for their own purposes: as arguments about Harrington's theory they are without foundation.

Take first Harrington's worth as a witness. We are told

---

[1] Ibid., p. 133.   [2] *Art of L.*, p. 419.
[3] *Valerius*, pp. 449–50. See below, p. 183.
[4] 'Harrington's Interpretation of His Age', p. 212.
[5] Ibid., p. 216; and 'The Rise of the Gentry', *Econ. Hist. Rev.* xi (1941), 5.
[6] *The Gentry*, 1540–1640, *Econ. Hist. Rev. Supplement*, no. 1 (1953).

that a consistent doctrine was expressed or referred to by Harrington, Neville, Chaloner, Baynes, Ludlow, and others, and that it included the proposition that a shift in the balance of property between social classes had taken place in England, that 'the Crown and nobility had lost their property and "the gentry have all the lands"'.[1] This doctrine is then discredited as evidence for the rise of the gentry between 1540 and 1640, on two grounds. First, these commentators 'were often obscure and sometimes self-contradictory' about the period in which the shift had occurred: its beginning was sometimes put two hundred or more years ago, sometimes in the reign of James I or even later. Hence the commentators could not be said to have been describing an historical process of 1540–1640; what they were doing was 'generalizing, over a vague tract of time, a process of which their only evidence is the violent change of the last decade' (i.e. 1640–50). Secondly, the commentators were not several independent observers but 'a group, almost a coterie, of active Republican politicians, who took their views from Harrington and Neville, themselves an inseparable combine'; their statements 'represent not a concurrence of observation but a repetition of dogma: the dogma of *Oceana*'.[2]

We may wonder how a coterie, repeating a dogma, could have been so vague and self-contradictory about the dates of the alleged shift, for Harrington was quite clear about it. The shift began about 1489 with Henry VII's legislation, was accelerated in 1536 with the dissolution of the monasteries, and had visibly tipped the balance by Elizabeth's reign.[3] It was not recently but in their great-grandfathers' time that the gentry had worn the blue coats of the nobility.[4] The reference to the nobility and clergy having the balance 'under the late monarchy' is to the time of the barons' wars.[5] True, when Harrington wants to show that a change in the balance can happen so sudden', he says that it had moved from

[1] *The Gentry*, p. 45.   [2] Ibid., pp. 45–46.
[3] *Oceana*, pp. 64–65; *Art of L.*, pp. 364–6.
[4] *Prerogative*, p. 281.   [5] Ibid., p. 246.

monarchical to popular 'between the reign of Henry the Seventh, and that of Queen Elizabeth, being under fifty years',[1] and when he wants to argue that it was not sudden he says that the government has been changing from aristocratical to popular for a hundred and forty years.[2] But there is no serious inconsistency here: the change in the balance starts about the beginning of the sixteenth century, the balance is tipped about the middle of the century, and it goes on moving down for another century. Harrington himself, then, was clear enough about the dates. And Harrington is not to be reproached with having generalized over that tract of time a process of which his only evidence was the violent change of 1640–50: the evidence on which he most relies he takes from Bacon's *History*, which had been published in 1622.

Harrington at any rate must be left out of the coterie. Whatever his disciples and those who made use of him said from time to time, Harrington did not say that 'the gentry have all the lands'. The shift he found was not from king and nobility to gentry but from king and nobility to the people, and in his usage the people always included the yeomanry and sometimes excluded the gentry.

The identification of Harrington's doctrine with the dicta of some of his followers leads Trevor-Roper even more unfortunately to describe Harrington's doctrine as false. The doctrine, he argues, providentially supplied just what the 'mere gentry' needed, and so became their slogan 'in their last losing struggle against the Court. The fact that they lost in that struggle is evidence of the falsity of the doctrine.'[3] But it was not Harrington's doctrine that property had shifted to, and power should therefore be vested in, the 'mere' gentry. He held, indeed, that property had shifted from nobility to gentry and people, and that power should shift accordingly. But even if we leave the people out of it, the gentry whom Harrington would invest with power included the 'greater gentry' and the 'improving gentry' as well as the

---

[1] *Art of L.*, p. 408.   [2] *Pian Piano*, p. 528.   [3] *The Gentry*, pp. 49–50.

mere or lesser or declining gentry. The greater or rising
gentry, with incomes up to £2,000 or £3,000 a year,[1] would
not be cramped by Harrington's agrarian limit of £2,000
a year lands in England (£4,500 in the British Isles, and
possibly twice as much again in colonies) plus unlimited
amounts from trade, and something from offices;[2] and the
improving gentry are recognized in Harrington's endorsement of racking of rents.[3] Had Harrington postulated a pre-
ponderance of property in the mere gentry, their actual
failure to win power would be evidence either that his factual
postulate was wrong or that his theory was false. Trevor-
Roper would have it both that Harrington's facts were wrong
and that the theory was false. But since these were not
Harrington's facts, neither conclusion follows.

There remains the question why Harrington was so ambiguous in placing the gentry now with the nobility and now
with the people. Why did he use two different definitions of
'the few or a nobility', one excluding and one including the
gentry, and was he inconsistent in doing so? It will be
recalled that he used the narrow definition in describing the
change from the Gothic to the modern balance, and the broad
definition in discussing the position in 1656. The difference
in usage is intelligible, and the two uses consistent, in view
of the difference between feudal and post-feudal land tenure.
When land was held on military tenure, it was only the
nobility proper whose titles to land gave them the military
power on which the balance of government depended; the
knights and gentlemen who held of them were subordinate.
But with the disappearance of feudal tenures the nobility
proper got no more military benefit from their lands, acre
for acre, than did any other landowner. Nobles and gentry,
and even freeholders below the rank of gentry, were, in
respect of the military potential given by land ownership,
co-ordinate; each acre was of equal value in feeding an army.

---

[1] *The Gentry*, p. 52.
[2] *Oceana*, p. 100; *Prerogative*, p. 280, quoted below, p. 179.
[3] *Oceana*, p. 165; see below, p. 178.

With this change, which was concurrent with the acquisition of a lot of land by the gentry and yeomanry, the old nobility was reduced so decisively that it became an insignificant class in calculations of the balance of property and power. But the nobles still had qualities of leadership which were needed. So had the gentry. Thenceforth, nobles and gentry, as leisured rentiers able to give political leadership, could be treated as essentially the same class. The newly significant dividing line for Harrington was that between the 'nobility or gentry' and the freeholders below that rank, who, working their land for a living, were by their way of life incapable of political leadership and so were classed with the mechanic 'people'.

It was not Harrington who moved the gentry from 'people' to 'nobility'; they moved themselves, by achieving independence of feudal status and acquiring substantial lands in their own right. In that sense at least, the gentry did in fact rise, and Harrington's double usage reflects that rise. This is not to say that Harrington made any such defence of his double usage. He made no defence of it at all. There is no indication that he was conscious of anything needing to be defended. He may well have assumed that the gentry readers for whom he was writing would not misunderstand his assessment of the facts, namely, that for purposes of government the gentry had, in the last century and a half, moved up a class. There is, after all, nothing odd in the fact that Harrington, in his main analyses, never referred to the gentry as a separate class but always included them in another. The gentry had in fact never been a class capable of ruling on its own. It could share rule with the nobility and court, or with the yeomanry, but that was all. Harrington's double treatment of the gentry recognizes this, as does his proposal of a commonwealth in which gentry and yeomanry would share the power.

On one of the rare occasions when Harrington did refer to the gentry as a separate class, it was to insist that they were still not capable of ruling on their own. In a pamphlet of

July 1659 he argues that the House of Commons 'as hath been hitherto usual in *England*', being 'for the most part gentlemen', had stood in between the interest of the king and the interest of the people 'while they were under a nobility; but since, through the natural decay of that order, they came to a greater height, it hath been to endure no check [from a king]'. The gentry had risen to fill a power vacuum created by the decay of the nobility. But Harrington warns that the gentry House of Commons of 1659, if not reformed so as to admit the people to a share of power, 'will be addicted unto the introduction of monarchy, through the check they apprehend from the people'.[1] Such an attempt, he argued, could lead to nothing but continuous instability; only the joint rule of the gentry and the people would work.

3. *The Bourgeois Society*

We have seen that Harrington's ambiguous use of 'the few', or ambiguous placing of the gentry, is intelligible on his own terms of reference. The gentry had shared with the people a common subordination to the nobility; now, all landowners being co-ordinate, the gentry had more in common with the nobility than with the people. But to leave the analysis there would be to leave a misleading impression of Harrington's view of his own society. If he took an aristocratic view of the seventeenth-century gentry he also took, to a surprising extent, a bourgeois view of the seventeenth-century aristocracy. Before we go on to look at the second central ambiguity in his theory we shall examine the extent to which he saw his England as a bourgeois society.

The orthodox post-Tawney view has credited Harrington with some insight into the nature of the change from feudal to bourgeois relations of production. Against this view Mr. Pocock has entered a strong dissent. Harrington, he writes,

---

[1] *A Discourse Shewing That the Spirit of Parliaments . . . is not to be trusted,* p. 575.

has no conception whatever that there exists a complex web of economic relationships between men which can be studied in itself and which
determines the distribution of power among them. Compared to the
best Tudor writers on social reform he is not so much ignorant of as
uninterested in the realities of an agrarian political economy, and it has
not occurred to him that the exchange of goods and services on an
agrarian basis either can be studied in order to determine its own laws,
or ought to be studied in its relation to political power. . . . His sole
comment on the economic relations between men—and the sole
foundation of all that he has to say about property as the basis of power
—is, 'an army is a beast that hath a great belly and must be fed'; he
that has the land can feed the soldiers.[1]

The vigour of this attack is welcome. Some corrective was
needed to the over-simple view that was coming to be taken
of Harrington. It was improper to infer that because Harrington saw the fundamental political role of changes in the
distribution of property between Henry VII and the Civil
War, he also saw the nature of the change in the economic
relations between men and classes that had taken place at the
same time. To see the political effect of the disappearance of
the system of dependent tenures—which Pocock holds to be
Harrington's claim to originality as a political thinker, and
one entitling him to high esteem—is not necessarily to see
at all into the system of market relationships which was
replacing it.

Yet Pocock's corrective goes too far. There is evidence
that Harrington was aware of the pervasiveness of market
relations, even in the use of land; 'he that has the land can
feed the soldiers' was not Harrington's sole comment on the
economic relations between men. And, perhaps more important, Harrington's main defence of his political proposals
rests on the assumption that the gentry are sufficiently bourgeois to administer an entrepreneurial society acceptably to
the entrepreneurs.

Take first the evidence of Harrington's awareness and
acceptance of market motivations and relationships. There

[1] J. G. A. Pocock, *The Ancient Constitution and the Feudal Law* (1957), pp. 128-9.

is his defence of usury, based on the postulates that private accumulations of capital should be made available for commercial enterprise, and that no man will venture his money but through hope of some gain. In a country as large as England, where money cannot overbalance land, usury 'is so far from being destructive that it is necessary'; it is 'of profit to the commonwealth', 'a mighty profit to the public', because it brings money into commercial circulation.[1] Moreover, accumulation is honourable and respectable. Estates are got by industry, not by 'covetousness and ambition'.[2] 'Industry of all things is the most accumulative, and accumulation of all things hates levelling: the revenue therfore of the people being the revenue of industry . . . [no people in the world] may be found to have bin levellers.'[3] The desire to accumulate, and the possibility of honest accumulation, are not of course presented as new in the seventeenth century, but one has only to compare the moral position revealed in these statements with the views of the seventeenth-century traditionalists to see how far Harrington has accepted bourgeois values.

His specific observations on the social economy of England recognize its fluid character. Upward class mobility based on commercial or industrial profits is commonplace: there are 'innumerable trades wherupon men live, not only better than others upon good shares of lands, but becom also purchasers of greater estates'; 'the revenue of industry in a nation, at least in this, is three or fourfold greater than that of the mere rent'.[4] The same postulate of mobility appears in the defence of the agrarian law, one of the merits of which is that under it the rich cannot 'exclude [the people's] industry or merit from attaining to the like estate, power, or honor'; to which he adds as a matter of course that the people will assume that the riches of the commonwealth should 'go according to the difference of mens industry'.[5]

[1] *Prerogative*, p. 229.
[2] *Ibid.*, p. 278; cf. Locke's treatment of covetousness, below, ch. V, pp. 236-7; and contrast Hobbes's treatment, above, ch. II, p. 38.
[3] *System of Politics*, p. 471.   [4] *Oceana*, p. 154.   [5] *Prerogative*, pp. 242-3.

To such indications that Harrington recognized the prevalence of bourgeois standards among 'the people' we may
add that he had some notion of the elements of the market
economy, and was not hostile to its social implications. He
was not to be frightened by the prospect of a great increase
in the size of mercantile cities : it would not disrupt but would
strengthen the existing economy, for urban and rural were
complementary parts of a single market society. Urban
growth leads to rural growth and vice versa; in each case it is
the natural operation of a law of supply and demand for
commodities and labour that brings the secondary growth.
Where the city grows first,

the more mouths there be in a city, the more meat of necessity must be
vented by the country, and so there will be more corn, more cattel, and
better markets; which breeding more laborers, more husbandmen, and
richer farmers, bring the country so far from a commonwealth of
cottagers, that . . . the husbandman, . . . his trade thus uninterrupted,
in that his markets are certain, gos on with increase of children, of
servants, of corn, and of cattel. . . . The country then growing more
populous, and better stock'd with cattel, which also increases manure
for the land, must proportionably increase in fruitfulness.

Likewise a populous countryside leads to a more populous
city,

for when the people increase so much, that the dug of earth can do no
more, the overplus must seek som other way of livelihood: which is
either arms, such were those of the *Goths* and *Vandals*; or merch-
andize and manufacture, for which ends it being necessary that they
lay their heads and their stock together, this makes populous citys.[1]

If this shows no mastery of political economy it does suggest
some grasp of the essentials of a market economy; his remarks about the comparative advantages of English and
Dutch trade[2] point in the same direction.

Harrington had, then, some idea of the market relations
that prevailed among 'the people'. Yet for all we have seen
so far he seems to have thought of the nobility and gentry as

[1] *Ibid.*, p. 279.   [2] *Oceana*, p. 165.

untouched by those relations. It is usually the contrast between the two ways of life, and between the two sources of income, that he emphasizes. Incomes derived from trade, manufacture, and husbandry come from effort intelligently applied to the production of commodities for the market, the incentive being the desire of accumulation. Income derived from ownership of land just flows in: 'that the rents and profits of a man's land in feesimple or property, com in naturally and easily, by common consent or concernment, that is, by virtue of the law founded upon the public interest, and therfore voluntarily establish'd by the whole people, is an apparent thing'.[1] No effort is required; the rentiers seem detached from the market society around them. But Harrington knew that their income did not arise from a traditional relation between landlord and tenant remote from the market relation. He knew that a capitalist relation had penetrated to the land, in the form of racking of rents, and he accepted it in principle, deploring only its excess: 'racking of rents is a vile thing in the richer sort, an uncharitable one to the poorer, a perfect mark of slavery, and nips your commonwealth in the fairest blossom. On the other side, if there should be too much ease given in this kind, it would occasion sloth, and so destroy industry, the principal nerve of a commonwealth.'[2] He professes himself insufficiently expert to say how far racking of rents should be allowed to go, but he is clear on the principle: far enough to keep the tenant yeomen from being slack but not so far as to destroy them, for they are the main strength of a commonwealth and 'the least turbulent or ambitious' of any class. Where upholders of traditional society could see nothing but evil and dissolvent effects in the racking of rents, Harrington saw its necessity as an incentive to industrious production. The economic function of the landlord was to enforce the industry of the tenant; by doing so he would keep alive, not destroy, a commonwealth of husbandmen.

Equally revealing of Harrington's view of the place of the

---

[1] *Prerogative*, p. 231.　　　　　[2] *Oceana*, p. 165.

landowner in capitalist society is his treatment of the advantages to be gained by military subjection of 'provinces'. He subsumes under one general theory of appropriation the labour of the entrepreneur and the labour of the armed nobility and gentry conquering lands and peoples for their private gain. In Harrington's labour justification of property, the labour that gives title to property is indifferently military or pacific. 'This donation of the earth to man', he writes, quoting the Psalms and Genesis, 'coms to a kind of selling it for INDUSTRY . . . . From the different kinds and successes of this industry, whether in arms, or in other exercises of the mind or body, derives the natural equity of dominion or property. . . .'[1] Oceana is to be

a commonwealth for increase: the trade of a commonwealth for increase, is arms; arms are not born by merchants, but by noblemen and gentlemen. The nobility therfore having these arms in their hands, by which provinces are to be acquir'd, new provinces yield new estates; so wheras the merchant has his returns in silk or canvas, the soldier will have his return in land. . . . if ever the commonwealth attains to five new provinces (and such a commonwealth will have provinces enow) it is certain, that (besides honors, magistracys, and the revenues annex'd) there will be more estates in the nobility of *Oceana*, of fourteen thousand pounds land a year, than ever were, or can otherwise be of four. . . .[2]

The acquisition of such large estates by nobles and gentlemen who already had the maximum estates in England (and Ireland and Scotland)[3] would not endanger the popular balance of property or power at home, for the subjugated people were to be producers of revenue for, rather than potential military servitors of, their conquerors.

The trade of the nobility and gentry is arms, the labour by which they entitle themselves to their shares of God's donation of the earth to man is the labour of arms. The difference

---

[1] *Art of L.*, p. 363. [2] *Prerogative*, p. 280.
[3] Under Harrington's agrarian law a man could hold up to £2,000 a year of land in England and as much again in Ireland, as well as £500 a year in Scotland (*Oceana*, p. 100).

between the nobility-gentry and the people, of which Harrington makes so much when he is thinking of their political qualities, comes down to this: they have different trades, both accumulative, both yielding returns that increase the real capital of the nation. This is not to say that Harrington had in his own mind entirely assimilated the nobility-gentry into a bourgeois order, but it is at least to say that the contrast he so often draws between them and the mercantile and mechanic people is perfectly consistent with his seeing them as components of a bourgeois society.

We can go farther. A policy of colonial subjugation is, of course, not peculiar to a bourgeois or capitalist society: it had been a normal method of building empires in the non-bourgeois states of the ancient world. But colonial subjugation, by which the surplus product of a people's labour could be made to flow in one form or another (as rents, or as profits of trade in the goods they produced) into the hands of the new owners, was in the sixteenth and seventeenth centuries one of the means by which the accumulations of wealth required to initiate modern capitalism were being provided. While we cannot be sure how clearly Harrington saw this, his views on Ireland are suggestive. He approved of its subjugation, regretted that it was not producing nearly as much revenue for England as it could do, and would have liked to see it repopulated with a more industrious and enterprising people, the Jews, whom he thought capable of improving Ireland's agriculture and increasing its trade to levels which produce £4 million a year 'dry rents', i.e. net surplus product over and above the wages of labour and the profits of enterprise. Of this surplus he modestly proposed that only £2 million a year (plus customs duties sufficient to maintain an army in Ireland) should be paid as tribute to England.[1] The scheme was unusual in that it involved granting the conquered lands to another outside people in return for an annual tribute. Harrington thought this unusual feature necessary because of the peculiar languor of the Irish

[1] *Oceana*, pp. 33–34.

climate, which had not only made the Irish people inveter-
ately slothful but had similarly softened the English who had
been planted there. Unique measures were needed to bring
the cash returns to England up to a reasonable level. But it
is clear from the remarks quoted above about the new estates
to be yielded by new provinces, that in the lands still to
be conquered Harrington envisaged the appropriation of
the surplus taking place through the then more usual
channels, chiefly as rents paid to the private English
landlords.

We may say, then, that while Harrington certainly had
no Marxian theory of 'primary accumulation' he saw plainly
enough that the function of colonial peoples was to produce
a surplus which would flow into English hands as disposable
wealth. His models of the 'commonwealth for increase' came
indeed from the ancient world. But if his head was stuffed
with 'ancient prudence' his feet were on seventeenth-century
ground. He saw the nobility and gentry making an economic
as well as a political contribution to seventeenth-century
England. In adding to their own wealth they would add very
substantially to the wealth of the nation, for their new
revenues could either be used to improve their estates or be
lent at interest, in either case to the benefit of the commonwealth. So the nobility and gentry fitted usefully and smoothly
into a society of predominantly free industrious entrepreneurs—husbandmen, tradesmen, and merchants—in
whom the balance now lay.

Before we leave Harrington's picture of his own society
we should notice that he put one class right out of the
picture. Wage-earners or 'servants' are not only denied
citizenship (on the ground that they are not freemen and
therefore are incapable of participating in the government
of a commonwealth);[1] they are treated less as a class within
the commonwealth than as a people outside it. No account
is to be taken of them in constructing the balance of classes
within the commonwealth: 'The causes of commotion in a

[1] Ibid., p. 77; *Art of L.,* p. 409.

commonwealth are either external or internal. External are from enemys, from subjects, or from servants.'[1]

4. *The Equal Commonwealth and the Equal Agrarian*

Upon this society Harrington proposed to erect a commonwealth that would last for ever. He calls it an 'equal commonwealth' and he makes its permanence depend ultimately on the agrarian law which he calls an 'equal agrarian'. But when we examine the proposals we find that the structure incorporates two legislative bodies, each with a veto in effect, made up of different social classes though both elected by the whole citizen body; that the two classes are, or may be, very unequal in their total landed wealth; and that the balance of property need not lie in that class which is numerically far the larger and which therefore can control the election of both legislative bodies. His attempts to explain why in spite of this the system will be everlasting— he scarcely tries to explain why it would work well from month to month or from year to year—are wildly confusing. We shall have to move a little way into this confusion in order to conjecture how Harrington could have thought he was being so clear. The argument essentially is that the commonwealth could not be overthrown as long as the agrarian law held, and that the agrarian law would hold because no class strong enough to alter it would have an interest in doing so. We shall see that neither of these propositions can be sustained without the assumption that both gentry and people are bourgeois; that he does in the course of the argument come close to stating this assumption but does not state it clearly or seem to see that it is needed; and that he is consequently involved in some striking contradictions. We shall first look briefly at the proposed constitutional structure, then at the more difficult problem of the agrarian.

---

[1] *Oceana*, p. 138; cf. Locke's treatment of the labouring class as not full members of civil society, below, ch. V, p. 248.

The essentials of the constitutional structure are: (1) a Senate of 300 members and a Representative of 1,050, both filled by indirect annual elections (one-third of the members elected each year for a three-year term, no member being eligible for successive terms) by secret ballot, the electors for both Senate and Representative being all men above the age of thirty, not servants or spendthrifts; candidacy for the Senate and for three-sevenths of the places in the Representative having a substantial property qualification; (2) a strict separation of powers between the two legislative bodies, the Senate debating and proposing legislation, the Representative approving or rejecting those proposals without debate; (3) election of civil, military, and judicial officers, no incumbent being eligible for successive terms. A system so constituted (with the agrarian to fix its property basis) would be immune from internal dissolution. It met the test of 'the perfection of government', namely, 'that no man or men in or under it can have the interest; or having the interest, can have the power to disturb it with sedition'.[1]

Where did the nobility-gentry and the people fit into this scheme? The nobility and gentry would fill the Senate, three-sevenths of the Representative, and the more important offices. They would fill them not as of right but elected by the whole people. The property qualification for these places (£100 a year in land, goods or money) would admit wealthier yeomen and townsmen as well as gentry. It was not on the property qualification but on the habitual deference of the people that Harrington relied to fill these places with gentry. Indeed, the point of the property qualification (which was unusual in that it worked in both directions) was, he said, to ensure that the majority of the places in the Representative would be filled by men of under £100 a year.[2] To these men of 'the meaner sort', who made up the bulk of the people, were allotted four-sevenths of the places in the Representative, and the less important offices.

[1] *Oceana*, p. 49; cf. *Prerogative*, p. 247; *Art of L.*, p. 433.
[2] *Valerius*, pp. 449–50; cf. *Oceana*, p. 133; *Art of L.*, p. 419.

We thus have careful provision for two legislative bodies made up predominantly of two different classes. The argument by which the separation of powers between them is justified implies that they have to some extent different interests: just as two girls having to divide a cake between them, each wanting the most, will be equally served if one divides and the other chooses, so the Senate and the people, each wanting the most, will be equally served if one proposes legislative measures and the other chooses. Now it is not self-evident that a system which requires the concurrence of two such bodies would work harmoniously. Both, it is true, were to be elected by the whole citizen body, but there were to be no parties, no canvassing,[1] by which the people could make their wishes prevail; and the property qualification for the Senate would make it impossible for the middle and lower ranges of the people to put their own men in. Nor can the habitual deference of the people be treated as a sufficient condition for the harmonious operation of the system. The deference to which Harrington refers is an effect rather than a cause of harmony of interests: the people are deferential only when they do not feel themselves injured, and he assumes throughout that the people know their own interests.[2] He simply asserts that where the Senate is not confined to an hereditary order but is elected by the people, the interests of the Senate and the people are the same.[3]

In fact Harrington offered no proofs that the system would work. Presumably he thought that this was covered by his proofs of the more important proposition, i.e. that the system could never be overthrown by sedition. These proofs all come down to proof of the ability of the agrarian law to prevent any class having the interest and the power to overthrow the commonwealth.

It is here that Harrington's argument becomes almost inexplicably confused. For the agrarian, by Harrington's own account, would not prevent gross inequality of property.

[1] *Oceana*, p. 144.   [2] e.g. *Prerogative*, p. 246; *Valerius*, p. 459.
[3] *Prerogative*, p. 244.

The agrarian limit of £2,000 a year in land would, on his computation, allow all the land of England to fall into the hands of 5,000 men, leaving the rest of the 500,000 citizens with no land at all.[1] While he regarded it as highly improbable that the land would ever come into the hands of as few as 5,000 owners—'as improbable as any thing in the world that is not altogether impossible'—he held that even in that case there would still be a popular state and an equal balance:

the land coming to be in the possession of five thousand, falls not into a number that is within the compass of the few, or such a one as can be princes, either in regard of their number, or of their estates; but to such a one as cannot consent to abolish the agrarian, because that were to consent to rob one another: nor can they have any party among them, or against their common interest, strong enough to force them, or to break it; which remaining, the five thousand neither are nor can be any more than a popular state, and the balance remains every whit as equal, as if the land were in never so many more hands.[2]

That the 5,000 would not consent to abolish the agrarian may be granted, for if 5,000 had the whole £10 million a year of land, each of the 5,000 would under the agrarian have exactly £2,000 a year of land, and if the agrarian were abolished or raised any owner's gain would be another's loss. Yet the argument as a whole appears to be circular. The agrarian would ensure the preservation of an equal balance, it is said, because the maximum concentration of ownership permitted by the agrarian would not lead the owners to destroy the agrarian. But this would only ensure the preservation of the equal balance if it was already assumed that the balance is equal as long as the agrarian is unbroken.

Harrington has in fact already made and stated virtually this assumption:

where the rich are so bounded by an agrarian that they cannot overbalance (and therfore neither oppress the people, nor exclude their industry or merit from attaining to the like estate, power, or honor) the whole people have the whole riches of the nation already equally divided among them; for that the riches of a commonwealth should not

<hr />

[1] See Note M, p. 298.   [2] *Prerogative*, p. 247.

go according to the difference of mens industry, but be distributed by the poll, were inequal.[1]

Equality of riches, in Harrington's view, is not arithmetical equality, it is equality of opportunity of increasing one's riches. It is hence a sufficient basis for an 'equal commonwealth' that the rich should not be able to check the upward mobility of the middle class. The agrarian is supposed to prevent them checking that mobility. Therefore, as long as the agrarian is unbroken, the balance is 'equal'.

Thus when Harrington's concept of equality is brought into the reckoning the argument no longer appears circular. But the argument still involves an unstated assumption. For the agrarian by itself would not prevent the rich from checking the upward mobility of the people. It would only do so on the assumption that any future class of the landed rich would be more interested in maintaining the market economy (which would incidentally permit industrious men from 'the people' to continue to accumulate and rise) than in banding together to oppose the people. Harrington's defence of the agrarian as a sufficient guarantee of an equal balance against attacks from the few rests, then, on a concept of equality that is characteristically bourgeois (equality of riches is equal opportunity to accumulate unequal amounts), and a concept of the gentry as sufficiently bourgeois to put first, in their own interests, the maintenance of a market economy.

The demonstration that the agrarian is immune from attack from the other side rests on the same concept of equality and on some rudimentary concepts of capitalist economics. Why might not the people who had little land (or none at all, in the case of 5,000 having it all) seek to level the wealth, either seizing it by civil war or in effect confiscating it by legislation reducing the agrarian limit? Harrington's most general answer is that they will not do it because they already have equal opportunity of accumulation, 'the whole riches of the nation already equally divided among them'. He reinforces this with an arithmetical

[1] *Prerogative*, pp. 242–3.

argument designed to show that they would not wish to level because it would be against their own interest. The whole value of the land, as it is or might be rented, is £10 million a year. If the land were seized and divided equally among the one million heads of families it would bring each only £10 a year. But the meanest labourer at a shilling a day gets more than this already, and if the land were levelled he would lose his present income for 'there would be no body to set him on work'. The more prosperous tradesmen would lose even more, for the revenue of industry is three or four times greater than that of rent, and they would lose that revenue by raising civil war or even by constitutional levelling.[1]

The arithmetic does not seem very convincing. Why might not the labourer turned smallholder enjoy the £10 a year (which was the measure of the supposed productivity of his land over and above the yield of the labour on it) and the revenue of his labour as well? Why might not the tradesman, whose revenue from his industry had been enough to allow him to accumulate, continue to enjoy that revenue, which had never depended on his title to land? And why might not the middling yeoman, who indeed needed more land than he would get by complete levelling, still profit from a partial confiscation of the great estates by reducing the maximum from £2,000 to £1,000 or less? Harrington saw no such difficulties. But the questions answer themselves if some rudimentary bourgeois economic notions are being assumed. The first objection disappears when it is assumed that the productivity of small holdings is much less than that of land worked as capital for a profit, or, which comes to the same thing, that the wage-labour structure is essential to maintain existing productivity. The second disappears when it is assumed that the profitability of trades depends on the profitable use of land. These assumptions are very much the ones we have already seen implied in Harrington's remarks on racking of rents and on the growth of cities. The third objection disappears when it is assumed (as we have seen

[1] *Oceana*, pp. 154-5; *Prerogative*, p. 247.

Harrington does assume) that the equality the people want is equality of opportunity of profiting according to their enterprise: they would not risk weakening the sanctity of property by any confiscatory measures.

The whole of Harrington's defence of the agrarian as a sufficient guarantee of an equal balance and a sufficient basis for a popular or equal commonwealth depends, we conclude, on a concept of the economy which takes for granted the necessity or at least the superiority of capitalist relations of production, and a concept of equality which is essentially bourgeois.

5. *The Self-cancelling Balance Principle*

It is only on these concepts that Harrington's extraordinary shift of meaning of the term overbalance makes any sense. In his general statements of the principle of the balance, and in his many examples of different historical balances and changes in balances, Harrington equates overbalance with possession of more than half the land. The prerequisite of a commonwealth is stated indifferently as possession of three-quarters (or two-thirds) of the land by the people, or where neither one man nor the few overbalance the people in land.[1] Yet now we find him saying that if all the land were to come into the hands of 5,000 proprietors (a tiny minority of the 500,000 citizens) the balance would still be a popular one; and not only that, but even that the agrarian of Oceana, which would permit 5,000 to get all the land, would not permit 'the few or the richer' (here defined as the 5,000) to overbalance the people (defined as 'the many or the poorer sort').[2]

It is hard to find any consistency in this. Everything seems to change its meaning. The few here are the 5,000; within a few pages it is said that 5,000 is not 'a number that is within the compass of the few'.[3] The balance is said to be

[1] e.g. *Oceana*, p. 37; *Prerogative*, pp. 227, 270; *Art of L.*, p. 363; *System of Politics*, p. 467.   [2] *Prerogative*, p. 243; cf. p. 242.

[3] Ibid., p. 247, as quoted above, p. 185.

in the people when all the land is in the 5,000-strong few. Overbalance does not mean what it did, for now the few, who would certainly have the overbalance of property, are 'not able to overbalance the people', in the sense of not having 'any power to disturb the commonwealth'.[1] Why not? Because even if they had an interest in doing so (which Harrington says they could not have, since they already have all the riches, all the liberty they want, and more power at the head of a commonwealth of a million men than they could have by excluding the million and thus reducing themselves to a commonwealth of 5,000,[2] or thus spoiling their militia[3]), they would lack the power to do so, 'the people being equally possest of the government, of the arms, and far superior in number'.[4] The last vestige of the principle that the balance of power depends on the balance of property seems to have disappeared. Political power still depends on military power, but military power is now divorced from ownership of property.

What has happened to the principle of the balance? One thing is clear: however we may account for the inconsistency in the use of overbalance, and the apparent abandonment of the whole principle, the term overbalance is used in this contradictory sense only when Harrington is considering a hypothetical future condition that might arise after the establishment of the equal commonwealth. His use of overbalance in this special sense does not, therefore, invalidate the inference we made earlier[5] about his view of the distribution of land in 1656.

But how could Harrington have failed to see that he had contradicted himself in basing the need for the commonwealth on the principle of the balance, and then defending the very citadel of the commonwealth—the agrarian—by arguments which deny the operation of the principle? He could do so if he was assuming that in any future condition in which 5,000 might come to have all the land, the 5,000

---

[1] Ibid., p. 243.   [2] Ibid.   [3] *Oceana*, p. 99.
[4] *Prerogative*, pp. 243-4.   [5] Above, p. 168.

would differ in quality as well as in quantity from the few who had upheld the oligarchies of the ancient and feudal worlds. Assume that the English gentry are, and will be, substantially committed to the market economy, that they are bourgeois in their outlook, and the inconsistencies are no longer apparent. Such a 5,000 would not wish to impose institutions that would be oppressive to the people (who are only those above the level of wage-earners). They would have no interest in overbalancing the people in the sense of denying them co-ordinate political authority. Nor would they have the power to do so, for the people (who, at the outset of the commonwealth, enjoyed a wider diffusion of land and were armed to maintain the popular or equal balance) were still armed, and would use their arms to repel any attempt to exclude them from political authority (which they could only interpret as an attack on the 'equality' of property that they enjoyed as long as they were able to accumulate and to rise).

Harrington's unawareness of any inconsistency in his use of the principle of the balance is understandable, then, if he was thinking of the present gentry and the proposed commonwealth as essentially bourgeois. And the evidence we examined earlier suggests that that was how he thought of them. But to say this is still to accuse Harrington of contradiction. For the principle of the balance, asserted as universal, turns out to operate only down to the time the bourgeois commonwealth is established, when it is cancelled by that very step. In the past the balance had worked in every direction: as it moved it had brought down monarchies, oligarchies, and commonwealths. But as soon as it has brought into being a bourgeois commonwealth it ceases to operate. Overbalance of land in a bourgeois few would not lead to overbalance of their political power. If Harrington's commonwealth were established, history would stop. Harrington was content that it should. His whole object was to stop it.

6. *Harrington's Stature*

What becomes then of Harrington's high claims? 'The doctrine of the balance', he boasted, 'is that principle which makes the politics, not so before the invention of the same, to be undeniable throut, and . . . the most demonstrable of any whatsoever.'[1] He insisted that it was not merely an historical generalization but also a necessary principle. He denied that he was a mere empirical reasoner. While he was scornful of Hobbes's hanging a system by geometry,[2] it was not the deductive method he disdained. Deductive reasoning he thought the more 'honourable' argument, though it is by no means clear that he understood it.[3] He agreed with the geometricians of politics that law proceeds from the will, and that the mover of will is interest.[4] Where he quarrelled with them was in their imputing undifferentiated interests, and hence undifferentiated wills, to all men. Throughout history the few and the many had had different kinds of interests. Each had wanted to secure its own way of life. Class interests (i.e. the interests men had, as members of different classes, in attaining security for different ways of life and thus for different systems of property) were more important than the undifferentiated interests all men had in security *per se*. This was why you could not make kings (or commonwealths) merely by constructing a geometry of men's wills without constructing an anatomy of their property.[5] Whenever two classes wanted different kinds of security, different systems of property, each would have an interest in imposing its rule on the other, and would seek to do so. Whichever class got the bulk of the property would have the ability, as well as the will, to impose itself on the other, and would therefore do so. The principle of the balance was probably intended to state this necessary relation. Put in these terms, the principle is not contradicted by the divorce between class power and class property in the commonwealth. It simply ceases to be

[1] *Prerogative*, p. 226.   [2] *Oceana*, p. 65.   [3] *Politicaster*, p. 560.
[4] Ibid., p. 553.   [5] *Art of L.*, pp. 402–3.

applicable because there are not now two classes who want different systems of property. But Harrington did not put it in these terms, and did contradict himself.

I have argued (1) that the reason Harrington was unaware of the inconsistencies between his principle of the balance and his defence of the agrarian was that he was all along assuming that both the few and the many citizens were now essentially bourgeois; and (2) that if he had made this assumption clearly, and if he had been as good a deductive thinker as he pretended to be, he could have avoided the contradiction (by formulating the principle as operating only between two classes who wanted different systems of property).

To argue thus is to credit Harrington with a little more insight into seventeenth-century society, and with rather less logical ability, than has been customary. The weakness of his logic when he tries to turn an historically valid relationship into a necessary and universal principle is surely sufficiently demonstrated. The degree of his insight into seventeenth-century society is more open to question. Those who see Harrington as essentially a classical republican might argue that he was so enchanted with ancient prudence that he could easily force his own society into the ancient categories without seeing the illogic involved. If that were the case, it would be improper to infer that he could have failed to see the illogic only because he was taking for granted the bourgeois nature of seventeenth-century society. We have, however, seen evidence, apart from such inference, that Harrington thought of his society in what would now be called bourgeois concepts.

And it must be remembered also that Harrington took his ancient prudence from that learned disciple of the ancients, Machiavelli, 'the only politician of later ages',[1] and that the master had already seen that a bourgeois class was no threat to a commonwealth.[2] Starting from Machiavelli, Harrington was already half way into the modern age. And

---

[1] *Oceana*, p. 36. [2] Machiavelli, *Discourses*, bk. i, ch. 55.

in understanding the modern age he made his own way somewhat farther. Where Machiavelli had drawn the line between those 'gentlemen' who were great landed proprietors and those whose wealth was in money and movable capital, and had allowed only the latter to be compatible with a commonwealth, Harrington had seen that a non-feudal landed gentry was also compatible with a commonwealth. In Machiavelli's Italy the moneyed men had been the bearers of capitalism; in Harrington's England the gentry were even more important in that role than were the merchants and financiers, and Harrington at least glimpsed this. The functions he saw the English gentry performing were capitalist functions, by which private accumulation would increase national wealth without at all endangering the 'equal' commonwealth. Private gain was public benefit.

Harrington had nothing like the insight of Hobbes into the nature of bourgeois society. He did not resolve all relations between men into relations of the market. If Harrington's gentry were bourgeois they were still gentry, with a sufficiently different way of life and code of behaviour that a separate place had to be found for them. Harrington found it, at the cost of some theoretical confusion. He cannot rank with Hobbes as a thinker. But just because he was less penetrating, because he abstracted less from the complexity of a society not yet entirely bourgeois, he may be counted the more realistic analyst of the transitional period.

V

LOCKE: THE POLITICAL THEORY OF APPROPRIATION

1. *Interpretations*

LOCKE has suffered as much as anyone, and more than most, from having had modern liberal-democratic assumptions read into his political thought. His work invites this treatment, for it seems to have almost everything that could be desired by the modern liberal democrat. Government by consent, majority rule, minority rights, moral supremacy of the individual, sanctity of individual property—all are there, and all are fetched from a first principle of individual natural rights and rationality, a principle both utilitarian and Christian. Admittedly there was some confusion and even self-contradiction in the whole doctrine, but this could be viewed indulgently in one who, after all, stood nearly at the beginning of the liberal tradition: he could not be expected to have come up to the perfection of nineteenth- and twentieth-century thought.

But to treat Locke's political theory in this way is to miss much of its significance. Neither its strength nor its weakness, nor even its meaning, are apt to be understood until we stop reading back into it the assumptions of a later age. It is not easy to stop doing so, especially as one must then conjecture what unstated assumptions Locke may have carried into his theory from his understanding of his own society. Yet the attempt must be made if we are to hope to resolve difficulties in Locke's theory which do not readily yield either to the usual liberal or constitutional approach or to abstract philosophical analysis.

It is not that all interpreters of Locke's political theory have neglected its social content. Some notable modern writers have inferred, from the central place Locke gives to property rights, that Locke's whole theory of limited and conditional government was essentially a defence of property. The view of Locke's state as in effect a joint-stock company whose shareholders were the men of property has won considerable acceptance. This was the view taken by Leslie Stephen, Vaughan, Laski, and Tawney.[1] But there is one great difficulty in this view. Who were the members of Locke's civil society? If they were only the men of property, how could Locke make the civil society oblige everyone? How could the social contract be an adequate basis of political obligation for all men? Yet undoubtedly the purpose of the social contract was to find a basis for all-inclusive political obligation. Here is an outstanding difficulty. That eminent historians of thought did not see it as such was perhaps due to the fact that in most cases their interpretation was still in the constitutional tradition;[2] it emphasized the limits Locke put on government in the interests of property, rather than the very great power Locke gave to the political community (his 'civil society') as against individuals.

Another view, which puts Locke outside the constitutional tradition, has been offered by Willmoore Kendall.[3] He has made a strong case that Locke's theory confers something very close to complete sovereignty on civil society, that is, in effect, on the majority of the people (though not, of course, on the government, which has only fiduciary power). Against this sovereignty of the majority, it is said, the individual has no rights. Impressive evidence can be shown for this reading of Locke. It leads to the striking conclusion that Locke was not an individualist at all, but

[1] Leslie Stephen, *English Thought in the Eighteenth Century* (1876); C. E. Vaughan, *Studies in the History of Political Philosophy* (1925); H. J. Laski, *Political Thought from Locke to Bentham* (1920) and *Rise of European Liberalism* (1936); and R. H. Tawney, *Religion and the Rise of Capitalism* (1926).

[2] Professor Tawney's was not so, and he did draw attention to a decisive seventeenth-century assumption, the view that the labouring class was a race apart (to which reference is made below, p. 228). But the implications of this for the political theory of the period, not being central to his argument, were not explored.

[3] Willmoore Kendall, *John Locke and the Doctrine of Majority-Rule* (Urbana, Illinois, 1941).

a 'collectivist' in that he subordinated the purposes of the individual to the purposes of society. Locke is made a forerunner of Rousseau and the General Will.[1] The case is a strong one. But in concluding that Locke was a 'majority-rule democrat', it overlooks all the evidence that Locke was not a democrat at all. It reads into Locke a concern with the democratic principle of majority rule which was to be the focus of much American political thinking in the late eighteenth and early ninteenth centuries, and again now, but which was not Locke's concern. And it leaves a major problem: does not majority rule endanger that individual property right which Locke was plainly out to protect? Moreover, it proposes a resolution of Locke's many inconsistencies by imputing to Locke an assumption ('that the chances are at least 50 plus out of 100 that the average man is rational and just')[2] which Locke certainly did not hold unambiguously and which he specifically contradicted more than once.[3]

More recently, attempts have been made, notably by J. W. Gough,[4] to bring Locke back into the liberal-individualist tradition. But these efforts are not conclusive. In trying to rescue Locke from the analytical treatment he has had at some hands, and to restore his theory to its historical context, the emphasis is again put on Locke's constitutionalism. But the context of political history overshadows that of social and economic history. At most, what is proposed is a compromise between Locke's individualism and his 'collectivism', and major inconsistencies are left unexplained.

Indeed, all these interpretations leave unexplained a radical contradiction in Locke's postulates. Why should Locke have said, and what could he have meant by saying, both that men on the whole are rational and that most of them are not; both that the state of nature is rational, peaceable,

---

[1] Kendall, op. cit., pp. 103–6.
[2] Ibid., pp. 134–5.
[3] See below, pp. 240–1.
[4] *John Locke's Political Philosophy, Eight Studies* (Oxford, 1950).

and social, and that it is not.[1] If we cannot explain this we can scarcely claim to have understood Locke's political theory.

All these, and more, contradictions and ambiguities in the theory can be explained, I shall argue, by Locke having read back into the nature of men and society certain preconceptions about the nature of seventeenth-century man and society which he generalized quite unhistorically, and compounded, rather unsystematically, with traditional conceptions such as those to which he assented in his frequent invocations of Hooker.[2]

Of these preconceptions, which we shall call the social assumptions of his political thinking, some are explicit in the *Second Treatise*, some are implicit there but explicit, though incidentally, in some of his other works. Of the social assumptions that are explicit in the *Second Treatise*, the most important is contained in his famous chapter 'Of Property'. And it is in the course of that chapter that the scarcely less important implicit assumptions can be seen to have entered into the political theory. Before we can begin to unravel Locke's theory of civil government, we must, therefore, look closely at his doctrine of property.

2. *The Theory of Property Right*

i. *Locke's purpose*

Everyone sees that Locke's assertion and justification of a natural individual right to property is central to his theory of civil society and government. 'The great and *chief end* therefore, of Mens uniting into Commonwealths, and putting

---

[1] Rational is used here in Locke's sense of governing oneself by the law of nature or reason (e.g. *Second Treatise*, sect. 6: reason *is* the law of nature; sect. 8: to transgress the law of nature is to live by another rule than that of reason and common equity). For Locke's contradictory views of man's rationality, see below, pp. 232–8.

[2] The view that Locke was unsystematic in his use of traditional conceptions has been challenged by R. H. Cox, *Locke on War and Peace* (Oxford, 1960) who argues that Locke's use (generally a misuse) of Hooker was part of a highly systematic attempt to disguise or soften his real (Hobbesian) position, and that Locke's contradictory statements about the state of nature were deliberately contrived as part of the same attempt. Cf. p. 243, and Note R, p. 300.

themselves under Government, *is the Preservation of their Property*.[1] It is from this proposition, repeated in many variations throughout the *Second Treatise*[2] that most of Locke's conclusions about the powers and limits of civil society and government are drawn. And that proposition clearly requires the postulate that men have a natural right to property, a right prior to or independent of the existence of civil society and government.

It is true that Locke somewhat confused matters by sometimes defining that property whose preservation is the reasons for entering civil society in unusually wide terms. 'Man . . . hath by Nature a Power . . . to preserve his Property, that is, his Life, Liberty and Estate'.[3] Men's 'Lives, Liberties and Estates . . . I call by the general Name, *Property*'.[4] 'By *Property* I must be understood here, as in other places, to mean that Property which Men have in their Persons as well as Goods.'[5]

But he does not always use the term property in such a wide sense. In his crucial argument on the limitation of the power of governments[6] he is clearly using property in the more usual sense of lands and goods (or a right in land and goods), as he is throughout the chapter 'Of Property'. The implications of this ambiguity need not detain us here;[7] we need only notice that both when he used property in the broad sense and in the narrow he was still classing estate with life and liberty as objects of men's natural right, objects for the preservation of which they set up governments. In either usage of property, Locke had to show a natural right to estate.

But to say that Locke had to show a natural individual right to possessions or estate is not to see very far into what he was doing in the chapter 'Of Property'. Locke had already, at the beginning of the *Treatise*, set it down as self-evident that every man had a natural right to possessions.

---

[1] *Second Treatise*, sect. 124. Quotations are from Peter Laslett's edition of the *Two Treatises of Government* (Cambridge, 1960).

[2] e.g. sects. 94, 134, 138, 222.

[3] sect. 87.

[4] sect. 123.

[5] sect. 173.

[6] sects. 138–9.

[7] See below, pp. 220, 247 ff.

The condition all men are naturally in is 'a *State of perfect Freedom* to order their Actions, and dispose of their Possessions, and Persons as they think fit, within the bounds of the Law of Nature, without asking leave, or depending upon the Will of any other Man'.[1]

The bounds of the law of nature require of men that 'being all equal and independent, no one ought to harm another in his Life, Health, Liberty, or Possessions'.[2] These propositions, which take for granted a natural right to possessions, as well as to life, health, and liberty, seemed to Locke to require little demonstration; they followed from the axiomatic proposition that all men are naturally equal in the sense that no one has natural jurisdiction over another: 'there being nothing more evident, than that Creatures of the same species and rank promiscuously born to all the same advantages of Nature, and the use of the same faculties, should also be equal one amongst another without Subordination or Subjection. . . .'[3]

The chapter on property, in which Locke shows how the natural right to property can be derived from the natural right to one's life and labour, is usually read as if it were simply the supporting argument for the bare assertion offered at the beginning of the *Treatise* that every man had a natural right to property 'within the bounds of the Law of Nature'. But in fact the chapter on property does something much more important: it removes 'the bounds of the Law of Nature' from the natural property right of the individual. Locke's astonishing achievement was to base the property right on natural right and natural law, and then to remove all the natural law limits from the property right. We must now see how this was done.

ii. *The initial limited right*

Locke begins by accepting, as the dictate both of natural reason and of Scripture, that the earth and its fruits were originally given to mankind in common. This was of course

---

[1] *Second Treatise,* sect. 4.   [2] sect. 6.   [3] sect. 4.

the traditional view, found alike in medieval and in seventeenth-century Puritan theory. But Locke accepts this position only to refute the conclusions previously drawn from it, which had made property something less than a natural individual right.

But this [that the earth was given to mankind in common] being supposed, it seems to some a very great difficulty, how any one should ever come to have a *Property* in any thing... I shall endeavour to shew, how Men might come to have a *property* in several parts of that which God gave to Mankind in common, and that without any express Compact of all the Commoners.[1]

The early stages of his argument are so familiar as to require little comment. 'Men, being once born, have a right to their Preservation, and consequently to Meat and Drink, and such other things, as Nature affords for their Subsistence.'[2] The earth and its produce were given to men 'for the Support and Comfort of their being', and though they belonged to mankind in common, 'yet being given for the use of Men, there must of necessity be a means *to appropriate* them some way or other before they can be of any use, or at all beneficial to any particular Man'.[3] Before any man can use any of the natural produce of the earth for his nourishment or support he must appropriate it; it 'must be his, and so his, *i.e.* a part of him, that another can no longer have any right to it, before it can do him any good for the support of his Life'.[4] There must therefore be some rightful means of individual appropriation, i.e. some individual right to appropriate. What is this right? The right, and the initial extent and limits of the right, Locke derives from the further postulate that 'every Man has a *Property* in his own *Person*. This no Body has any Right to but himself. The *Labour* of his Body, and the *Work* of his Hands, we may say, are properly his.'[5] Whatever a man removes out of its natural state, he has mixed his labour with. By mixing his labour with it, he makes it his property, 'at least where

---

[1] *Second Treatise,* sect. 25.   [2] sect. 25.   [3] sect. 26.
[4] sect. 26.   [5] sect. 27.

there is enough, and as good left in common for others'.[1] No consent of the others is needed to justify this kind of appropriation: 'If such a consent as that was necessary, Man had starved, notwithstanding the Plenty God had given him'.[2] Thus from two postulates, that men have a right to preserve their life, and that a man's labour is his own, Locke justifies individual appropriation of the produce of the earth which was originally given to mankind in common.

Now the individual appropriation justified by this argument has certain limitations; two of them are explicitly and repeatedly stated by Locke, a third has been taken (though wrongly, I shall argue) to have been necessarily implied by the logic of Locke's justification. First, a man may appropriate only as much as leaves 'enough, and as good' for others;[3] this limit, explicitly stated by Locke, is clearly required by the justification, for *each* man has a right to his preservation and hence to appropriating the necessities of his life.

Secondly: 'As much as any one can make use of to any advantage of life before it spoils; so much he may by his labour fix a Property in. Whatever is beyond this, is more than his share, and belongs to others. Nothing was made by God for Man to spoil or destroy'.[4] Barter of the surplus perishable produce of one's own labour was permitted within this limit; no injury was done, no portion of the goods that belonged to others was destroyed, so long as nothing perished uselessly in the appropriator's hands.[5] Thirdly, the rightful appropriation appears to be limited to the amount a man can procure with his own labour; this seems necessarily implied in the justification, for it is 'the *Labour* of his Body, and the *Work* of his Hands' which, being mixed with nature's products, makes anything his property.

So far Locke has justified only appropriation of the fruits of the earth.

But the *chief matter of Property* being now not the Fruits of the Earth, and the Beasts that subsist on it, but the *Earth it self*; . . . I

---

[1] sect. 27. [2] sect. 28. [3] sect. 27; cf. sect. 33. [4] sect. 31. [5] sect. 46.

think it is plain, that *Property* in that too is acquired as the former. *As much Land* as a Man Tills, Plants, Improves, Cultivates, and can use the Product of, so much is his *Property*. He by his Labour does, as it were, inclose it from the Common.[1]

No consent of the others is needed for this appropriation. For God commanded man to labour the earth, and so entitled him to appropriate whatever land he mixed his labour with; and besides, the original appropriation was not 'any prejudice to any other Man, since there was still enough, and as good left' for others.[2]

The same limits to the appropriation of land as to the appropriation of its natural produce are implied in this justification. A man is entitled by these arguments to appropriate only as much as leaves 'enough and as good' for others, 'as much as he can use the product of', and as much as he has mixed his labour with.

It is instructive that Locke, speaking here mainly of the appropriation of land 'in the first Ages of the World, when Men were more in danger to be lost, by wandering from their Company, in the then vast Wilderness of the Earth, than to be straitned for want of room to plant in',[3] reads back into primitive society the institution of individual ownership of land, taking it for granted that that was the only way land could then be cultivated. His disregard of communal ownership and labour in primitive society allows him to say that 'the Condition of Humane Life, which requires Labour and Materials to work on, necessarily introduces *private Possessions*'.[4]

If Locke had stopped here he would have had a defence of limited individual ownership, though the argument would have had to be stretched pretty far even to cover the property right of the contemporary English yeoman, for it would have to be shown that his appropriation left enough and as good for others. Locke does suggest such a defence in arguing that, 'full as the World seems', a man may still find enough and as good land in 'some in-land, vacant places

[1] *Second Treatise*, sect. 32.   [2] sect. 33.   [3] sect. 36.   [4] sect. 35.

of *America*'.[1] But he does not base his case on this. When we examine how he does make his case, we shall see that it is a case not for such limited appropriation, but for an unlimited natural right of appropriation, a right transcending the limitations involved in his initial justification.

iii. *The limitations transcended*

The crucial argument has so often been misunderstood that it is necessary to examine it closely. The transition from the limited right to the unlimited right is first stated in sect. 36. After saying that by including the vacant lands of America there may still be enough land in the world for everyone to have as much as he could work and use, Locke continues:

> But be this as it will, which I lay no stress on; This I dare boldly affirm, That the same *Rule of Propriety*, (*viz.*) that every Man should have as much as he could make use of, would hold still in the World, without straitning any body, since there is Land enough in the World to suffice double the Inhabitants had not the *Invention of Money*, and the tacit Agreement of Men to put a value on it, introduced (by Consent) larger Possessions, and a Right to them. . . .[2]

This is quite explicit. The natural law rule, which by its specific terms limited the amount anyone could appropriate so that everyone could have as much as he could use, does *not* now hold; it 'would hold . . . had not . . . Money . . . introduced (by Consent) larger Possessions, and a Right to them'. The reason the rule does not now hold is not that the land has run out: there is enough in the whole world to suffice double the inhabitants, but only by including those parts of the world where money has never been introduced. There, where the old rule still holds, there are '*great Tracts* . . . which . . . *lie waste*', but 'this can scarce happen amongst that part of Mankind, that have consented to the Use of Money'.[3] Wherever money has been introduced there ceases to be unappropriated land. The introduction of money by

---

[1] sect. 36.   [2] sect. 36.   [3] sect. 45.

tacit consent has removed the previous natural limitations of rightful appropriation, and in so doing has invalidated the natural provision that everyone should have as much as he could make use of. Locke then proceeds to show in more detail how the introduction of money removes the limitations inherent in his initial justification of individual appropriation.

(a) *The spoilage limitation.* Of the two limitations he had explicitly recognized, the second (as much as a man can use, or use the product of, before it spoils) seemed to Locke to be obviously transcended by the introduction of money. Gold and silver do not spoil; a man may therefore rightfully accumulate unlimited amounts of it, 'the *exceeding of the bounds of his* just *Property* not lying in the largeness of his Possession, but the perishing of any thing uselessly in it'.[1] Not only is the limit thus inapplicable to durable movable property; it is inapplicable by the same token to land itself: 'a man may fairly possess more land than he himself can use the product of, by receiving in exchange for the overplus, Gold and Silver, which may be hoarded up without injury to any one, these metals not spoiling or decaying in the hands of the possessor'.[2]

Locke saw no difficulty about this. But the fact that he left certain questions unasked is itself revealing. Why would anyone want to appropriate more than he could make use of for the support and conveniency of life? Locke had shown that before the introduction of money no one would want more.[3] Why should he want it after? What is 'the desire of having more than Men needed'[4] which Locke finds to have entered with the introduction of money?

At first sight Locke might seem to be speaking merely of a desire for useless hoarding: the terms he uses for this accumulation are 'heap up'[5] and 'hoard up'.[6] But since Locke is thinking throughout of men whose behaviour is rational in the ordinary utilitarian sense of that word (as well

---

[1] *Second Treatise*, sect. 46. [2] sect. 50. [3] sect. 36.
[4] sect. 37. [5] sect. 46. [6] sects. 48, 50.

as the moral sense), the presumption is against such a meaning. And we have only to refer to Locke's economic treatises to see that he was a mercantilist to whom the accumulation of gold was a proper aim of mercantile policy not as an end in itself but because it quickened and increased trade. His main concern in *Considerations on . . . Money* is the accumulation of a sufficient supply of money to 'drive trade'; both exporting and hoarding (i.e. accumulating money without using it as capital) injure this.[1] The aim of mercantile policy and of individual economic enterprise was to Locke the employment of land and money as capital; the money to be laid out in trading stock or materials and wages, the land to be used to produce commodities for trade. That this was what Locke had in mind in the *Treatise* as the new reason for larger appropriation after the introduction of money is suggested by sect. 48, where the introduction of money is shown to provide both the opportunity and the reason (which could not have existed previously) for a man 'to enlarge his Possessions beyond the use of his Family, and a plentiful supply to its Consumption, either in what their own Industry produced, or they could barter for like perishable, useful Commodities, with others'. It is 'Commerce . . . to draw *Money* to him by the Sale of the Product' that provides the reason for appropriation of land in excess of what would provide 'a plentiful supply to [his family's] Consumption'.

The desire to accumulate beyond plentiful consumption requirements, 'the desire of having more than Men needed', which entered with the introduction of money, is not, then, merely the miser's desire to hoard.

Another possible meaning of the desire to accumulate may equally be shown to be inappropriate. It could be thought that Locke was here merely saying that money, by enlarging trade past the simple barter stage, enabled those who had money to consume more various and gratifying

---

[1] *Some Considerations of the Consequences of the Lowering of Interest and Raising the Value of Money* (1691); in *Works*, ed. 1759, vol. ii, pp. 22–23.

commodities. But that interpretation can scarcely be sustained when we notice Locke's concept of money. In the *Considerations* he identifies money and capital, and assimilates both to land. 'Money therefore, in buying and selling, being perfectly in the same condition with other commodities, and subject to all the same laws of value, let us next see how it comes to be of the same nature with land, by yielding a certain yearly income, which we call use, or interest'.[1] Money, Locke emphasizes, is a commodity; it has a value because it is a commodity which can enter into exchange with other commodities. But its purpose is not merely to facilitate the exchange of things produced for consumption, that is, to enlarge, beyond the scale of barter, exchange between producers of goods intended for consumption. The characteristic purpose of money is to serve as capital. Land itself Locke sees as merely a form of capital.

We may notice incidentally how modern was Locke's attitude towards money. In arguing that the taking of interest for the loan of money is equitable, as well as 'by the necessity of affairs, and the constitution of human society, unavoidable', he disposed of the medieval view without seeming to deny it. Land, he says, 'produces naturally something new and profitable, and of value to mankind; but money is a barren thing, and produces nothing . . .'. How then, he asks, has money come to be 'of the same nature with land', as it has done in yielding a yearly income (interest) akin to the rent of land? Simply by compact between those of unequal possessions. Money

by compact transfers that profit, that was the reward of one man's labour, into another man's pocket. That which occasions this, is the unequal distribution of money; which inequality has the same effect too upon land, that it has upon money. . . . For as the unequal distribution of land, (you having more than you can, or will manure, and another less) brings you a tenant for your land; . . . the same unequal distribution of money, (I having more than I can, or will employ, and another less) brings me a tenant for my money. . . .[2]

[1] *Works* (1759), ii. 19.   [2] Ibid.

The barren quality traditionally assigned to money is not explicitly denied; it is neatly transcended by the concept of consent between unequals. The value of money, as capital, is created by the fact of its unequal distribution. Nothing is said about the source of the inequality; it is simply taken to be part of 'the necessity of affairs and the constitution of human society'.

But what is relevant here is that Locke saw money as not merely a medium of exchange but as capital. Indeed its function as a medium of exchange was seen as subordinate to its function as capital, for in his view the purpose of agriculture, industry, and commerce was the accumulation of capital. And the purpose of capital was not to provide a consumable income for its owners, but to beget further capital by profitable investment. Mercantilist that he was, when Locke discussed the purpose of economic activity, it was generally from the point of view of the nation's rather than the individual's wealth. In some notes written in 1674, on 'trade', in which term he included agriculture and industry as well as commerce, his expression is almost Hobbesian:

The chief end of trade is Riches & Power which beget each other. Riches consists in plenty of mooveables, that will yield a price to foraigner, & are not like to be consumed at home, but espetially in plenty of gold & silver. Power consists in numbers of men, & ability to maintaine them. Trade conduces to both these by increasing y^r stock & y^r people. & they each other.[1]

If Locke does not recognize as clearly as Hobbes that the goal of individual activity is wealth and power, it is at least clear in the *Considerations* that he assumes the same goal for the individual estate as for the national: consume less than the revenue and so accumulate capital; for the nation's wealth consisted of the capitals accumulated by private industry and commerce.

Enough has now been said to show that 'the desire of having more than Men needed', or the desire 'to enlarge his

[1] Bodleian Library, MS. Locke c. 30, f. 18.

possessions beyond the use of his family and a plentiful supply to its consumption', which Locke found to have entered with the introduction of money and governed men's actions since, was in his view neither a desire for miserly hoarding nor merely a desire to consume more various and gratifying commodities, but was a desire to accumulate land and money as capital.

What Locke has done, then, is to show that money has made it possible, and just, for a man to accumulate more land than he can use the product of before it spoils. The original natural law limit is not denied. It is still contrary to natural law to appropriate a quantity of produce any of which (or any of the other things obtainable for it by barter) will spoil before they can be consumed. And it is still contrary to natural law to appropriate a quantity of land any of whose produce (or its barter yield) will spoil before it can be consumed. But now that it is possible to exchange any amount of produce for an asset which never spoils, it is neither unjust nor foolish to accumulate any amount of land in order to make it produce a surplus which can be converted to money and used as capital. The spoilage limitation imposed by natural law has been rendered ineffective in respect of the accumulation of land and capital. Locke has justified the specifically capitalist appropriation of land and money.

And it is to be noticed that he has justified this as a natural right, as a right in the state of nature. For while the introduction of money is by tacit consent, the consent which introduces money is not the same as the consent which brings men into civil society. The consent to money is independent of and prior to the consent to civil society:

... it is plain, that Men have agreed to disproportionate and unequal Possession of the Earth, they having by a tacit and voluntary consent found out a way, how a man may fairly possess more land than he himself can use the product of, by receiving in exchange for the over-plus, Gold and Silver, which may be hoarded up without injury to any one, these metals not spoileing or decaying in the hands of the possessor. This partage of things, in an inequality of private possessions, men have made practicable *out of the bounds of Societie, and without compact*, only by putting a value on gold and silver and tacitly agreeing in the use of Money.[1]

Locke thus specifically puts into the state of nature, money, the consequent inequality of possession of land, and the supersession of the initial spoilage limit on the amount of land a man can rightfully possess. And since he has just explained, in the two preceding paragraphs, that the way money leads to this unequal possession of land beyond the spoilage limit is by its introducing markets and commerce beyond the level of barter, it must be presumed that Locke is ascribing such commerce also to the state of nature.

If this at first sight seems incredible, it must be remembered that Locke's state of nature is a curious mixture of historical imagination and logical abstraction from civil society. Historically, a commercial economy without civil society is indeed improbable. But as an abstraction it is readily conceivable. Given Locke's opening postulate of the *Treatise*, that men are naturally rational creatures, largely governing themselves by the law of nature, and naturally free 'to order their Actions, and dispose of their Possessions, and Persons as they think fit, within the bounds of the Law of Nature, without asking leave, or depending upon the Will of any other Man',[2] it is perfectly intelligible that such men should agree not only to put a value on money but also to abide by a code of commercial honesty which would make possible an extensive commercial economy, without setting up a formal civil power. Men in the state of nature are capable of 'other Promises and Compacts' than the one that establishes civil society, 'for Truth and keeping of Faith belongs to Men, as Men, and not as Members of Society'.[3] To postulate, as Locke does, that men are by nature rational enough—both in the sense of seeing their own interest and in the sense of acknowledging moral obligation—to make the more difficult agreement to enter civil society, is to presume that men are rational enough to make the less

[1] *Second Treatise*, sect. 50 (italics added).   [2] sect. 4.   [3] sect. 14.

difficult agreements required to enter into commerce. Thus if men are taken abstractly rather than historically—and Locke initially presents the state of nature as an inference from Creation and from man's observed rational capacities, not as an inference from history or from primitive society—men can be assumed to have a commercial economy quite independently of having a formal civil society.[1] To put it more simply, Locke can assume that neither money nor contracts owe their validity to the state; they are an emanation of the natural purposes of men and owe their validity to man's natural reason. It is, on this view, the postulated moral reasonableness of men by nature, not the authority of a government, that establishes the conventional value of money and the obligation of commercial contracts.

There are, then, two levels of consent in Locke's theory. One is the consent between free, equal, rational men in the state of nature, to put a value on money, which Locke treats as accompanied by conventional acceptance of the obligation of commercial contracts. This consent is given 'out of the bounds of society, and without compact'; it leaves men still in the state of nature, and entitles them to larger possessions there than they could otherwise rightfully have had. The other level of consent is the agreement of each to hand over all his powers to the majority; this is the consent that establishes civil society. The first kind of consent is valid without the second. But although the institutions of property that are established in the state of nature by the first kind of consent are morally valid, they are practically difficult to enforce in the state of nature. This difficulty of enforcement is the main reason Locke finds for men moving to the second level of consent and entering civil society. When the move out of the state of nature into civil society is treated—as

[1] This seems to answer the question raised by Gough who, agreeing that Locke had put money and wage-labour in the state of nature, adds: 'Locke's state of nature thus becomes more incredible than ever. Did he really think that a sophisticated commercial economy could exist, without political government, in the state of nature?' (Gough, op. cit., 2nd edition, 1956, p. 92, Additional Note). Cf. below, pp 217-18.

Locke does treat it—as a temporal sequence, it is treated as coming *after* the consent to money. The temporal sequence involves three stages in all: two stages of the state of nature (one before, and one after, consent to money and unequal possessions), followed by civil society.

(*b*) *The sufficiency limitation*. We may now look at the limit on individual appropriation that Locke mentions first, i.e. that every appropriation must leave enough and as good for others. This limit is less obviously overcome by reference to the introduction of money by consent, yet there is no doubt that Locke took it to be overcome. The initial natural law rule, 'that every Man should have as much as he could make use of', does not hold after the invention of money.[1] In the first editions of the *Treatise* Locke provided no specific arguments on this point. Perhaps he thought it sufficiently evident to need no separate argument. His chain of thought seems to have been that the automatic consequence of the introduction of money is the development of a commercial economy, hence the creation of markets for the produce of land hitherto valueless, hence the appropriation of land not hitherto worth appropriating.[2] And by implication, consent to the use of money is consent to the consequences.[3] Hence an individual is justified in appropriating land even when it does not leave enough and as good for others.

While a case for the removal of the sufficiency limitation can be made out by inference in this way, Locke apparently felt that a more direct argument was needed, for in a revision of the third edition of the *Treatises* he added a new argument following the first sentence of sect. 37.[4]

To which let me add, that he who appropriates land to himself by his labour, does not lessen but increase the common stock of mankind. For the provisions serving to the support of humane life, produced by one acre of inclosed and cultivated land, are (to speak much within

---

[1] *Second Treatise*, sect. 36.   [2] sects. 45, 48.   [3] sect. 36.

[4] The new passage was first published in the fourth edition of the *Two Treatises* (1713), and appeared in all the subsequent standard editions of the *Treatises* and the *Works*, but is unfortunately not reproduced in some modern reprints of the *Second Treatise*, which are based on earlier editions.

compasse) ten times more, than those, which are yeilded by an acre of Land, of an equal richnesse, lyeing wast in common. And therefor he, that incloses Land and has a greater plenty of the conveniencys of life from ten acres, than he could have from an hundred left to Nature, may truly be said, to give ninety acres to Mankind. For his labour now supplys him with provisions out of ten acres, which were but the product of an hundred lying in common.

Thus, although more land than leaves enough and as good for others may be appropriated, the greater productivity of the appropriated land more than makes up for the lack of land available for others. This assumes, of course, that the increase in the whole product will be distributed to the benefit, or at least not to the loss, of those left without enough land. Locke makes this assumption. Even the land-less day-labourer gets a bare subsistence.[1] And bare subsistence, at the standard prevailing in a country where all the land is appropriated and fully used, is better than the standard of any member of a society where the land is not appropriated and fully worked: 'a King of a large and fruitful Territory there [among 'several nations of the *Americans*'] feeds, lodges, and is clad worse than a day Labourer in *England*'.[2] Private appropriation, in this way, actually increases the amount that is left for others. No doubt at some point, there is no longer as much left for others. But if there is not then enough and as good *land* left for others, there is enough and as good (indeed a better) *living* left for others. And the right of all men to a living was the fundamental right from which Locke had in the first place deduced their right to appropriate land. Not only is as good a living provided for others after the appropriation of all the land; it is *by* the appropriation of all the land that a better living is created for others. So, when the results of appropriation beyond the initial limit are measured by the fundamental test (provision of the necessities of life for all others) rather than by the instrumental test (availability of enough land

---

[1] *Considerations, Works* (1759), ii. 29. Cf. *First Treatise*, sects. 41–42, on the right of propertyless men to the means of subsistence.

[2] *Second Treatise*, sect. 41.

for others to get the necessities of life from), appropriation beyond the limit takes on a positive virtue.

Thus the initial sufficiency limitation has been transcended. Or, if one prefers, the sufficiency limitation remains valid in principle but now operates differently. The original rule that no one may appropriate so much of the fruits of the earth as would not leave as much and as good for others still holds, for each man still has a right to his preservation and hence a right to appropriate the necessities of life. But this right does not now entail a right to as much and as good land, which was never more than a derived right; hence the sufficiency rule does not, after the first ages of the world, require that every appropriation of land should leave enough and as good land for others.

In short, the appropriation of land in excess of what leaves enough and as good for others is justified both by the implied tacit consent to the necessary consequences of the introduction of money, and by the assertion that the standards of those without land, where it is all appropriated and used, are higher than the standards of any where it is not generally appropriated.

It may be thought that Locke's justification of larger possessions on these grounds, however plausible or acceptable it may be, is strictly inconsistent with his assertion that the right to appropriate is limited to what leaves enough and as good for others. That would be so if the original assertion had been made absolutely. But it was not. It was asserted as a consequence of a prior principle, namely, the natural right of every man to get the means of subsistence by his labour, which was a right to appropriate the means of subsistence in Locke's original sense of ingest.[1] That right can be satisfied in either of two ways. One way is to stipulate that everyone is entitled to appropriate land. This way entails the original limitation on the amount of land anyone may appropriate. Where there is still plenty of unappropriated land, this is the obvious way to satisfy the right, for no one

[1] sect. 26.

is inconvenienced by the limit. And it is only in the context of still plentiful land that Locke asserts the limitation.[1] But there is another way in which the natural right to subsistence can be satisfied, a way which can operate when there is no longer plenty of land: that is, by stipulating or assuming an arrangement which ensures that those without land can get a subsistence by their labour. Such an arrangement Locke found to be a natural consequence of the introduction of money. Thus in saying that men, after the introduction of money, have a right to more land than leaves enough for others[2] Locke is not contradicting his original assertion of the natural right of all men to the means of subsistence.

(c) *The supposed labour limitation*. The third apparently implied limitation on individual appropriation (only as much as one has mixed one's own labour with) seems the most difficult to transcend or remove, for it seems to be absolutely required by the very labour justification Locke has given for any appropriation. Surely, we may think, the onus is on Locke to show how this limitation, as well as the other two, may be considered to be overcome as a consequence of the introduction of money. But Locke did not think so. He offered no explicit argument to this purpose. He did not need to do so, if all along he was assuming the validity of the wage relationship, by which a man may rightfully acquire a title to the labour of another. We must now inquire whether there is any reason to presume that Locke was assuming this relationship as rightful and natural.

We may notice first that Locke's emphasis that 'every Man has a *Property* in his own *Person*. This no Body has any Right to but himself', and that, when he mixes his labour with nature, 'this *Labour* being the unquestionable Property of the Labourer, no Man but he can have a right to what that is once joyned to',[3] is not at all inconsistent with the assumption of a natural right to alienate one's labour in return for a wage. On the contrary, the more emphatically labour is asserted to be a property, the more it is to be

---

[1] *Second Treatise*, sects. 27, 33.   [2] sect. 36.   [3] sect. 27.

understood to be alienable. For property in the bourgeois sense is not only a right to enjoy or use; it is a right to dispose of, to exchange, to alienate. To Locke a man's labour is so unquestionably his own property that he may freely sell it for wages. A freeman may sell to another 'for a certain time, the Service he undertakes to do, in exchange for Wages he is to receive'.[1] The labour thus sold becomes the property of the buyer, who is then entitled to appropriate the produce of that labour.[2] A strong presumption that Locke was taking this for granted from the beginning of his labour justification of property can be established on two grounds.

(1) Immediately after, and in support of, his argument that the natural right to appropriate something from what was given to mankind in common is established solely by a man's mixing his labour with it, and that this right does not depend at all on consent of others but is a natural right, Locke points to the acknowledged right of individuals to appropriate the natural produce of 'commons which remain so by compact'. Here as in the state of nature, the right is established simply by the expenditure of labour. But it does not occur to Locke that one man's right can be established only by the labour of his own body; it is equally established by the labour he has purchased:

Thus the Grass my Horse has bit; the Turfs my Servant has cut; and the Ore I have digg'd in any place where I have a right to them in common with others, become my *Property*, without the assignation or consent of any body. The *labour* that was mine, removing them out of that common state they were in, hath *fixed* my *Property* in them.[3]

Had Locke not been taking the wage relationship entirely for granted, his inclusion of 'my servant's' labour in 'the labour that was mine', the labour whose expenditure gave me by natural right a title to the product, would have been a direct contradiction of the case he was making.[4]

---

[1] sect. 85.   [2] See Note N, p. 298.   [3] *Second Treatise*, sect. 28.

[4] Laslett (op. cit., p. 104, n. ‡) objects that this passage does not demonstrate that a man can own his servant's labour. I do not see how Locke could have been more specific: the labour performed by my servant *is* 'the labour that was mine'. The only possible question, which I discuss immediately below, is whether Locke was assuming this relationship to be natural as well as civil.

This passage by itself does not establish certainly that Locke was assuming the wage relationship as natural, i.e. as existing in the state of nature. For while the principle that my servant's labour entitles me to appropriate is asserted for 'any place where I have a right [to the natural produce] in common with others', the assertion is there made in the context of common lands in civil society.

The passage would, however, probably be allowed as presumptive evidence that Locke was assuming the wage relationship to be natural, were it not that the idea of wage-labour in a state of nature seems too patent an absurdity to attribute to Locke. But the presumption is that Locke did, rather than that he did not, think of wage-labour in the state of nature. We have seen that he did attribute to the state of nature a commercial economy, developed to the point where large estates (of thousands of acres) are privately appropriated for the production of commodities for profitable sale. Such an economy could scarcely have been understood by Locke or the men of his time except as implying production by wage-labour.

Because Locke does not in the *Treatise* dwell on the role of wage-labour, but talks mainly about the savage individualist and the self-sufficient cultivator, it has often been assumed that Locke was reading back into his state of nature not the England of substantial estates and wage-labour but an England of yeomen who worked their land themselves. But in fact, however confused Locke may have been, he was not confused about the class structure of his own England. When he addressed himself to questions of economic policy, as in the *Considerations*, he treated wage-labourers as a normal and substantial class in the contemporary economy, and assumed as self-evident that of necessity wages are normally at a bare subsistence level, and that the wage-labourer has no other property than his labour. These assumptions are quite explicit in three of his technical economic arguments. When he estimates the velocity of circulation of money the only three classes he considers

significant are labourers, landowners and 'brokers', i.e.
merchants and shopkeepers; and the labourers are assumed
to be 'living generally but from hand to mouth', and to have
no resources other than their wages.[1] Again, in tracing the
incidence of taxation he says taxes cannot fall on 'the poor
labourer or handicraftsman . . . for he just lives from hand to
mouth already'; if a tax raises the price of his food, clothing,
or utensils 'either his wages must rise with the price of
things, to make him live; or else, not being able to maintain
himself and family by his labour, he comes to the parish'.[2]
And when, in a period of deflation, economic classes struggle
to retain the same money income, 'this pulling and contest
is usually between the landed-man and the merchant. For
the labourer's share, being seldom more than a bare subsistance, never allows that body of men, time, or opportunity
to raise their thoughts above that, or struggle with the richer
for theirs. . . .'[3]

For Locke, then, a commercial economy in which all the
land is appropriated implied the existence of wage-labour.
And since Locke was reading back into the state of nature
the market relations of a developed commercial economy,
the presumption is that he read back the wage relation along
with the other market relations. The normality and justice
of the market in labour was as much a commonplace of
seventeenth-century thinking as the normality and justice of
the markets in commodities and capital. They were equally
seen to be required for capitalist production. Supporters of
capitalist production, of whom Locke was one, were not yet
troubled in their consciences about any dehumanizing effects
of labour being made into a commodity; in the absence of
such moral qualms there was no reason for them not to
think of the wage relation as natural.

The ascription of wage-labour to a state of nature is no
less intelligible than the ascription of a developed commercial
economy to the state of nature.[4] Locke is consistent enough:

---

[1] *Works* (1759), ii. 13–16.   [2] Ibid., p. 29.
[3] Ibid., p. 36.   [4] See above, pp. 209–10.

his view is that each institution owes nothing to civil society but is based on simple agreement or consent between individuals governed only by natural law. Thus (*a*) accumulation of capital through the medium of money is based only on consent of individuals to put a value on money; and (*b*) the wage relationship is based only on the free contract of the individuals concerned. That neither of these propositions has historical warrant is beside the point. Both propositions are fully intelligible, given Locke's initial postulates that men are by nature free and rational.[1]

(2) The presumption that Locke was attributing the wage relation to the state of nature is further strengthened when we notice how he relates natural rights and natural law to civil society. The agreement to enter civil society does not create any new rights; it simply transfers to a civil authority the powers men had in the state of nature to protect their natural rights. Nor has the civil society the power to override natural law; the power of civil society and government is limited to the enforcement of natural law principles.[2] It is just because of this that Locke was so concerned to show that the right to unequal property is a right men bring with them into civil society; that it is individual consent in the state of nature, not the agreement to establish civil society, that justifies property in excess of the initial natural limits. Now since civil society cannot override natural law, and since both the appropriation of more land than a man can work by himself, and the purchase of the labour of others, are lawful in civil society, both must have been in accordance with natural law. Or, to take it from the point of view of natural rights: since the agreement to enter civil society creates no new individual rights, and since the appropriation of more land than a man can work by himself is rightful in civil society, it must have been assumed to be a natural right; and since the alienation of one's labour for a wage is rightful in civil society, it must have been assumed to be a natural right.

[1] For the full meaning of 'rational' in this context, see below, pp. 235–6
[2] *Second Treatise*, sect. 135.

It may seem strange that Locke, who derives the right to appropriate land and goods from the right to preserve one's own life and from the natural property in one's labour, should assume a natural right to alienate one's labour while denying a natural right to alienate one's life.[1] Yet he does make a distinction between property, including the property in one's own labour, and life. In chapter ii of the *Second Treatise* the distinction is not yet made: men have a natural right to 'dispose of their Possessions, and Persons as they think fit, within the bounds of the Law of Nature'.[2] But after he had established the natural right to unequal possessions, a distinction appears, as we would expect: in the state of nature, he asserts, 'no Body has an absolute Arbitrary Power over himself, or over any other, to destroy his own Life, or take away the Life or Property of another'.[3] Thus while no one has a natural right to alienate his own life, which is God's property, or to take arbitrarily the life or property of another, he is left with a natural right to alienate his own property. That Locke's law of nature gives a man's wife and children a claim on his estate in the event of his death or his subjection by conquest[4] does not seem to be a limit on his disposal of it while he is a free agent.

Indeed any property right less than this would have been useless to Locke, for the free alienation of property, including the property in one's labour, by sale and purchase is an essential element of capitalist production. And the alienation of one's own labour is sharply distinguished from the granting of arbitrary power over one's life, in Locke's distinction between the slave and the free wage-earner.[5]

In emphasizing that a man's labour is his own Locke marked out the extent of his departure from the medieval view and of his acceptance of the bourgeois view expressed so tersely by Hobbes. But Locke fell short of Hobbes in his acceptance of bourgeois values. To Hobbes not only was labour a commodity but life itself was in effect reduced to a

---

[1] Cf. below, p. 231, and compare the Leveller position, above, ch. III, pp. 145 ff.
[2] *Second Treatise,* sect. 4.   [3] sect. 135.   [4] sects. 182–3.   [5] sect. 83.

commodity;[1] to Locke life was still sacred and inalienable, though labour, and one's 'person' regarded as one's capacity to labour,[2] was a commodity. Locke's distinction between life and labour is a measure of his retention of the traditional values. His confusion about the definition of property, sometimes including life and liberty and sometimes not, may be ascribed to the confusion in his mind between the remnant of traditional values and the new bourgeois values.[3] It is this, no doubt, which makes his theory more agreeable to the modern reader than the uncompromising doctrine of Hobbes. Locke did not care to recognize that the continual alienation of labour for a bare subsistence wage, which he asserts to be the necessary condition of wage-labourers throughout their lives, is in effect an alienation of life and liberty.

I conclude that Locke took it for granted, throughout his justification of the natural right to property, that labour was naturally a commodity and that the wage relationship which gives me the right to appropriate the produce of another's labour was a part of the natural order. It follows that the third supposed limitation on the natural right to appropriate (i.e. as much as one can work with one's own natural labour) was never entertained by Locke. There is then no question of Locke's removing this limitation; it was not present in his mind but has been read into his theory by those who have approached it in the modern tradition of humane liberalism.

iv. *Locke's achievement*

When Locke's assumptions are understood as presented here, his doctrine of property appears in a new light, or, rather, is restored to the meaning it must have had for Locke and his contemporaries. For on this view his insistence that a man's labour was his own—which was the essential novelty of Locke's doctrine of property—has almost the

---

[1] 'The *Value*, or WORTH of a man, is as of all other things, his Price' (*Leviathan*, ch. 10, p. 67); 'a mans Labour also, is a commodity exchangeable for benefit, as well as any other thing' (ibid., ch. 24, p. 189); cf. above ch. II, sect. 2, iii.

[2] *Second Treatise*, sect. 27.   [3] Cf. below, p. 247.

opposite significance from that more generally attributed to it in recent years; it provides a moral foundation for bourgeois appropriation. With the removal of the two initial limitations which Locke had explicitly recognized, the whole theory of property is a justification of the natural right not only to unequal property but to unlimited individual appropriation. The insistence that a man's labour is his own property is the root of this justification. For to insist that a man's labour is his own, is not only to say that it is his to alienate in a wage contract; it is also to say that his labour, and its productivity, is something for which he owes no debt to civil society. If it is labour, a man's absolute property, which justifies appropriation and creates value, the individual right of appropriation overrides any moral claims of the society. The traditional view that property and labour were social functions, and that ownership of property involved social obligations, is thereby undermined.

In short, Locke has done what he set out to do. Starting from the traditional assumption that the earth and its fruits had originally been given to mankind for their common use, he has turned the tables on all who derived from this assumption theories which were restrictive of capitalist appropriation. He has erased the moral disability with which unlimited capitalist appropriation had hitherto been handicapped.[1] Had he done no more than this, his achievement would have to be accounted a considerable one. But he does even more. He also justifies, as natural, a class differential in rights and in rationality, and by doing so provides a positive moral basis for capitalist society.

3. Class Differentials in Natural Rights and in Rationality

To see how Locke did this we must notice two further assumptions he made, which rank in importance with the explicit postulate that a man's labour is his own. These are, first, that while the labouring class is a necessary part of the

[1] Cf. below, pp. 235–8.

nation its members are not in fact full members of the body politic and have no claim to be so; and secondly, that the members of the labouring class do not and cannot live a fully rational life. 'Labouring class' is used here to include both the 'labouring poor' and the 'idle poor', that is, all who were dependent on employment or charity or the workhouse because they had no property of their own by which, or on which, they might work. These ideas were so generally prevalent in Locke's day that it would be surprising if he had not shared them. But since their importance in Locke's thinking has generally been so completely overlooked it will be well to establish that he did share them. Direct evidence that Locke was taking these propositions for granted is to be found in several of his writings. After we have seen how fully he was taking them for granted as propositions about the labouring class in seventeenth-century England we shall consider how far he generalized them and how they enter into the argument of the *Treatise*.

i. *Locke's assumption of the differentials in seventeenth-century England*

Locke's proposals for the treatment of the able-bodied unemployed are fairly well known, although when they are mentioned by modern writers it is usually to deprecate their severity and excuse it by reference to the standards of the time. What is more to the point is the view they afford of Locke's assumptions. Masters of workhouses ('houses of correction') were to be encouraged to make them into sweated-labour manufacturing establishments, justices of the peace were to be encouraged to make them into forced-labour establishments. The children of the unemployed 'above the age of three' were unnecessarily a burden on the nation; they should be set to work, and could be made to earn more than their keep. All this was justified on the explicit ground that unemployment was due not to economic causes but to moral depravity. The multiplying of the un-

employed, Locke wrote in 1697 in his capacity as a member
of the Commission on Trade, was caused by 'nothing else
but the relaxation of discipline and corruption of manners'.[1]
There was no question in Locke's mind of treating the unemployed as full or free members of the political community;
there was equally no doubt that they were fully subject to
the state. And the state was entitled to deal with them in this
way because they would not live up to the moral standard
required of rational men.

Locke's attitude towards the employed wage-earning class
has been less often noticed, though it is plain enough in
various passages of his economic writings, particularly in
the *Considerations*. There, as we have already seen, incidentally to his technical arguments, Locke takes for granted that
the wage-labourers are a normal and sizeable class in the
nation, that the wage-labourer has no property to fall back
on but is entirely dependent on his wages, and that, of
necessity, wages are normally at a bare subsistence level.
The wage-labourer 'just lives from hand to mouth'. One passage, already quoted in part, deserves fuller consideration
here:

... the labourer's share [of the national income], being seldom more
than a bare subsistance, never allows that body of men, time, or
opportunity to raise their thoughts above that, or struggle with the
richer for theirs, (as one common interest) unless when some common
and great distress, uniting them in one universal ferment, makes them
forget respect, and emboldens them to carve to their wants with armed
force: and then sometimes they break in upon the rich, and sweep all
like a deluge. But this rarely happens but in the male-administration of
neglected, or mismanaged government.[2]

It would be hard to say which part of these remarks is the
most revealing. There is the assumption that the labourers
are normally kept too low to be able to think or act politically.
There is the assumption that on the rare occasions when
they do raise their thoughts above bare subsistence, the only

---

[1] Quoted in H. R. Fox Bourne, *The Life of John Locke* (1876), vol. ii, p. 378.
[2] *Works* (1759), ii. 36.

kind of political action they will take is armed insurrection. There is the assumption that maladministration consists not of leaving the poor at bare subsistence, but of allowing such unusual distress to occur as will unite them in armed revolt. And there is the conviction that such revolt is improper, an offence against the respect they owe to their betters.

Now the question who are to have the right of revolution is a decisive question with Locke: the right of revolution is with him the only effective test of citizenship, as he made no provision for any other method of exercising the right to turn out an unwanted government. Although he insists, in the *Treatise*, on the majority's right to revolution, it does not seem to cross his mind here that the labouring class might have the right to make a revolution. And indeed there is no reason why it should have crossed his mind, for to him the labouring class was an object of state policy, an object of administration, rather than fully a part of the citizen body. It was incapable of rational political action, while the right to revolution depended essentially on rational decision.

The assumption that the members of the labouring class are in too low a position to be capable of a rational life— that is, capable of regulating their lives by those moral principles Locke supposed were given by reason—is evident again in *The Reasonableness of Christianity*. The whole argument of that work is a plea that Christianity be restored to a few simple articles of belief 'that the labouring and illiterate man may comprehend'. Christianity should thus again be made

a religion suited to vulgar capacities; and the state of mankind in this world, destined to labour and travel. . . . The greatest part of mankind have not leisure for learning and logick, and superfine distinctions of the schools. Where the hand is used to the plough and the spade, the head is seldom elevated to sublime notions, or exercised in mysterious reasoning. 'Tis well if men of that rank (to say nothing of the other sex) can comprehend plain propositions, and a short reasoning about things familiar to their minds, and nearly allied to their daily

experience. Go beyond this, and you amaze the greatest part of mankind. . . .[1]

This is not, as might be thought, a plea for a simple
rationalist ethical religion to replace the disputations of the
theologians. On the contrary, Locke's point is that without
supernatural sanctions the labouring class is incapable of
following a rationalist ethic. He only wants the sanctions
made clearer. The simple articles he recommends are not
moral rules, they are articles of faith. They are to be believed.
Belief in them is all that is necessary, for such belief converts
the moral rules of the Gospel into binding commands.
Locke's problem is simply to frame the articles so that they
will appeal directly to the experience of the common people,
who will thus be enabled to believe.[2] The greatest part of
mankind, Locke concludes, cannot be left to the guidance of
the law of nature or law of reason; they are not capable of
drawing rules of conduct from it. For 'the day-labourers and
tradesmen, the spinsters and dairy-maids, . . . hearing plain
commands, is the sure and only course to bring them to
obedience and practice. The greatest part cannot know, and
therefore they must believe.'[3]

Locke was, of course, recommending this simplified Christianity for all classes, as may be seen in his ingenuously
mercantile observations on the surpassing utility of the
Christian doctrine of rewards and punishments.

The [ancient] philosophers, indeed, shewed the beauty of virtue;
. . . but leaving her unendowed, very few were willing to espouse her.
. . . But now there being put into the scales on her side, 'an exceeding
and immortal weight of glory;' interest is come about to her, and virtue
now is visibly the most enriching purchase, and by much the best
bargain. . . . The view of heaven and hell will cast a slight upon the
short pleasures and pains of this present state, and give attractions and
encouragements to virtue, which reason and interest, and the care of
ourselves, cannot but allow and prefer. Upon this foundation, and
upon this only, morality stands firm, and may defy all competition.[4]

[1] *Works* (1759), ii. 585–6. Cf. *Human Understanding*, bk. iv, ch. 20, sects. 2–3.
[2] See Note O, p. 299.   [3] *Works* (1759) ii. 580.   [4] Ibid. 582.

Locke's readers would appreciate this recommendation of Christianity more than would the labourers, who were not in a position to think in terms of making 'the most enriching purchase'. But the ability of his fundamental Christian doctrine to satisfy men of higher capacities Locke regards as only a secondary advantage. His repeated emphasis on the necessity of the labouring class being brought to obedience by believing in divine rewards and punishments leaves no doubt about his main concern. The implication is plain: the labouring class, beyond all others, is incapable of living a rational life. One can detect a shade of difference in his attitude towards the employed and the unemployed. The idle poor he seems to have regarded as depraved by choice; the labouring poor as simply incapable of a fully rational life because of their unfortunate position. But whether by their own fault or not, members of the labouring class did not have, could not be expected to have, and were not entitled to have, full membership in political society; they did not and could not live a fully rational life.

These were not only Locke's assumptions, they were also his readers'. When he makes these assumptions, as in the passages we have quoted from the *Considerations* and *The Reasonableness of Christianity*, he does not argue them. The presumption is that he saw no need to argue them. He could safely take them for granted, for they were well established in the prevailing view. Ever since there had been wage-labourers in England their political incapacity had been assumed as a matter of course. Both the employed and the unemployed had been the object of much state concern by the Tudor and early Stuart governments, but neither the labouring nor the idle poor had been considered capable of political rights. Puritan individualism, to the extent that it superseded the paternalism of the Tudor and early Stuart state, did nothing to raise the estimation of the political capacity of the dependent working class. On the contrary, the Puritan doctrine of the poor, treating poverty as a mark of moral shortcoming, added moral obloquy to the political disregard in which the poor had always been held. The poor might deserve to be helped, but it must be done from a superior moral footing. Objects of solicitude or pity or scorn, and sometimes of fear, the poor were not full members of a moral community. Here was a further reason—if any was needed—for continuing to think of them as less than full members of the political community. But while the poor were, in this view, less than full members, they were certainly subject to the jurisdiction of the political community. They were in but not of civil society.

There is a suggestive similarity between this view of the poor and the Calvinist view of the position of the non-elect. The Calvinist church, while claiming to include the whole population, held that full membership could be had only by the elect. The non-elect (who were mainly, though not entirely, coincident with the non-propertied) were thus at once members and not members of the church: not full members sharing in the government of the church, but sufficiently members to be subject, rightfully, to its discipline.[1] How far the Puritan view of the moral and civil position of the poor was a secularization of the strict Calvinist doctrine we need not try to estimate. The Calvinist doctrine of election was less widely held than the Puritan doctrine of the poor, but it is not improbable that some residue of the strict Calvinist position was carried into the broader Puritan tradition. In any case, the Puritan doctrine reinforced the previously accepted view of the political incapacity of the working class. Even at the height of political Puritanism, during the Civil War and Commonwealth, when the idea that the dependent poor should have political rights was briefly canvassed, it won no support even from the Levellers, though the Levellers based themselves on the unfreedom rather than any moral inferiority of the poor.

With the Restoration the idea of political right for the poor dropped out of sight again, and the idea of their moral

[1] For expressions of this view in English Calvinism, see Christopher Hill, *Puritanism and Revolution* (1958), pp. 228–9.

inadequacy was raised to the status of economic orthodoxy. Writers on economic policy after the Restoration, though not conspicuously Puritan, fully embraced the Puritan view of the poor. The moral delinquency of the labouring class is a constant theme of their writings. Not merely the idle poor, who had been treated as outcasts from Tudor times, but the labouring poor as well, were now treated almost a race apart, though within the state. Tawney has observed that the prevailing attitude of English economic writers after 1660 'towards the new industrial proletariat [was] noticeably harsher than that general in the first half of the seventeenth century, and . . . has no modern parallel except in the behaviour of the less reputable of white colonists towards coloured labour'.[1] The working class were regarded not as citizens but as a body of actual and potential labour available for the purposes of the nation. The economic writers admitted, even insisted, that the labouring poor were the ultimate source of any nation's wealth, but held that they were so only if they were encouraged and compelled to continuous labour. The existing arrangements for extracting this labour were generally thought to be inadequate in that they did not cope with the moral failings of the poor. Whatever the remedies proposed—and many of them were in the direction of greater severity—the common assumption was that the labouring class was something that was to be managed by the state to make it productive of national gain. It was not that the interests of the labouring class were subordinated to the national interest. The labouring class was not considered to have an interest; the only interest was the ruling-class view of the national interest. The general view was nicely put by William Petyt:

People are . . . the chiefest, most fundamental and precious commodity, out of which may be derived all sorts of manufactures, navigation, riches, conquests and solid dominion. This capital material being of itself raw and indigested is committed into the hands of the supreme

[1] R. H. Tawney, *Religion and the Rise of Capitalism*, ch. iv, sect. iv, Penguin edition, 1948, p. 267.

authority in whose prudence and disposition it is to improve, manage and fashion it to more or less advantage.[1]

The view that human beings of the labouring class were a commodity out of which riches and dominion might be derived, a raw material to be worked up and disposed of by the political authority, was typical of Locke's period. So was the political corollary, that the labouring class was rightly subject to but without full membership in the state. And so was the moral foundation, that the labouring class does not and cannot live a rational life. Locke did not have to argue these points. He could assume that his readers would take them for granted, as he did. When he did mention them, as in the passages we have quoted from the *Considerations* and *The Reasonableness of Christianity*, it was only to establish a technical religious or economic argument by reminding his readers of something they already knew but had not correctly applied.

It is clear enough, then, that when Locke looked at his own society he saw two classes with different rights and different rationality. We must now consider the extent to which he read back, into the very nature of man and society, the differentials he saw in his own society.

ii. *Differential rights and rationality generalized*

We may begin by observing that Locke's unhistorical habit of mind would present no obstacle to his transferring assumptions about seventeenth-century society into a supposed state of nature, and generalizing some attributes of seventeenth-century society and man as attributes of pre-civil society and of man as such. And as he took his assumptions about his own society so much for granted that he felt no need to argue them, they could easily be carried into his premisses without his being conscious of a problem of

---

[1] William Petyt, *Britannia Languens* (1680), p. 238. This and similar passages from various writers of the period are quoted in E. S. Furniss, *The Position of the Laborer in a System of Nationalism* (New York, 1920), pp. 16 ff. Cf. Sir William Petty: *Political Arithmetic*, in *Economic Writings*, ed. Hull, i. 307, 108, 267.

consistency. The question is, where if at all did the assumptions about differential rights and rationality get into his premisses about society and man?

In Locke's initial statement of his postulates in the *Treatise* (and in his analysis of human nature in the *Essay Concerning Human Understanding*, which has to be considered along with the *Treatise* for a full statement of his general theory of human nature), there is nothing to suggest an assumption of class differentiation. But before he uses these postulates to deduce the necessary character of civil society he has put forward other arguments, especially in his treatment of property rights, which imply that he had already generalized his differential assumptions about his own society into abstract implicit assumptions of differential human nature and natural rights.

(*a*) *Differential rights*. We have seen that Locke recognized in seventeenth-century society a class differentiation so deep that the members of the labouring class had very different effective rights from the classes above them. They lived, and must live, 'from hand to mouth', could never 'raise their thoughts above that', and were unfit to participate in political life. Their condition was a result of their having no property on which they could expend their labour; and their having no property was one aspect of the prevailing inequality which was grounded in 'the necessity of affairs, and the constitution of human society'.[1]

All this Locke saw in his own society and took to be typical of all civil society. But how did this become an assumption of differential *natural* rights, and where does it, as such an assumption, enter into the argument of the *Treatise*? It is certainly not present in the opening statements about natural rights; there the emphasis is all on the natural equality of rights.[2]

The transformation of equal into differential natural rights comes to light in the working out of the theory of property. In the chapter on property in the *Treatise*, Locke went out

---

[1] *Considerations*, Works (1759), ii. 19.   [2] *Second Treatise*, sects. 4, 5.

of his way, as we have seen, to transform the natural right of every individual to such property as he needed for subsistence, and as he applied his labour to, into a natural right of *unlimited* appropriation, by which the more industrious could rightfully acquire all the land, leaving others with no way to live except by selling the disposal of their labour.

This is not an aberration in Locke's individualism but an essential part of it. The core of Locke's individualism is the assertion that every man is naturally the sole proprietor of his own person and capacities[1]—the absolute proprietor in the sense that he owes nothing to society for them—and especially the absolute proprietor of his capacity to labour.[2] Every man is therefore free to alienate his own capacity to labour. This individualist postulate is the postulate by which Locke transforms the mass of equal individuals (rightfully) into two classes with very different rights, those with property and those without. Once the land is all taken up, the fundamental right not to be subject to the jurisdiction of another is so unequal as between owners and non-owners that it is different in kind, not in degree: those without property are, Locke recognizes, dependent for their very livelihood on those with property, and are unable to alter their own circumstances. The initial equality of natural rights, which consisted in no man having jurisdiction over another[3] cannot last after the differentiation of property. To put it in another way, the man without property in things loses that full proprietorship of his own person which was the basis of his equal natural rights.[4] And Locke insists that the differentiation of property is *natural*, that is, that it takes place 'out of the bounds of Societie, and without compact'.[5] Civil society is established to protect unequal possessions, which have already in the state of nature given rise to unequal rights. In this way Locke has generalized the assumption of a class differential in rights in his own society,

---

[1] sects. 4, 6, 44, 123.   [2] sect. 27.   [3] sect. 4.
[4] Cf. above, p. 219; also ch. III, pp. 145 ff.
[5] *Second Treatise*, sect. 50.

into an implicit assumption of differential *natural* rights. The implicit assumption, as we shall see, did not replace the initial assumption of equality; rather it appears that both were in Locke's mind at the same time.

(*b*) *Differential rationality*. We have seen that Locke assumed in his own society a class differential in rationality which left the labouring class incapable of a fully rational life, i.e. incapable of ordering their lives by the law of nature or reason. The question is, how did this become an assumption of differential rationality in general, and where did this enter the argument of the *Treatise*? It is not present in the opening statements of postulates. There, rationality and depravity are dealt with in abstraction, and although a distinction[1] is made between rational men, who stay within the bounds of the law of nature, and depraved men, who transgress that law, there is no suggestion that this distinction is correlated with social class. The same may be said of the distinction Locke makes in the first stage of the state of nature, when there was still plenty of land, between 'the Industrious and Rational', who followed the law of nature which commanded men to subdue the earth by their labour (and whose labour on it gave them a title to it), and 'the Quarrelsom and Contentious' whose covetousness led them instead 'to meddle with what was already improved by another's Labour'.[2] In the first stage of the state of nature, man confronts his natural environment in such a way that rational behaviour consists in subduing nature by labour, and appropriating in order to subdue. The essence of rational behaviour is industrious appropriation. But in the course of the chapter on property the essence of rational behaviour undergoes a change. It shifts from industrious appropriation of that modest amount of land that a man could use to produce what he and his family needed, to appropriation of amounts greater than could be used for that purpose. And when this unlimited accumulation becomes rational, full rationality is possible only for those who can so accumulate.

---

[1] Discussed below, pp. 239–40.　　　　[2] *Second Treatise*, sect. 34.

This change in the concept of rationality is important enough to merit closer scrutiny. In the first stage of the state of nature, the essence of rational conduct was to subdue and improve the earth.

God, when he gave the World in common to all Mankind, commanded Man also to labour, and the penury of his Condition required it of him. God and his Reason commanded him to subdue the Earth, *i.e.* improve it for the benefit of Life, and therein lay out something upon it that was his own, his labour.[1]

God gave the World to Men . . . for their benefit, and the greatest Conveniencies of Life they were capable to draw from it. . . . He gave it to the use of the Industrious and Rational, (and *Labour* was to be *his Title* to it;) not to the Fancy or Covetousness of the Quarrelsom and Contentious.[2]

In the beginning, then, reason commanded each man to subdue and improve some land for his own benefit. But no man could subdue and improve land unless he owned it: 'the Condition of Humane Life, which requires Labour and Materials to work on, necessarily introduces *private Possessions*'.[3] The essence of rational conduct therefore is private appropriation of the land and the materials it yields, and investment of one's energies in improving them for the greatest conveniences of life one may thereby get for oneself. The industrious and rational is he who labours and appropriates. Such behaviour is rational in the moral sense of being required by the law of God or law of reason, as well as in the expedient sense. And it is the moral rationality that Locke emphasizes: if nothing but expediency were in question, it could be just as rational to 'meddle with what was already improved by another's Labour'.[4] And in the first stage of the state of nature, before the introduction of money and the consequent taking up of all the land, everyone who laboured did appropriate.

But with the introduction of money in any territory, all the land therein is soon appropriated,[5] leaving some men without any. This, we must remember, is for Locke still the

[1] sect. 32.   [2] sect. 34.   [3] sect. 35.   [4] sect. 34.   [5] sect. 45.

state of nature: men agreed to disproportionate and unequal possession of the earth merely by their tacit consent to the use of money, which they gave out of the bounds of society, and without compact.[1] In the second stage of the state of nature, then, those who are left with no land cannot be industrious and rational in the original sense: they cannot appropriate and improve the land to their own benefit, which was originally the essence of rational behaviour.

Whereas in the first stage labouring and appropriating implied each other, and together comprised rational behaviour, in the second stage labouring no longer implied appropriating, though appropriating implied (someone's) labouring. At this point it became morally and expediently rational to appropriate land in amounts greater than could be used to produce a plentiful supply of consumption goods for oneself and one's family; that is, it became rational to appropriate land to use as capital, which involves appropriating the surplus product of other men's labour, i.e. of the labour of those who have no land of their own. In other words, at the point where labouring and appropriating became separable, full rationality went with appropriating rather than with labouring.

To see this we have only to notice that in Locke's view the only thing that had changed in passing from the first to the second stage of the state of nature was the scale on which appropriation was rational, in both the moral and expedient senses. Before the introduction of money, appropriation beyond the amount required for consumption was unreasonable, in both senses: 'it was a foolish thing, as well as dishonest, to hoard up more than [a man] could make use of'.[2] But it was unreasonable, in both senses, only because it involved spoiling or wasting, and it involved spoiling or wasting only because of the lack of the technical device of money. The moral law had nothing against large possessions, 'the *exceeding of the bounds of* [a man's] just *Property* not lying in the largeness of his Possession, but the perishing of any thing uselessly in it'.[1] The introduction of money, in its capacity as a store of value, removed the technical obstacle which was all that had prevented unlimited appropriation from being rational in the moral sense, i.e. being in accordance with the law of nature or law of reason. The introduction of money removed also the technical obstacle which had prevented unlimited appropriation from being rational in the expedient sense. Money, as a means of exchange and a store of value, made it profitable for a man to produce commodities for commercial exchange 'to draw *Money* to him by the Sale of the Product', and hence made it profitable for him to enlarge his possession of land 'beyond the use of his Family, and a plentiful supply to its Consumption', and far beyond the amount that would otherwise 'be worth the inclosing'.[2] Locke does not ask why men took to unlimited appropriation after the introduction of money; he simply explains why they would not be bothered to do it before then.

Locke has evidently started from the position that accumulation is morally and expediently rational *per se*, and then found that the only thing that prevented it being rational in man's original condition was the absence of money and markets. He also found that men were by nature sufficiently rational to be able to agree on the use of money and the conventions of commerce, without establishing a formal civil authority. What is more natural, then, than that rational men should have surmounted the technical barriers to unlimited accumulative behaviour, and so have enabled themselves to become fully rational, and all this in the state of nature?

In short, Locke has read back into man's original nature a rational propensity to unlimited accumulation, has shown that it is naturally checked in pre-monetary society, and has shown how the check can be removed by a device which he assumes to be well within the rational powers of natural man. The whole notion of a monetary and commercial state

[1] sect. 46.   [2] sect. 48.

of nature, which is nonsense historically, is intelligible hypothetically, but is so only if one attributes to man's nature, as Locke did, the rational propensity to accumulate. It is intelligible, that is to say, only if one reads back into the state of nature a relation between man and nature (i.e. between man and the land as the source of man's subsistence) which is typically bourgeois, as Locke does in his assertion that the condition of human life necessarily introduces private possession of land and materials to work on.[1] It was because Locke had always assumed fully rational behaviour to be accumulative behaviour that he could, at the point where labouring and appropriating became separable, find that full rationality lay in appropriating rather than in labouring.

It may be thought that the assumption of the rationality of the propensity to unlimited accumulation which we have found in Locke is contradicted by the fact that he sometimes denounces covetousness in quite traditional terms. He refers to 'the *Golden Age* (before vain Ambition, and *amor sceleratus habendi*, evil Concupiscence, had corrupted Mens minds into a Mistake of true Power and Honour) . . .'.[2] He tells us that it was the emergence of covetousness that made a full-fledged political society necessary. In 'the first Ages in *Asia* and *Europe*, whilst the Inhabitants were too few for the Country, and want of People and Money gave Men no Temptation to enlarge their Possessions of Land' there was 'little matter for Covetousness or Ambition' and no reason 'to apprehend or provide against it'.[3] 'The equality of a simple poor way of liveing confineing their desires within the narrow bounds of each mans smal propertie made few controversies and so no need of many laws to decide them: And there wanted not of Justice where there were but few Trespasses, and few Offenders.'[4] Such a people, Locke says, would require only a rudimentary political society, chiefly for protecting themselves against foreign force. Its rulers,

---

[1] *Second Treatise*, sect. 35.   [2] sect. 111.
[3] sects. 108, 107.   [4] sect. 107.

except in time of war, 'exercise very little Dominion, and
have but a very moderate Sovereignty'.[1] It is only after the
introduction of money, the appropriation of all the land,
and the appearance of large unequal properties, that covetousness comes to the fore and brings the need for a fully
sovereign civil society to protect property from the covetous.

Locke's disapproval of covetousness is plain enough. Yet
it is not at all inconsistent with his belief in the moral
rationality of unlimited accumulation. On the contrary, it
was rational, i.e. industrious, appropriation that required protection against the covetousness of the quarrelsome and contentious who sought to acquire possessions not by industry
but by trespass. It was not the industrious appropriator
who was covetous, but the man who would invade his appropriation. And rational industrious appropriation required
protection only after it had passed beyond the limits of simple
small properties and had become unlimited accumulation.
Locke's denunciation of covetousness is a consequence,
not a contradiction, of his assumption that unlimited
accumulation is the essence of rationality.[2] The contrast
with Hobbes's position is instructive. For Hobbes, 'Covetousnesse of great Riches, and ambition of great Honours, are
Honourable; as signes of power to obtain them.'[3] Here,
as in the treatment of man as a commodity,[4] Locke was
not prepared to go as far as Hobbes. For both thinkers,
unlimited accumulation was morally justified; but since
Hobbes had reduced society completely to a market, and
found no room for moral principles not deducible from
market relations, he made no distinction between covetousness and unlimited accumulation. Locke (and Harrington[5]),
retaining in some measure the traditional moral principles,
made the distinction but were not troubled by it.

We find, then, that Locke considered private appropriation to be natural and rational from the beginning, and
considered the propensity to accumulate beyond the limits

---

[1] sect. 108.   [2] See Note P, p. 299.   [3] *Leviathan*, ch. 10, p. 71.
[4] See above, pp. 219–20.   [5] See above, ch. IV, p. 176.

of consumption and barter to be natural and rational after the introduction of money, which is, on his own recognition, the stage at which all the land is taken up and some men have to begin to live without land of their own. From this time on, in the second stage of the state of nature, rational conduct consists in unlimited accumulation, and the possibility of accumulation is open only to those who succeed in getting possession of land or materials to work on.

It follows that there was in Locke's view a class differential in rationality in the state of nature. Those who were left without property after the land was all appropriated could not be accounted fully rational. They had no opportunity to be so. Like the day-labourer in civil society they were not in a position to expend their labour improving the gifts of nature; their whole energies were needed to keep alive, they could not 'raise their thoughts above that' for they just lived 'from hand to mouth'.

4. *The Ambiguous State of Nature*

We have seen how Locke read back into the state of nature, in a generalized form, the assumptions he made about differential rights and rationality in existing societies. The generalized assumptions could not but modify in his own mind the initial postulates of the *Treatise*. But they did not displace them. We can now see that Locke entertained both at the same time, so that the postulates on which he was operating were confused and ambiguous. All men were on the whole rational; yet there were two distinct classes of rationality. All men were equal in natural rights; yet there were two distinct orders of possession of natural rights. Here we have the source of the extraordinary contradiction in Locke's presentation of human nature.

We are accustomed to think that Locke held men to be essentially rational and social. Rational, in that they could live together by the law of nature, which is reason, or which at least (though not imprinted on the mind) is knowable by reason, without the help of revelation. Social, in that they could live by the laws of nature without the imposition of rules by a sovereign. This, indeed, is usually said to be the great difference between Locke's and Hobbes's view of human nature. If there is a significant difference it is here that one expects to find it, rather than in the theory of motivation. For Locke, like Hobbes, held that men are moved primarily by appetite and aversion; and that the appetites are so strong that 'if they were left to their full swing, they would carry men to the overturning of all morality. Moral laws are set as a curb and restraint to these exorbitant desires.'[1] The difference, it is said, between this and Hobbes's view, is that Locke thought men capable of setting these rules on themselves, by perceiving their utility, without setting up a sovereign.

The general theory presented at the opening of the *Treatise* is certainly to the effect that men are naturally able to govern themselves by the law of nature, or reason. The state of nature, we are told, has a law of nature to govern it, which is reason.[2] The state of nature is flatly contrasted to the state of war: the two are 'as far distant, as a State of Peace, Good Will, Mutual Assistance, and Preservation, and a State of Emnity, Malice, Violence, and Mutual Destruction are one from another. Men living together according to reason, without a common Superior on Earth, with Authority to judge between them, is *properly the State of Nature*'.[3]

It is no derogation from this view of the state of nature to allow, as Locke does, that there are in it some men who will not follow the law of nature. The law of nature teaches only those 'who will but consult it'; some men transgress it and, by doing so, declare themselves 'to live by another Rule,

---

[1] *Essay Concerning Human Understanding*, ed. Fraser (1894), bk. i, ch. 2, sect. 13. Cf. Locke's Hobbesian reflection in 1678 that 'the principal spring from which the actions of men take their rise, the rule they conduct them by, and the end to which they direct them, seems to be credit and reputation, and that which at any rate they avoid is in the greatest part shame and disgrace', and the consequences he draws for government. (Quoted from Locke's MS. journal, in Fox Bourne, op. cit. i. 403–4).   [2] *Second Treatise*, sect. 6.   [3] sect. 19.

than that of *reason* and common Equity' and so become 'dangerous to Mankind'; a man who violates the law of nature 'becomes degenerate, and declares himself to quit the Principles of Human Nature, and to be a noxious Creature'.[1] There are, then, some natural criminals amongst the natural law-abiding people of the state of nature. But Locke's description of these men as 'noxious', 'degenerate', and having 'quit the Principles of Human Nature' makes it apparent that he wants his readers to regard them as an exceptional few. The extravagance of his language might even be taken to suggest that Locke was anxious to convince himself of the prevailing decency of the state of nature. In any case he is definite that the existence of some transgressors in the state of nature does not affect the prevalence of the law of nature: it is the state of nature including transgressors that he describes as 'men living together according to reason', and 'a State of Peace, Good Will, Mutual Assistance, and Preservation'.[2]

But this is only one of two opposite pictures Locke has of the state of nature. As early as chapter 3 of the *Treatise*, only a page after the distinction between the state of nature and the state of war, we read that where there is no authority to decide between contenders 'every the least difference is apt to end' in the 'State of War', and that 'one great *reason of Mens putting themselves into Society*, and quitting the State of Nature' is 'to avoid this State of War'.[3] The difference between the state of nature and the Hobbesian state of war has virtually disappeared. We read further, some chapters later, that the state of nature is 'very unsafe, very unsecure', that in it the enjoyment of individual rights is 'very uncertain, and constantly exposed to the Invasion of others', and that it is 'full of fears and continual dangers'; and all this because 'the greater part [are] no strict Observers of Equity and Justice'.[4] What makes the state of nature unliveable, according to this account, is not the viciousness of the few

---

[1] *Second Treatise* sects. 6. 8. 10.   [2] sect. 19.   [3] See Note Q, p. 300.
[4] sect. 123. Cf. sects. 124–5, 'Men'; 131, 'unsafe and uneasie'; 137, 'terms of force'.

but the disposition of 'the greater part' to depart from the law of reason. The state of nature is now indistinguishable from the state of war. So it is in Locke's discussion of re-bellion as a dissolution of government: those who rebel, 'bring back again the state of War';[1] they take away 'the Umpirage, which every one had consented to, for a peace-able decision of all their Controversies, and a bar to the state of War amongst them', and *expose the People a new to the state of War*.[2] It is the state of war, not the peaceable state of nature, to which men are brought back again when civil society is dissolved.

The contradiction between Locke's two sets of statements about natural man is fundamental. The state of nature is sometimes the opposite of the state of war, sometimes identical with it. This is the central contradiction in the explicit postulates on which Locke's political theory is built. It will not do to say that it is simply an echo of the tradi-tional Christian conception of man as a contradictory mix-ture of appetite and reason. Locke no doubt accepted that view. And within it there is indeed room for a considerable variety of belief as to the relative weights (or potentialities) of the two ingredients of human nature. Different exponents of the Christian doctrine could take different views. But what has to be explained is how Locke took not one position in this matter but two opposite positions.

One might, of course, say that he had to take both in order to make his case as against Hobbes—that he had to make men so rational as not to require a Hobbesian sove-reign, yet had to make them contentious enough to require their handing over their natural rights and powers to a civil society. But to say this would be to accuse Locke, quite un-justly and unnecessarily, either of intellectual dishonesty or of extraordinary superficiality; and would, besides, imply an underestimate of the extent to which Locke did subordinate the individual to the state.[3]

Another explanation, less objectionable in its imputations,

[1] sect. 226.   [2] sect. 227.   [3] See below, pp. 255–8.

is suggested by a certain similarity that can be seen between Locke's two general pictures of the state of nature and the two stages of the state of nature (pre- and post-monetary) that we have seen to be implicit in his treatment of the introduction of money. Might not the pleasant picture of the state of nature, in which there are only a few degenerate men, be drawn from the rudimentary pre-monetary society 'where there were but few Trespasses, and few Offenders' and therefore no full civil authority?[1] The pleasant state of nature would thus correspond to the first of the two stages discussed in the chapter on property. The unpleasant state of nature, where 'the greater part' are so little observers of equity and justice that nobody's property is secure, would correspond to the post-monetary stage, when 'evil concupiscence' had made some headway and there were by implication many offenders.

But this explanation will not do. For Locke presents both the pleasant and unpleasant versions as pictures of the state of nature immediately preceding the establishment of civil society, i.e. of the second stage of the state of nature. There is no doubt that the unpleasant picture is of the second stage. And that the pleasant picture is also of the state of nature immediately preceding the establishment of civil society is evident from one of the arguments he uses to prove that no government can have arbitrary power. He has to postulate that the state of nature from which men enter civil society is one in which men do on the whole follow the law of nature, i.e. do not arbitrarily invade the lives, liberties, or properties of others. If they did so act, they would have arbitrary power in the state of nature. But Locke's case is that men have no arbitrary power in the state of nature and therefore cannot transfer it to civil society.[2]

What still has to be explained, then, is how Locke could say that the men who moved from the state of nature into civil society both were substantially governed by the law of nature and were not substantially governed by it; how these

[1] *Second Treatise*, sects. 107–8.   [2] sect. 135.

same men at the same time were for the most part rational and peaceable and were for 'the greater part' so contemptuous of natural law that nobody was at all secure.[1]

An explanation that does cover this is afforded by our analysis of Locke's social assumptions. I suggest that Locke was able to take both positions about human nature because he had in his mind at the same time two conceptions of society, which, although logically conflicting, were derived from the same ultimate source. One was the notion of society as composed of equal undifferentiated beings. The other was the notion of society as composed of two classes differentiated by their level of rationality—those who were 'industrious and rational' and had property, and those who were not, who laboured indeed, but only to live, not to accumulate. Locke would not be conscious of the contradiction between these two conceptions of society, because both of them (and not merely, as we have already seen, the second one) were carried over into his postulates from his comprehension of his own society.

The first concept, though Locke presents it as the traditional Christian natural law view, has in it a considerable admixture of the atomistic view that was typical of seventeenth-century materialism. The traditional concept of the natural moral equality of men, their equal entitlement to the benefits of natural law and their equal capacity of recognizing its obligations, is of course in the forefront of Locke's presentation: men are 'Creatures of the same species and rank promiscuously born to all the same advantages of Nature, and the use of the same faculties', and it is Hooker, who carried the Christian natural law tradition into the seventeenth century, who is quoted in support of 'this *equality* of Men by Nature'.[2] This equality of rights is at the same time an equality of reason: men are equally capable of comprehending the law of nature: 'Reason, which is that Law, teaches all Mankind, who will but consult it. . . .'[3]

But what we have to notice now is that Locke's assumption of natural equality goes beyond this traditional Christian

[1] See Note R, p. 300. [2] *Second Treatise*, sects. 4, 5. [3] sect. 6.

view. The reason why all just government must be based on consent is not only that men are created free and equal in the sense that they are equally God's creatures and so have equal moral rights. It is also, as Locke emphasizes in his argument against paternalism, that men are assumed to be equally capable of shifting for themselves in the practical matter of managing their lives.

Locke's whole case against those who would base political authority on an analogy between political and paternal power rests on the proposition that paternal power is by nature valid only until the children are old enough to be assumed able both to know the law of nature and to manage the business of day-to-day living for themselves. All men, except lunatics and idiots, are then free of parental authority because they are presumed equally able both to recognize the law of nature and 'to shift for themselves'.[1] Similarly the only natural foundation Locke finds for the conjugal estate is that it is necessary for the protection and sustenance of the offspring until they can 'shift for themselves'.[2] Again when Locke sums up the limits of '*Paternal* or *Parental Power*' he describes that power indifferently as 'nothing but that, which Parents have over their Children, to govern them for the Childrens good, till they come to the use of Reason, or a state of Knowledge, wherein they may be supposed capable to understand that Rule, whether it be the Law of Nature, or the municipal Law of their Country they are to govern themselves by',[3] and as the power which nature gives to parents 'for the Benefit of their Children during their Minority, to supply their want of Ability, and understanding how to manage their Property . . . [i.e.] that Property which Men have in their Persons as well as Goods'.[4]

The assumption that men are by nature equally capable of shifting for themselves was not an idle one. It enabled Locke in good conscience to reconcile the great inequalities of observed society with the postulated equality of natural

---

[1] *Second Treatise*, sect. 60. [2] sect. 83; cf. sect. 80.
[3] sect. 170. [4] sect. 173.

right. If men are by nature equally rational, in the sense of equally capable of looking after themselves, those who have fallen permanently behind in the pursuit of property can be assumed to have only themselves to blame. And only if men are assumed to be equally capable of shifting for themselves, can it be thought equitable to put them on their own, and leave them to confront each other in the market without the protections which the old natural law doctrine upheld. The assumption that men are equally rational in capacity of shifting for themselves thus makes it possible to reconcile the justice of the market with the traditional notions of commutative and distributive justice.

Locke's doctrine of equal rationality was, we may say, by Hobbes out of Hooker. The assumption of equal capacity to shift for themselves was necessary for anyone who wanted to justify market society and who yet was unwilling, as Locke was, to go the whole way with Hobbes in reducing all justice to the justice of contractors in the market. In other words, it was necessary, at least for any bourgeois theory which claimed continuity with traditional natural law, to conceive man in general in the image of rational bourgeois man, able to look after himself and morally entitled to do so.

Now when man in general is thus conceived in the image of bourgeois rational man, the natural condition of man is eminently rational and peaceable. This, I suggest, is the source of the first of Locke's two concepts of the state of nature, and it owes as much to his comprehension of bourgeois society as to the tradition of Christian natural law.

Locke's other concept of the state of nature is more directly related to a concept of society which is more markedly bourgeois, namely the concept of human society in which there is an inherent class differential in rationality. The seventeenth-century bourgeois observer could scarcely fail to see a deep-rooted difference between the rationality of the poor and that of the men of some property. The difference was in fact a difference in their ability or willingness to order their own lives according to the bourgeois moral code.

But to the bourgeois observer this appeared to be a difference in men's ability to order their lives by moral rules as such. We have seen that this was Locke's view. When this class differential in rational morality is read back into the nature of man, it results in a state of nature that is unsafe and insecure. For to say, as Locke did, that the greater part of men are incapable of guiding their lives by the law of reason, without sanctions, is to say that a civil society with legal sanctions (and a church with spiritual sanctions) is needed to keep them in order. Without these sanctions, i.e. in a state of nature, there could be no peace.

I have called Locke's concept of differential rationality a bourgeois concept. It had nothing in common with the Aristotelian notion of two classes—masters and slaves—whose relative positions were justified by a supposed inherent difference in rationality. With Locke the difference in rationality was not inherent in men, not implanted in them by God or Nature; on the contrary, it was socially acquired by virtue of different economic positions. But it was acquired in the state of nature; it was therefore inherent in civil society. Once acquired, that is to say, it was permanent, for it was the concomitant of an order of property relations which Locke assumed to be the permanent basis of civilized society. Locke's notion of differential rationality justified as natural, not slavery,[1] but the subordination of one part of the people by their continual contractual alienation of their capacity to labour. The differentiation came about because men were free to alienate their freedom. The difference in rationality was a result, not a cause, of that alienation. But the difference in rationality, once established, provided a justification of differential rights.

Both of Locke's views of the state of nature, then, flow from a bourgeois conception of society. And their common source obscured their contradictory quality. In the last

[1] Locke did, of course, justify slavery also, but not on grounds of inherently different rationality. Enslavement was justified only when a man had 'by his fault, forfeited his own Life, by some Act that deserves Death' (sect. 23). Locke appears to have thought of it as a fit penalty for his natural criminals.

analysis it was Locke's comprehension of his own society that was ambiguous and contradictory. It could scarcely have been otherwise. It reflected accurately enough the ambivalence of an emerging bourgeois society which demanded formal equality but required substantive inequality of rights. The leaders of that society were not prepared, as the chilly reception of Hobbes's doctrine on all sides had shown, to abandon traditional moral law in favour of a fully materialist doctrine of utility. Rightly or wrongly, such a doctrine was thought to be too dangerous to the fabric of society. As long as it was thought so, it was necessary to profess the natural equality of men and to clothe that equality in natural law, and equally necessary to find a natural justification of inequality. Locke did both, to the general satisfaction of his contemporary readers. And if this left at the heart of his theory an ambiguity which pervaded all the rest of it, that made the theory no less serviceable to his own society.

5. The Ambiguous Civil Society

We may now inquire how Locke's ambiguous position on natural rights and rationality comes out in his theory of the formation of civil society. Men enter into civil society, Locke tells us, to protect themselves from the inconveniences, insecurity, and violence of the state of nature. Or, as he says repeatedly, the great end of men's uniting into civil society and putting themselves under government is the preservation of their property, by which, he says, he means their 'Lives, Liberties and Estates'.[1] When property is so defined, everyone has a reason to enter civil society, and everyone is capable of entering it, having some rights which he can transfer. But Locke did not keep to this definition. He used the term in two different senses at points where its meaning was decisive in his argument. The property for the protection of which men oblige themselves to civil society is sometimes[2] stated to be life, liberty, and estate, and

---

[1] *Second Treatise*, sect. 123.   [2] e.g. sects. 123, 131, 137.

sometimes[1] it is clearly only goods or land. The upshot of this is that men without estate or goods, that is, without property in the ordinary sense, are rightfully both in and not in civil society.

When the property for the protection of which men enter civil society is taken to be life, liberty, and estate, all men (except slaves) are eligible for membership; when it is taken to be goods or estate only, then only men who possess them are eligible. Locke takes it both ways, without any consciousness of inconsistency. What has happened is understandable in the light of our analysis. Locke's recognition of differential class rights in his own society, having been carried into his postulates as an implicit assumption of differential natural rights and rationality, but without there displacing the formal assumption of general rationality and equal rights, has emerged at the level of the social contract in a crucial ambiguity about who are parties to the contract.

The question whom Locke considered to be members of civil society seems to admit of only one answer. Everyone, whether or not he has property in the ordinary sense, is included, as having an interest in preserving his life and liberty. At the same time only those with 'estate' can be full members, for two reasons: only they have a full interest in the preservation of property, and only they are fully capable of that rational life—that voluntary obligation to the law of reason—which is the necessary basis of full participation in civil society. The labouring class, being without estate, are subject to, but not full members of, civil society.[2] If it be objected that this is not one answer but two inconsistent answers, the reply must be that both answers follow from Locke's assumptions, and that neither one alone, but only the two together, accurately represent Locke's thinking.

The ambiguity as to who are members of civil society by virtue of the supposed original contract allows Locke to

[1] e.g. *Second Treatise*, sects. 138–40, 193.
[2] Cf. Harrington's assumption that wage-earners are outside the commonwealth; above, ch. IV, p. 182.

consider all men as members for purposes of being ruled and only the men of estate as members for the purposes of ruling. The right to rule (more accurately, the right to control any government) is given to the men of estate only: it is they who are given the decisive voice about taxation, without which no government can subsist.[1] On the other hand, the obligation to be bound by law and subject to the lawful government is fixed on all men whether or not they have property in the sense of estate, and indeed whether or not they have made an express compact. When Locke broadens his doctrine of express consent into a doctrine of tacit consent he leaves no doubt as to who are obliged:

every Man, that hath any Possession, or Enjoyment, of any part of the Dominions of any Government, doth thereby give his *tacit Consent*, and is as far forth obliged to Obedience to the Laws of that Government, during such Enjoyment, as any one under it; whether this his Possession be of Land, to him and his Heirs for ever, or a Lodging only for a Week; or whether it be barely travelling freely on the Highway; and in Effect, it reaches as far as the very being of any one within the Territories of that Government.[2]

Locke is explicit that the tacit consent which is assumed to be given by all such men does not make them full members of the society: 'Nothing can make any Man so, but his actually entering into it by positive Engagement, and express Promise and Compact'.[3] And the only men who are assumed to incorporate themselves in any commonwealth by express compact are those who have some property, or the expectation of some property, in land:

every Man, when he, at first, incorporates himself into any Commonwealth, he, by his uniting himself thereunto, annexed also, and submits to the Community those Possessions, which he has, or shall acquire, that do not already belong to any other Government. For it would be a direct Contradition, for any one, to enter into Society with others for the securing and regulating of Property: And yet to suppose his Land, whose Property is to be regulated by the Laws of the Society,

---

[1] *Second Treatise*, sect. 140. Cf. sect. 158.   [2] sect. 119.   [3] sect. 122.

should be exempt from the Jurisdiction of that Government, to which he himself the Proprietor of the Land, is a Subject.[1]

Not every proprietor of land is necessarily a full member of the society—foreigners[2] and even natives who have not actually incorporated themselves in the society[3] may possess land there—but every full member is assumed to be a proprietor of land. Thus, the native with no estate or expectation of estate is not admitted to full membership by the back door of tacit consent; like the resident foreigner, he is simply subject to the jurisdiction of the government.[4] The reason Locke introduced the concept of tacit consent was presumably the impossibility of showing express consent in the case of all present citizens of an established state. But his doctrine of tacit consent has the added convenience that it clearly imposes obligation, reaching to their 'very being', on those with no estate whatever.

From the whole foregoing analysis it appears that the result of Locke's work was to provide a moral basis for a class state from postulates of equal individual natural rights. Given the seventeenth-century individualist natural rights assumptions, a class state could only be legitimized by a doctrine of consent which would bring one class within but not make it fully a part of the state. This is just what Locke's theory did do. The doing of it required the implicit assumptions we have seen he did have in his mind. The assumptions were such as to involve him in the ambiguities and contradictions that pervade his argument. And it is difficult to see how he could have persisted in such contradictions had he not been taking the class state as one desideratum and equal natural rights as another.

It is not suggested that Locke deliberately twisted a theory of equal natural rights into a justification of a class state. On the contrary, his natural rights assumptions, honestly held, were such as to make it possible, indeed almost to guarantee, that his theory would justify a class state

[1] *Second Treatise*, sect. 120.   [2] sect. 122.   [3] sect. 121.
[4] Cf. Ireton's position; above, ch. III, pp. 151-2.

without any sleight of hand. The decisive factor was that the equal natural rights Locke envisaged, including as they did the right to unlimited accumulation of property, led logically to differential class rights and so to the justification of a class state. Locke's confusions are the result of honest deduction from a postulate of equal natural rights which contained its own contradiction. The evidence suggests that he did not realize the contradiction in the postulate of equal natural right to unlimited property, but that he simply read into the realm of right (or the state of nature) a social relation which he accepted as normal in civilized society. In this view, the source of the contradictions in his theory is his attempt to state in universal (non-class) terms, rights and obligations which necessarily had a class content.

6. *Unsettled Problems Reconsidered*

When Locke's theory is understood in the sense here ascribed to it, some outstanding difficulties of its interpretation may be resolved.

i. *The joint-stock theory*

The problem inherent in the joint-stock interpretation of Locke's state is now no problem, for we have seen how Locke could consider the state to consist both of property-owners only and of the whole population. He would have no difficulty, therefore, in thinking of the state as a joint-stock company of owners whose majority decision binds not only themselves but also their employees. The labouring class, whose only asset is their capacity to labour, cannot take part in the operations of the company at the same level as the owners. Nevertheless, the labouring class is so necessary to the operations of the company as to be considered an organic part of it. For the purpose of the company is not only to preserve what property it has, but also to preserve the right and conditions to enable it to enlarge its property; and one of these conditions is a labour force effectively submitted to its jurisdiction. Perhaps the closest analogue of Locke's state is the joint-stock company of merchants trading to or planting in distant lands, whose charter gives them, or allows them to take, such jurisdiction over the natives or the transplanted labour force as the character of the trade requires.

ii. *Majority rule* v. *property right*

The implicit contradiction in that interpretation of Locke's theory which emphasizes the supremacy of the majority is also cleared. The contradiction, it will be remembered, was between the assertion of majority rule and the insistence on the sanctity of individual property. If the men of no property were to have full political rights, how could the sanctity of existing property institutions be expected to be maintained against the rule of the majority? This was no fanciful problem. When it had been raised during the Civil War all the men of property had seen the impossibility of combining real majority rule and property rights. And Locke assumed, correctly, that the propertyless were a majority in England at the time he wrote.[1] But we can now see that there is no conflict between Locke's two assertions, of majority rule and of property right, inasmuch as Locke was assuming that only those with property were full members of civil society and so of the majority.

iii. *The equation of individual and majority consent*

Even when it is recognized that Locke's consent of the majority is consent of the majority of property-owners, there is a further difficulty in his treatment of consent. This is most clearly seen in his discussion of consent to taxation. Locke first asserts, in the strongest possible terms, that 'The *Supream Power cannot take* from any Man any part of his *Property* without his own consent', on the ground that without this provision individuals would have 'no *Property*

---

[1] For Locke's assumption, *Reasonableness of Christianity* as quoted above, pp. 224–5: for its accuracy, King's estimates, as quoted below, Appendix.

at all' and so would 'lose that by entring into Society, which was the end for which they entered into it, too gross an absurdity for any Man to own'.[1] Here is a clear statement of an extreme individualist position. Two paragraphs later Locke acknowledges that 'Governments cannot be supported without great Charge, and 'tis fit every one who enjoys his share of the Protection, should pay out of his Estate his proportion for the maintenance of it. But still it must be with his own Consent, *i.e.* the Consent of the Majority, giving it either by themselves, or their Representatives chosen by them'.[2] This equation of the consent of each individual property-owner with the consent of the majority of property-owners, or of their representatives, seems difficult to reconcile with the strong individualist position Locke had just asserted. Gough asks, for instance, whether Locke can 'really have thought that the consent of a majority of representatives was the same as a man's own consent, from which it is, in fact, twice removed?',[3] and finds no satisfactory answer. Locke's equation of the two consents seems even more curious when we notice that Locke was very well aware that there were differences of interest between the landed men, the merchants, and the moneyed men, and that these differences came out particularly sharply in contests between them about the incidence of taxation.[4] Yet Locke's awareness of these differences provides a clue to his thinking about consent. The fact that Locke could, knowing the conflict of individual interests, equate individual and majority consent, indicates that he was thinking of the function of government as the defence of property as such. He could assume, as a man of property himself,[5] that the common

---

[1] *Second Treatise*, sect. 138.   [2] sect. 140.
[3] Gough, op. cit., p. 69.   [4] *Considerations*, *Works* (1759), ii. 36, 29.
[5] The extent and variety of Locke's holdings have been brought to light recently. In the 1670's he had land bringing in £240 a year, substantial investments in the silk trade, the slave trade, and other overseas ventures, as well as money out on short-term loans and on mortgage. In 1694 he took £500 of the first issue of Bank of England stock; in 1699 he is asking for advice about investing £1,500 he had 'lying dead'. His estate at his death was about £20,000. Maurice Cranston, *John Locke, a Biography* (1957), pp. 114–15, 377, 448, 475.

interest that propertied men had in the security of property was more important, and could be seen by any rational self-interested man of property to be more important, than their divergent interests as owners of land, of money, or of mercantile stock. On this assumption, and only on this, is it consistent to equate (rational) individual and (rational) majority consent. Differences between individual interests will still exist—every rational man will not come to the same conclusion about the merits of any tax, so their rational decisions will not be unanimous on every proposal; but every rational man will see that he must consent to whatever is acceptable to the majority, for without this there can be no adequate government revenue, hence no adequate protection of the institution of property. His self-interested rational will is to submit to the will of the majority of rational property-owners; by ellipsis, his will *is* the will of the majority.

Locke's equation of individual and majority consent to taxation is only one case, perhaps the most revealing one, of his equation of the two consents. He can say, of every man who enters civil society 'for the preservation of the property of all the Members of that Society, as far as is possible', that 'the Judgments of the Commonwealth . . . are his own Judgments, they being made by himself, or his Representative'.[1] He can say that when the people, finding their properties not secure under the government of one man, established a collective legislative body for the preservation of property, 'every single person became subject, equally with other the meanest Men, to those Laws, which he himself, as part of the Legislative had established'.[2]

Indeed the equation of the consent of the individual and the consent of the majority follows from the terms of the agreement that is necessary to establish civil society. The consent which *every* individual who wishes to enter civil society must give in order to enter it, is the consent to be bound by the decisions of the majority 'which is the *consent of the majority*';[3] without this, there could be no society.

[1] *Second Treatise*, sect. 88.   [2] sect. 94.   [3] sect. 96.

When Locke is demonstrating that civil society requires majority rule, he does distinguish between individual consent and majority consent, but only in order to demonstrate that individual consent is an impossible requirement.[1] He who wills the end wills the means: the end is preservation of his property, the means is acceptance of the majority will as his will: 'it would be a direct Contradiction, for any one, to enter into Society with others for the securing and regulating of Property: And yet to suppose his Land, whose Property is to be regulated by the Laws of the Society, should be exempt from the Jurisdiction of that Government, to which he himself the Proprietor of the Land, is a Subject.'[2] The rational proprietor has to consent to majority consent. Because of this, it is allowable to equate the consent of the individual proprietor with the consent of the majority of proprietors. This leads us into a still larger question.

iv. *Individualism* v. *Collectivism*

The debate whether Locke was an individualist or a 'collectivist', whether he put the purposes of the individual or the purposes of society first, now appears in a new light. When the fundamental quality of Locke's individualism is kept in mind the debate becomes meaningless. Locke's individualism does not consist entirely in his maintaining that individuals are by nature free and equal and can only be rightfully subjected to the jurisdiction of others by their own consent. To leave it at that is to miss its main significance. Fundamentally it consists in making the individual the natural proprietor of his own person and capacities, owing nothing to society for them.

Such an individualism is necessarily collectivism (in the sense of asserting the supremacy of civil society over every individual). For it asserts an individuality that can only fully be realized in accumulating property, and therefore only realized by some, and only at the expense of the individuality

---

[1] sects. 97–98.   [2] sect. 120.

of the others. To permit such a society to function, political authority must be supreme over individuals; for if it is not, there can be no assurance that the property institutions essential to this kind of individualism will have adequate sanctions. The individuals who have the means to realize their personalities (that is, the propertied) do not need to reserve any rights as against civil society, since civil society is constructed by and for them, and run by and for them. All they need do is insist that civil society, that is, the majority of themselves, is supreme over any government, for a particular government might otherwise get out of hand. Locke had no hesitation in allowing individuals to hand over to civil society all their natural rights and powers[1] including specifically all their possessions and land[2] or, what comes to the same thing, to hand over all the rights and powers necessary to the ends for which society was formed,[3] the majority being the judge.[4] The wholesale transfer of individual rights was necessary to get sufficient collective force for the protection of property. Locke could afford to propose it because the civil society was to be in control of the men of property. In these circumstances individualism must be, and could safely be, left to the collective supremacy of the state.

The notion that individualism and 'collectivism' are the opposite ends of a scale along which states and theories of the state can be arranged, regardless of the stage of social development in which they appear, is superficial and misleading. Locke's individualism, that of an emerging capitalist society, does not exclude but on the contrary demands the supremacy of the state over the individual. It is not a question of the more individualism, the less collectivism; rather, the more thorough-going the individualism, the more complete the collectivism. Of this the supreme illustration is Hobbes's theory; but Hobbes's denial of traditional natural law, and his failure to provide guarantees for property as against a

---

[1] *Second Treatise*, sects. 128, 136.   [2] sect. 120.
[3] sects. 99, 129, 131.   [4] sect. 97.

self-perpetuating sovereign did not recommend his views to those who thought property the central social fact. Locke was more acceptable because of his ambiguity about natural law and because he provided some sort of guarantee of property rights. When the specific quality of seventeenth-century bourgeois individualism is seen in this way it is no longer necessary to search for a compromise between Locke's individualist and collectivist statements; in the circumstances, they imply each other.

v. *Locke's constitutionalism*

Locke's constitutionalism also now falls into a more intelligible place; it need neither be minimized nor be emphasized to the exclusion of all else. It becomes possible to see it for what it is, a defence of the rights of expanding property rather than of the rights of the individual against the state.

That this is the real meaning of Locke's constitutionalism is suggested by the significant fact that Locke did not think it desirable (whereas the Levellers in the *Agreement of the People* had thought it essential) to reserve some rights to the individual as against any parliament or government. No individual rights are directly protected in Locke's state. The only protection the individual has against arbitrary government is placed in the right of the majority of civil society to say when a government has broken its trust to act always in the public good and never arbitrarily. Locke could assume that this supremacy of the majority was a sufficient safeguard of the rights of each, because he assumed that all who had the right to be consulted were agreed on one concept of the public good, ultimately the maximization of the nation's wealth, and thereby (as he saw it) of the nation's welfare. He could assume this agreement only by virtue of his assumption that the labouring class was not among those who had the right to be consulted. Locke's constitutionalism is essentially a defence of the supremacy of property—and not that of the yeoman only, but more especially that of the men of substance to whom the security of unlimited accumulation was of first importance.

Locke's insistence that the authority of the government ('the legislative') is limited and fiduciary, dependent on the consent of the majority of taxable persons, or on that majority's interpretation of the government's faithfulness to its trust, is only one part of his whole theory, and not the primary part. It was necessary (and possible) for him to develop limitations on government because he had first constructed the other part, i.e. the total subordination of the individual to civil society. Both parts were necessary to any theory which would protect and promote the property institutions, and thereby the kind of society, which a civil war, a restoration, and a further revolution had been needed to secure. If in 1689 the confinement of arbitrary government had a more obvious immediacy, the subordination of the individual to the state had at least as lasting a significance. The Whig Revolution not only established the supremacy of parliament over the monarchy, it also consolidated the position of the men of property—and specifically of the men who were using their property in the new way, as capital employed to yield profit—over the labouring class.[1] Locke's theory was of service to the Whig state in both respects.

We may notice incidentally that there is less difference than recent writers have suggested[2] between the position Locke took in 1660 on the supremacy of the state and his position in 1689. Locke's unpublished treatise of 1660 on the civil magistrate contains some remarkably authoritarian passages, the most extreme being his statement in the Preface that 'the *Supreme Magistrate* of every Nation what way soever created must necessarily have an *absolute & arbitrary* power over all the indifferent actions of his people'.[3] This

---

[1] Cf. H. J. Habbakuk, 'English Landownership, 1680–1740', *Econ. Hist. Rev.* Feb. 1940.

[2] Gough, op. cit., p. 178; Locke, *Essays on the Law of Nature*, ed. W. von Leyden (Oxford, 1954), pp. 15, 27; Cranston, op. cit., p. 67; Locke, *Two Treatises of Government*, ed. Laslett, pp. 19–20.

[3] Bodleian Library, MS. Locke, c. 28, f. 3ʳ.

sounds very unlike his insistence, three decades later, that neither the civil society nor any government can possibly have arbitrary power over the life, liberty, or property of any subject. But in fact the power he allows to the civil authority is the same in both cases. The 'absolute and arbitrary power' of 1660 is only over 'indifferent actions', i.e. actions that are neither required nor prohibited by the law of nature or the revealed law of God. It is in respect of those actions, and those alone, that man is naturally free, and therefore it is over those actions alone that he has any power that he can transfer to society. This is precisely the same limited natural power that in the *Second Treatise* Locke has the individual hand over to the supreme civil authority (there the civil society itself).

The essential identity of the two doctrines may be seen by comparing the familiar doctrine of the *Second Treatise* with a passage from the 1660 manuscript, where, after premissing that no man has natural or original freedom from God's law or the law of nature, Locke writes:

4°. That all things not comprehended in that Law are perfectly indifferent, & as to them man is naturally free, but yet soe much master of his own liberty, that he may by compact convey it over to an other, & invest him with a power over his actions there being noe Law of God forbidding a man to dispose of his liberty & obey another, But on the other side there being a law of God inforceing fidelity & truth in all Lawfull contracts, it obliges him after such a resignation & agreement to submitt.

5°. That supposeing man naturally owner of an entire liberty, & soe much master of himself as to owe noe subjection to any other but God alone (which is the freest condicen we can phancy him in) it is yet the unalterable condicon of Society & Govermt that every particular man must unavoidably part with his right to his liberty & intrust the magistrate with as full a power over all his actions as he himself hath, it being otherwise impossible that any one should be subject to the commands of an other who retains the free disposure of himself, & is master of an equall liberty. . . .[1]

This is exactly the doctrine of the *Second Treatise* as to the

---

[1] Ibid., e. 7, ff. 1–2.

extent of the power of the civil authority.[1] In both doctrines, individuals hand over all their natural power. In both, their natural power is limited to what is allowed by natural law. In both, the civil authority has absolute power within the law of nature but none beyond it. In 1660 Locke called this power 'absolute and arbitrary'; in 1689 he reserved the term 'arbitrary' for power that contravened natural law.

There is of course a substantive difference in the two doctrines as to the *locus* of power. In 1660 Locke was willing to consider an absolute monarchy, or a king in parliament, or the elected assembly of a pure commonwealth, as eligible bearers of civil authority. The 'magistrate' whose power is asserted in the passage just quoted, Locke defines in a side-note, in which he also makes his own preference clear:

By magistrate I understand the supreme legislative power of any society not considering the forme of govermt or number of persons wherein it is placd. Only give me leave to say that the indelible memory of our late miserys, & the happy returne of our ancient freedome & felicity, are proofs sufficient to convince us where the supreme power of these nations is most advantageously placd, without the assistance of any other arguments.

Locke will not, he says in the Preface, 'meddle with the Quest. whether the magistrates crowne drops down on his head immediately from heaven or be placed there by the hands of his subjects';[2] the magistrate's power must be the same on either supposition. And a commonwealth is no different from an absolute monarchy in the extent of the magistrate's power:

Nor doe men as some fondly conceive injoy any greater share of this [their natural] freedome in a pure common wealth if any where to be found than in an absolute monarchy the same arbitrary power being there in the Assembly (wch acts like one person) as in a Monarch: wherein each particular man hath noe more power, (bating the inconsiderable addition of his single vote) of him self to make new or dispute old Laws than in a Monarchy, all he can doe (wch is noe more

---

[1] *Second Treatise*, sects. 135, 136.
[2] Bodleian Library, MS. Locke c. 28, f. 3^r.

than Kings allow petitioners) is to persuade the Majority which is the Monarch.[1]

Thus in 1660 Locke's preference is for the restored Stuart monarchy, and he would allow it supreme power, i.e. absolute power within the limits of the law of nature. In the *Second Treatise* Locke reserves the supreme civil authority to the civil society itself; he would admit the supremacy of a king in parliament, but with narrow limits on the power of the king and always with the proviso that the people may 'remove or *alter the Legislative*, when they find the *Legislative* act contrary to the trust reposed in them'.[2]

The difference in the two positions is not as great as it might seem, since the supreme power in both is supposed to be only within the limits of natural law. But the difference is still substantial, for it is only in the *Second Treatise* that the people are given the right to impose their interpretation of natural law on the constituted civil authority. We need not, however, infer from this difference that there was any change in Locke's fundamental principles. He was consistent throughout in wanting a civil authority which could secure the basic institutions of a class society. In 1660 this required the recall of the Stuarts and the doctrine of the magistrate's absolute and arbitrary power in things indifferent; in 1689 it required the dismissal of the Stuarts and the doctrine of the *Second Treatise*.

We have seen how Locke, by carrying into the postulates of the *Second Treatise* the implicit assumptions of class differential rationality and rights (derived from his comprehension of his own society), reached an ambiguous theory of differential membership in civil society, a theory which justified a class state from postulates of equal individual natural rights. The ambiguity about membership concealed (from Locke himself, I have suggested) the contradiction in his individualism, in which full individuality for some was produced by consuming the individuality of others. Locke could not have been conscious that the individuality he

---

[1] Ibid., e. 7, f. 2.   [2] *Second Treatise*, sect. 149.

championed was at the same time a denial of individuality. Such consciousness was not to be found in men who were just beginning to grasp the great possibilities of individual freedom that lay in the advancement of capitalist society. The contradiction was there, but it was impossible for them to recognize it, let alone to resolve it. Locke was indeed at the fountain-head of English liberalism. The greatness of seventeenth-century liberalism was its assertion of the free rational individual as the criterion of the good society; its tragedy was that this very assertion was necessarily a denial of individualism to half the nation.

VI

POSSESSIVE INDIVIDUALISM AND
LIBERAL DEMOCRACY

1. *The Seventeenth-Century Foundations*

WE are now in a position to consider the extent to which some identifiable social assumptions are common to the main seventeenth-century political theories, and how they are relevant to the problems of later liberal-democratic society.

The assumptions which comprise possessive individualism may be summarized in the following seven propositions.

(i) What makes a man human is freedom from dependence on the wills of others.

(ii) Freedom from dependence on others means freedom from any relations with others except those relations which the individual enters voluntarily with a view to his own interest.

(iii) The individual is essentially the proprietor of his own person and capacities, for which he owes nothing to society.

Proposition (iii) may appear in a theory as an independent postulate, or as a deduction from (i) and (ii) plus a concept of property as an exclusive right. Thus: since the freedom, and therefore the humanity, of the individual depend on his freedom to enter into self-interested relations with other individuals, and since his ability to enter into such relations depends on his having exclusive control of (rights in) his own person and capacities, and since proprietorship is the generalized form of such exclusive control, the individual is essentially the proprietor of his own person and capacities.

(iv) Although the individual cannot alienate the whole of his property in his own person, he may alienate his capacity to labour.

(v) Human society consists of a series of market relations.

This follows from the assumptions already stated. Since the individual is human only in so far as free, and free only in so far as a proprietor of himself, human society can only be a series of relations between sole proprietors, i.e. a series of market relations.

Or proposition (v) may appear in a theory not as a deduced proposition but as the primary or even the sole social assumption. This is possible because propositions (i) to (iv) are contained in it. The concept of market relations necessarily implies individual freedom as defined in (ii) and proprietorship as defined in (iii) and (iv); and the postulate that human society consists of market relations necessarily implies that an individual's humanity is a function of his freedom (proposition i).

(vi) Since freedom from the wills of others is what makes a man human, each individual's freedom can rightfully be limited only by such obligations and rules as are necessary to secure the same freedom for others.

(vii) Political society is a human contrivance for the protection of the individual's property in his person and goods, and (therefore) for the maintenance of orderly relations of exchange between individuals regarded as proprietors of themselves.

These assumptions are present in one form or another in each of the theories that have been analysed. And it appears from the analysis that the strength of each theory is due to its having incorporated these assumptions, and the weakness of each to its having failed to deal with some of their implications.

The assumptions are clearest and fullest in Hobbes. His model of man, as the sum of a man's powers to get gratifications, reduces the human essence to freedom from others' wills and proprietorship of one's own capacities. His model of society, which follows from his model of man plus the assumption that every man's powers are opposed to every other man's, we have seen to be a full possessive market model. The political society whose necessity he deduced from these models is an artificial device, calculated to provide the maximum security that could by any means be provided for the individual's exercise of his capacities.

For Hobbes the model of the self-moving, appetitive, possessive individual, and the model of society as a series of market relations between these individuals, were a sufficient source of political obligation. No traditional concepts of justice, natural law, or divine purpose were needed. Obligation of the individual to the state was deduced from the supposed facts, as set out in the materialist model of man and the market model of society. The models contained the two suppositions of fact which Hobbes thought sufficient for the deduction of right and obligation: equality of need for continued motion, and equal insecurity because of equal liability to invasion by others through the market. The system, both mechanical and moral, was self-moving and self-contained. It needed no outside mover or outside standard of right.

I have argued that it was Hobbes's possessive market assumptions which gave his political theory its extraordinary strength and consistency. I have argued also that it was one flaw in his market model that made his political theory inapplicable to the possessive market society. The flaw was his failure to see that the market society generated a degree of class cohesion which made possible a viable political authority without a self-perpetuating sovereign body.

When we turn to the theory of the Levellers we find again the main assumptions of possessive individualism, but now differently formulated, and with their implications not as fully worked out. The human essence is freedom from the wills of others, and freedom is a function of proprietorship of one's person: 'every one as he is himselfe, so he hath a selfe propriety, else he could not be himselfe'.[1] Political

---

[1] Quoted above, ch. III, p. 140.

society is a contrivance for securing individual natural rights, that is, individual freedom and proprietorship. No individual can alienate the whole of his property in his person, but anyone can alienate his property in his own labour; in doing so he gives up his natural right to a voice in elections but not his natural right to civil and religious liberties.

The strength of the Leveller theory may be variously assessed. Its powerful appeal, for those in the Leveller movement, may be ascribed to its insistence on individual freedom, both religious and secular, and to the skill with which history and Scripture were marshalled in the cause of freedom for the men below the wealthy and above the dependent poor. Its theoretical strength is attributable in large measure to its realistic recognition of the position of the individual in a market society. The Leveller writers saw that freedom in their society was a function of possession. They could therefore make a strong moral case for individual freedom by defining freedom as ownership of one's person.

The theoretical weaknesses of the Leveller position can all be referred to their failure to see the full implications of their possessive individualist assumptions, which failure may in turn be referred to the limits of their vision as members of an intermediate class. They did not see that if you make individual freedom a function of possession, you must accept the full market society. If you insist that a man is human only as sole proprietor of himself, only in so far as he is free from all but market relations, you must convert all moral values into market values. But the Levellers wrote as if there were no difference between the market morality of possessive individualism and the Christian social ethic which they also upheld. They brought in, over and above the individual right of self-preservation and self-advancement, a concept of 'humane society, cohabitation or being' as 'the earthly sovereigne good of mankind', with a consequent obligation on everyone to work for 'communitive Happinesse'.[1] They wavered between a view of a man's labour as a commodity

[1] Quoted above, ch. III, pp. 156–7.

and a view of it as an integral part of his personality. They asserted the right of individual appropriation of land and goods, but denied the rightness of its consequence, the greatly unequal distribution of wealth.

While the Levellers treated the class structure of seventeenth-century society more seriously than did Hobbes, and so avoided the error into which Hobbes had been led by his neglect of class cohesion, their treatment of class was also faulty. In excluding wage-earners and alms-takers from political rights they recognized one of the prevailing class divisions, and in denouncing the conspiracy of the rich against themselves (the intermediate class of small independent producers) they recognized another. Their demand for a political voice for themselves was a demand that the second dividing line should be erased. The implied assumption was that all those above the dependent poor were capable of enough cohesion to support a single elective political authority. There was no such cohesion, as events were to show. This error of the Levellers, which appears as a fault of empirical judgement, may be traced to the imprecision of their theoretical grasp of market society. They did not see that a possessive market society necessarily puts in a dependent position not only the wage-earners but also all those without a substantial (and, by the natural operation of the market, an increasing) amount of capital.

Harrington's theory stands somewhat apart from the others. Less concerned with right and obligation than with empirical uniformities of political change and stability, Harrington gave less attention to moral principles than the Levellers, and less to psychological analysis than Hobbes. While his concern for civil and religious liberties puts him in the liberal tradition, he is not as pronounced an individualist as the others. Working mainly by comparative and historical analysis he does not appear to rely on postulates about the moral or behavioural nature of the individual. Yet as we have seen,[1] he did postulate that every man seeks power over

[1] Above, ch. IV, p. 163.

others, and that power is a function of property. He recognized that these postulates were necessary for his theory of the balance. And if he said little about human nature, it was because he fully endorsed Hobbes's analysis: 'his treatises of human nature, and of liberty and necessity, are the greatest of new lights, and those which I have follow'd, and shall follow'.[1]

What most clearly entitles us to describe Harrington as a possessive individualist is his assumption that seventeenth-century English society was a possessive market society. His whole case for erecting an 'equal commonwealth' in England depends, I have argued, on that assumption. He both assumed the existence and accepted the morality of bourgeois society. The behaviour of both gentry and people was brought under one general theory of possessive and accumulative motivation. The institutional balance he proposed between gentry and people would work, and the agrarian law which was to stabilize the balance would be indestructible, only because both classes accepted the market relations which Harrington assumed would henceforth permanently prevail.

He did not read market relations back into the very nature of man, as Hobbes had done. But though he did not penetrate as far as Hobbes into the nature of bourgeois man, he avoided the error into which Hobbes had been led by such a high degree of abstraction. Harrington saw the reality of class structure. He allowed for, indeed built upon, the possibility of class cohesion, as Hobbes did not. And he avoided the opposite error of the Levellers: he did not assume an improbable degree of cohesion or identity of interests between the greater and the meaner sort of freemen, but tried to arrange a balance of power between them.

The main weakness of Harrington's theory, I have suggested, was due to his insufficient logical ability, which led him to contradict himself in his use of the principle of the balance. Had he sharpened his assumptions and been more careful in his deduction he could have avoided those contradictions. Thus we may say of Harrington that the theoretical

---

[1] *Prerogative of Popular Government, Works* (1771), p. 241.

strength of his system lay in his recognition and acceptance of possessive market relations and motivation, and its theoretical weakness in his failure to see fully or state clearly all the assumptions that were involved.

With Locke we are again in the realm of moral rights and obligation derived from the supposed nature of man and society. As with Hobbes, Locke's deduction starts with the individual and moves out to society and the state, but, again as with Hobbes, the individual with which he starts has already been created in the image of market man. Individuals are by nature equally free from the jurisdiction of others. The human essence is freedom from any relations other than those a man enters with a view to his own interest. The individual's freedom is rightly limited only by the requirements of others' freedom. The individual is proprietor of his own person, for which he owes nothing to society. He is free to alienate his capacity to labour, but not his whole person. Society is a series of relations between proprietors. Political society is a contractual device for the protection of proprietors and the orderly regulation of their relations.

But the assumptions of possessive individualism are not unalloyed in Locke. He refused to reduce all social relations to market relations and all morality to market morality. He would not entirely let go of traditional natural law. He used both Hobbes and Hooker to establish his political obligation. His main theoretical weaknesses might be traced to his attempt to combine these two sources of morality and obligation. The weaknesses are better traced, I have suggested, to his inability to surmount an inconsistency inherent in market society. A market society generates class differentiation in effective rights and rationality, yet requires for its justification a postulate of equal natural rights and rationality. Locke recognized the differentiation in his own society, and read it back into natural society. At the same time he maintained the postulate of equal natural rights and rationality. Most of Locke's theoretical confusions, and most of his practical appeal, can be traced to this ambiguous position.

The ambiguity was less a result of his imperfect logic than of his trying to cope with a contradiction in market society of which he was not fully aware. He did not analyse that society as clearly as Hobbes but he did take into account a problem that Hobbes had neglected, that is, the complications raised by class differentiation in an atomized market society.

It may be too much to say that it was because Locke kept these complications in mind that he did not produce clear models of man and society, and reason from them as rigorously as Hobbes. But it may be said that the effective reception of Locke's theory owes much to his having kept the complications in mind and dealt with them, however confusedly. At least his having kept them in mind enabled him to avoid Hobbes's error, and to produce a political system without a self-perpetuating sovereign.

In making the one structural alteration in Hobbes's theoretical system that was required to bring it into conformity with the needs and possibilities of a possessive market society, Locke completed an edifice that rested on Hobbes's sure foundations. Locke's other contribution, his attaching to this structure a façade of traditional natural law, was by comparison unimportant. It made the structure more attractive to the taste of his contemporaries. But when tastes changed, as they did in the eighteenth century, the façade of natural law could be removed, by Hume and Bentham, without damage to the strong and well-built utilitarian structure that lay within. Hobbes, as amended by Locke in the matter of the self-perpetuating sovereign, thus provided the main structure of English liberal theory.

The basic assumptions of possessive individualism—that man is free and human by virtue of his sole proprietorship of his own person, and that human society is essentially a series of market relations—were deeply embedded in the seventeenth-century foundations. It was these assumptions that gave the original theory its strength, for they did correspond to the reality of seventeenth-century market society. The assumptions of possessive individualism have been retained in modern liberal theory, to an extent not always realized. Yet they have failed as foundations of liberal-democratic theory. The trouble is not that they have been kept after they had ceased to correspond to our society. They still do correspond to our society, and so must be kept. The trouble with some liberal theory is that it does not recognize this, and tries to do without them. But the real trouble is that one change in possessive market society—a change which does not alter the validity of possessive individualist assumptions, since it is a change in an aspect of market society that was not reflected in those assumptions —has made it impossible, on two counts, to derive a valid theory of obligation from the assumptions.

The change was the emergence of working-class political articulacy. It has not altered the validity of possessive individualist assumptions for possessive market societies, because those assumptions reflect or state the atomized rather than the class nature of that society. We have seen[1] that a possessive market society is necessarily class-divided. We have also seen[2] that a possessive market society is a series of competitive and invasive relations between all men, regardless of class: it puts every man on his own. It is this second aspect of possessive market society that was and still is accurately reflected in the assumptions of possessive individualism. The assumptions remain indispensable, but no sufficient principle of obligation can now be derived from them. We must now consider how this has happened, and what prospects are left for liberal-democratic theory.

2. *The Twentieth-century Dilemma*

The assumptions of possessive individualism are peculiarly appropriate to a possessive market society, for they state certain essential facts that are peculiar to that society. The individual in a possessive market society *is* human in his capacity as proprietor of his own person; his humanity does

[1] Above, ch. II, pp. 55-56.   [2] Above, ch. II, p. 57.

depend on his freedom from any but self-interested contractual relations with others; his society does consist of a series of market relations. England, and the other modern liberal-democratic nations, are still, in the twentieth century, possessive market societies. Why, then, should not modern liberal-democratic justificatory theory, to the extent that it contains these assumptions, be satisfactory? Why should not the possessive individualist theory of the English utilitarian tradition, which is essentially the theory of Hobbes as amended by Locke in the matter of the self-perpetuating sovereign, be a satisfactory demonstration of the political obligation of the individual to the liberal state? And why should not that theory, further amended as it was in the nineteenth century by the admission that wage-earners were free men, be adequate now for the liberal-democratic state? We can best deal with these questions by collecting from our earlier analysis the conditions on which a possessive individualist theory can be an adequate theory of political obligation.

I have argued[1] that to get a valid theory of political obligation without relying on any supposed purposes of Nature or will of God (which we may call an autonomous theory of political obligation), one must be able to postulate that the individuals of whom the society is composed see themselves, or are capable of seeing themselves, as equal in some respect more fundamental than all the respects in which they are unequal. This condition was fulfilled in the original possessive market society, from its emergence as the dominant form in the seventeenth century until its zenith in the nineteenth, by the apparent inevitability of everyone's subordination to the laws of the market. So long as everyone was subject to the determination of a competitive market, and so long as this apparently equal subordination of individuals to the determination of the market was accepted as rightful, or inevitable, by virtually everybody, there was a sufficient basis for rational obligation of all men to a political

---

[1] Above, ch. II, p. 83.

authority which could maintain and enforce the only possible orderly human relations, namely, market relations.

I have argued also[1] that in a possessive market society a further condition is required for a valid theory of obligation of the individual to a non-self-perpetuating sovereign body (and hence for a theory of obligation to any kind of liberal state). The further condition is that there be a cohesion of self-interests, among all those who have a voice in choosing the government, sufficient to offset the centrifugal forces of a possessive market society. This condition was fulfilled, in the heyday of the market society, by the fact that a political voice was restricted to a possessing class which had sufficient cohesion to decide periodically, without anarchy, who should have the sovereign power. As long as this condition was fulfilled there was a sufficient basis for an autonomous theory of obligation of the individual to a constitutional liberal state. This second condition, like the first, was fulfilled until about the middle of the nineteenth century.

Thereafter, both conditions ceased to be met. Although possessive market relations continued to prevail in fact, their inevitability became increasingly challenged as an industrial working class developed some class consciousness and became politically articulate. Men no longer saw themselves fundamentally equal in an inevitable subjection to the determination of the market. The development of the market system, producing a class which could envisage alternatives to the system, thus destroyed the social fact (acceptance of inevitability of market relations) which had fulfilled the first prerequisite of an autonomous theory of political obligation.

The second prerequisite condition was similarly affected. Although the society continued to be class divided, and the possessing class continued to be cohesive, its cohesion ceased to fulfil the prerequisite when the possessing class had to yield its monopoly of power by admitting the rest of the society to the franchise. With the democratic franchise,

[1] Above, ch. II, pp. 94–95.

there was no longer that assurance of cohesion, among all those with a political voice, which had been provided by class interest during the time when only one class had had the franchise.

It may be argued that the continued existence of liberal-democratic states in possessive market societies, since that time, has been due to the ability of a possessing class to keep the effective political power in its hands in spite of universal suffrage. But while this may suffice to keep a liberal state going, it savours too much of deception to be an adequate basis for a moral justification of liberal democracy.

It may be argued also that the continued existence of liberal-democratic states into the twentieth century, after the cohesion of a possessing governing class had given way to the uncertain cohesion of the democratic franchise, was made possible by a sort of class cohesion on an international level. The democratic franchise came in the nineteenth century in advanced capitalist countries. By the time it came, these countries stood, in relation to the backward peoples, in somewhat the same relation as the possessing class had stood towards the non-possessing class within the advanced market societies. But while the cohesion of a possessing nation may have provided some substitute for the previous cohesion of a possessing class, this too was an inadequate basis for a moral justification of liberal democracy. In any case, with the emergence of colonial peoples to national independence, this basis is now rapidly disappearing.

A temporary substitute for the old cohesion has sometimes been provided in our century by war. But, apart from the fact that the cost of this cohesion is a weakening of liberal institutions, few would rest a moral justification of liberal democracy on a premiss of continual war. In any case, the technical conditions of war are now such that war on a scale sufficient to bring the required cohesion within one warring nation would destroy the nation. Thus none of the factors which together may be said to have operated to keep liberal-democratic states going in possessive market societies, after the disappearance of the old basis of cohesion, has provided or can provide a satisfactory justifying theory.

The dilemma of modern liberal-democratic theory is now apparent: it must continue to use the assumptions of possessive individualism, at a time when the structure of market society no longer provides the necessary conditions for deducing a valid theory of political obligation from those assumptions. Liberal theory must continue to use the assumptions of possessive individualism because they are factually accurate for our possessive market societies. Their factual accuracy has already been noticed, but the point will bear repetition. The individual in market society *is* human as proprietor of his own person. However much he may wish it to be otherwise, his humanity does depend on his freedom from any but self-interested contractual relations with others. His society does consist of a series of market relations. Because the assumptions are factually accurate, they cannot be dropped from a justificatory theory. But the maturing of market society has cancelled that cohesion, among all those with a political voice, which is a prerequisite for the deduction of obligation to a liberal state from possessive individualist assumptions. No way out of the dilemma is to be found by rejecting those assumptions while not rejecting market society, as so many theorists from John Stuart Mill to our own time have done on the ground that the assumptions are morally offensive. If they are now morally offensive they are none the less still factually accurate for our possessive market societies. The dilemma remains. Either we reject possessive individualist assumptions, in which case our theory is unrealistic, or we retain them, in which case we cannot get a valid theory of obligation. It follows that we cannot now expect a valid theory of obligation to a liberal-democratic state in a possessive market society.

The question whether the actual relations of a possessive market society can be abandoned or transcended, without abandoning liberal political institutions, bristles with difficulties. In the measure that market society could be abandoned, the problem of cohesion would be resolved, for the problem was defined as the need for a degree of cohesion which would counteract the centrifugal force of market relations. But there would still be the problem of finding a substitute for that recognition of a fundamental equality which had originally been provided by the supposed inevitable subordination of everyone to the market. Could any conceivable new concept of fundamental equality, which would be consistent with the maintenance of liberal institutions and values, possibly get the wide acknowledgement without which, as I have argued, no autonomous theory of political obligation can be valid?

We may take some comfort from the fact that the two problems, of cohesion and of equality, do not now have to be solved in that order. The question whether the actual possessive market relations of a given liberal-democratic state can be abandoned or transcended has now become of secondary importance. For a further change in the social facts has supervened. The very factor, namely, technical change in the methods of war, that has made war an impossible source of internal cohesion, has created a new equality of insecurity among individuals, not merely within one nation but everywhere. The destruction of every individual is now a more real and present possibility than Hobbes could have imagined.

From this, the possibility of a new rational political obligation arises. We cannot hope to get a valid theory of obligation of the individual to a single national state alone. But if we postulate no more than the degree of rational understanding which it has always been necessary to postulate for any moral theory of political obligation, an acceptable theory of obligation of the individual to a wider political authority should now be possible. Given that degree of rationality, the self-interested individual, whatever his possessions, and whatever his attachment to a possessive market society, can see that the relations of the market society must yield to the overriding requirement that, in Overton's words, which now acquire a new significance, 'humane society, cohabitation or being, . . . above all earthly things must be maintained'.[1]

The new equality of insecurity has thus changed the terms of our problem. Twentieth-century technology has, so to speak, brought Hobbes and the Levellers together. The problems raised by possessive individualism have shrunk: they can perhaps now be brought to manageable proportions, but only if they are clearly identified and accurately related to the actual changes in the social facts. Those changes have driven us again to a Hobbesian insecurity, at a new level. The question now is whether, in the new setting, Hobbes can again be amended, this time more clearly than he was by Locke.

[1] Quoted above, ch. III, p. 156.

APPENDIX

Social Classes and Franchise Classes
in England c. 1648

THE following estimates are computed from Gregory King's estimates of the
population, income, and expenditure, of the people of England in 1688, by
ranks or occupational classes, together with his estimates of population by age,
sex, and marital status, and of tax yields and commodity consumption by
certain social classes.[1] King's estimates have come under close scrutiny by
modern economic historians and demographers, and have stood up remarkably well.[2]

We want estimates for the following franchise classes:

1. Freeholders and freemen of corporations.
2. Ratepaying householders not in (1).
3. Non-ratepayers not in (4).
4. Servants and alms-takers.

This will give us the extent of each of the four franchises in question: the
freeholder franchise is measured by (1); the ratepayer franchise by (1)+(2);
the non-servant franchise by (1)+(2)+(3); and manhood franchise by
(1)+(2)+(3)+(4).

King's main estimate is reproduced on the two following pages.

King's categories, it will be seen, cannot simply be grouped to get each of
our franchise classes. There are in the first place some problems of definition:
for instance, are his categories 'labouring people and out-servants' and 'cottagers and paupers' to be counted entirely in our class 'servants and alms-
takers'? With other categories the problem is less one of definition than of
making arbitrary assumptions: for instance, what proportions of King's
official, mercantile, and industrial categories are to be assumed to be freeholders, non-freehold ratepayers, and non-ratepayers? We must also transfer,

---

[1] Gregory King, *Natural and Political Observations and Conclusions upon the
State and Condition of England, 1696*, printed as an appendix to George Chalmers's
Estimate of the Comparative Strength of Great Britain. . . . (London, 1804). Many of
King's tables are printed (some with slight changes) in Charles Davenant's *Essay
upon the Probable Methods of Making a People Gainers in the Balance of Trade* (in
Davenant, *Works*, 1771, vol. ii). Davenant's presentation is in some respects more
useful than King's, for Davenant gives some account of the sources and methods of
King's estimates.

[2] D. C. Coleman, 'Labour in the English Economy of the Seventeenth Century',
Econ. Hist. Review, 2nd ser., viii. 3 (1956), p. 283, and authorities there cited.

Gregory King's

'A Scheme of the Income, and Expence, of the Several Families of England; calculated for the Year 1688'[1]

No. of families	Ranks, degrees, titles, and qualifications	Heads per family	No. of persons	Yearly income per family		Yearly income per head		Yearly expence per head	
				£	s.	£	s.	£	s.
160	Temporal lords	40	6,400	2,800	0	70	0	60	0
26	Spiritual lords	20	520	1,300	0	65	0	55	0
800	Baronets	16	12,800	880	0	55	0	51	0
600	Knights	13	7,800	650	0	50	0	46	0
3,000	Esquires	10	30,000	450	0	45	0	42	0
12,000	Gentlemen	8	96,000	280	0	35	0	32	10
5,000	Persons in offices	8	40,000	240	0	30	0	27	0
5,000	„ „	6	30,000	120	0	20	0	18	0
2,000	Merchants and traders by sea	8	16,000	400	0	50	0	40	0
8,000	Merchants and traders by land	6	48,000	200	0	33	0	28	0
10,000	Persons in the law	7	70,000	140	0	20	0	17	0
2,000	Clergymen	6	12,000	60	0	10	0	8	0
8,000	„	5	40,000	45	0	9	0	8	0
40,000	Freeholders	7	280,000	84	0	12	0	11	0
140,000	„	5	700,000	50	0	10	0	9	10
150,000	Farmers	5	750,000	44	0	8	15	8	10
16,000	Persons in sciences and liberal arts	5	80,000	60	0	12	0	11	10
40,000	Shopkeepers and tradesmen	4½	180,000	45	0	10	0	9	10
60,000	Artizans and handicrafts	4	240,000	40	0	10	0	9	10
5,000	Naval officers	4	20,000	80	0	20	0	18	0
4,000	Military officers	4	16,000	60	0	15	0	14	0
511,586		5¼	2,675,520	67	0	..		..	

[1] King in Chalmers, pp. 48–49. Three of King's columns, and some of his totals, are omitted as unnecessary for our purposes.

No. of families	Ranks, degrees, titles, and qualifications	Heads per family	No. of persons	Yearly income per family		Yearly income per head		Yearly expense per head	
				£	s.	£	s.	£	s.
50,000	Common seamen	3	150,000	20	0	7	0	7	10
364,000	Labouring people and outservants	3½	1,275,000	15	0	4	10	4	12
400,000	Cottagers and paupers	3¼	1,300,000	6	10	2	0	2	5
35,000	Common soldiers	2	70,000	14	0	7	0	7	10
849,000		3¼	2,795,000	10	10	2	0	3	0
	Vagrants		30,000	10	10	..		..	
849,000		3¼	2,825,000	10	10	..		..	

So the General Account is:

511,586	Increasing the wealth of the kingdom	5½	2,675,520	67	0	..	..
849,000	Decreasing the wealth of the kingdom	3¼	2,825,000	10	10	..	..
1,360,586	Nett totals	..	5,500,520	32	0	..	..

from the families to a separate sub-class, the servants living in the establishments of their masters. Once we have allotted the members of King's categories into our franchise classes, two further calculations are necessary. What we then have in most of the franchise classes is the number of 'families': these must be converted into the numbers of men aged 21 and over. And since the estimates we then have are for the year 1688 it will be desirable to reduce these to take account of population growth between 1648 and 1688.

It will be convenient to begin with a calculation of franchise class 'servants and alms-takers'.

Class 4. Servants and Alms-takers

(a) Servants

The term servant in seventeenth-century England meant anyone who worked for an employer for wages, whether the wages were by piece-rates or time-rates, and whether hired by the day or week or by the year.[1] Servants' rights and obligations were defined by statutes, their wage rates were from time to time determined in considerable detail by justices' assessments, and their place in the economy was noted in various contemporary economic writings.[2]

The most numerous group was the 'servants in husbandry', farm employees ranging from overseers and skilled ploughmen to 'plain labourers in husbandry' and women for 'out-work and drudgery'.[3] To have one or two such servants was not uncommon even for a modest yeoman, and more substantial yeomen would employ several; they were traditionally hired by the year, but an increasing proportion was coming to be hired for shorter periods at daily rates.[4] Servants in industry were a further large group. From skilled journeymen to barge hands, they comprised a substantial part of the productive force.

[1] The famous Statute of Artificers, 5 Eliz., c. 4, 1563, was drawn in terms that might suggest a distinction between 'servants' (sect. 7) and 'artificers and labourers being hired for wages by the day or week' (sect. 9), although sect. 11 lumps them together as 'servants, labourers and artificers, either by the year or day or otherwise', and as 'the said artificers, handicraftsmen, husbandmen, or any other labourer, servant or workman'. But whatever the intention of the statute, it is clear from the sources cited in the next four notes that 'servants' did not in seventeenth-century usage exclude 'labourers' or others employed for less than the year.

[2] For wage assessments see, for example, George Unwin, *Studies in Economic History*, ed. Tawney, 1927, p. 296 (wage-rates of specified categories of servants in the cloth industry in 1630); for an example of numerous servants employed by a clothier in 1615 at piece-work rates, Unwin, op. cit., p. 292; for seventeenth-century economic writers, see, for example, Andrew Yarranton, *England's Improvement by Sea and Land* (London, 1677), pp. 124–5, 127, 132, 164–71, 179–88; Thomas Firmin, *Some Proposals for the Imployment of the Poor* (London, 1681), pp. 9, 45; John Carey, *Essay on the State of England* (Bristol, 1695), p. 161. See also Note U.

[3] Mildred Campbell, *The English Yeoman under Elizabeth and the Early Stuarts* (New Haven, 1942), App. III, p. 398.   [4] Campbell, op. cit., pp. 212–14.

Hired by the year or less, paid by time or piece rates, they worked for a wide range of employers, from the large clothier to the single handicraftsman.[1]

Since, then, in seventeenth-century usage 'servants' included all sorts of wage-earners—labourers and piece-workers as well as yearly employees—it would appear that all King's 'labouring people and out-servants' would fall within the Leveller concept 'servants'.

There is, however, a possible disparity which should be considered. It might be argued that not all of King's 'labouring people and out-servants' would fall within the Levellers' meaning of servants, since some of the labouring people might be cottagers who worked for wages only intermittently and so would not be as dependent on their employers as were regular contractual servants; and dependence on the will of other men by virtue of employment was the Levellers' criterion of servant. But it must be observed, first, that such intermittent labourers are not likely to have been among King's 'labouring people and out-servants' but among his 'cottagers and paupers' (see below, pp. 286–7); and second, that no significant number of intermittent labourers was likely to have been economically independent enough to merit greater political consideration from the Levellers than did the yearly employees.[2]

It thus appears that all the 'labouring people and out-servants' are properly to be considered as falling within the Levellers' meaning of servants.

To estimate the size of the whole class of servants, we must add, to King's labouring people and out-servants, the in-servants. The seventeenth-century distinction between out-servants and in-servants was fairly plain. Servants in husbandry, and in many branches of industry, commonly lived in the household (which was generally also the working establishment) of the employer, until they married, and thereafter lived out.

The number of in-servants in industry, agriculture, and domestic service can be got from either of two of King's tables.

In Table III[3] King gives 'servants' as 560,000, of whom 260,000 are male. It may be inferred from the classification used in this table that these are in-servants not out-servants. For the classification is by households, the classes being 'husbands and wives, widowers, widows, children, servants, and sojourners and single persons'. Out-servants would mostly be married and would be classified as 'husbands and wives'. This inference is not certain. However, it is supported by a calculation from King's main table, the 'Scheme of the Income and Expence of the several families in England', reproduced above. In that table, in-servants are clearly included in the families, which range in size from 40 to 4 for the classes above the poverty line.

The number of in-servants, including apprentices, in the households of the

---

[1] Unwin, and the contemporary economic writers cited on p. 282, n. 2.
[2] Cf. Coleman's description of the under-employed rural labour force as 'a "reserve army of labour" if ever there was one'. *Econ. Hist. Review*, 2nd ser. viii. 3, p. 289.
[3] King in Chalmers, p. 39.

ranks above the poor can be calculated by subtracting from the total number in these households an estimated number of members of the families proper. Certain assumptions have to be made about the number of children, of bachelors, and of widows, in these families; these assumptions can be made largely though not entirely on the basis of King's Table III and his Table IV[1] which gives an age and sex distribution and some figures on marital status. A calculation based on assumptions which appear reasonable and consistent gives a total of in-servants of 540,000.[2]

This is sufficiently close to the figure for servants in King's Table III to substantiate our reading of 'servants' in Table III as in-servants. On the face of it, indeed, both figures appear rather low. For the total number of households in all the ranks which could employ servants is 511,586; which means an average of only slightly over one in-servant (of either sex and any age) in all the potentially employing households.

Using King's figure of 560,000 in-servants, of whom 260,000 are male, a deduction is needed to get the number of male in-servants of voting age (21 and over). The 260,000, while not including children, does include apprentices and servants less than 21 years old. There is no clear indication in King's figures what proportion these might be of all in-servants,[3] and other contemporary evidence shows such wide variations between trades and localities as to afford no basis for a general estimate. But the proportion of employed or apprenticed males in agriculture and industry together, who were under 21, seems unlikely to have been more than 50 per cent. If we therefore deduct one-half, the total of male in-servants of 21 years and over is 130,000.

Conversion from 'families' to men aged 21 and over. Only now that we have estimated the number of male in-servants are we in a position to reach a basis for converting the number of 'families' in any class to the number of men aged 21 and over. For as soon as the male in-servants of 21 or over are transferred from King's families to a separate sub-class, it becomes apparent that we cannot assume that all of King's families are headed by a man of 21 or over. For on that assumption the total of men aged 21 and over would be 1,360,586 (heads of families) plus 130,000 in-servants, plus the proportion of 'vagrants' who are adult males, which we may estimate conservatively at 10,000: a total of 1,500,586. But the total number of men aged 21 and over

---

[1] King in Chalmers, p. 40.

[2] It should be said that by varying the assumptions, while still keeping well within the bounds of probability, one can get a total of over 600,000 or one somewhat below 500,000. The calculations need not be reproduced here; it is enough to note that they yield results consonant with the figure in King's Table III.

[3] For the whole male population, the age-group 16–21 comprised 18 per cent. of the age group 21 and over (King, Table IV); the percentage for the in-servant class is presumably larger, since all the apprentices (who would be mainly in the age group 16–21) are bunched in the category of in-servants. The only other indication is that the average age of in-servants is 27 (Table IV), which is perhaps consistent with anything up to half the in-servants being under 21.

is given in King's Table IV (age and sex distribution of the total population) as 1,300,000.[1] It follows that the number of men aged 21 and over, in the families proper, i.e. other than in-servants, must be some 200,000 less than the whole number of families. In other words, 200,000 (or more) families are not headed by (indeed, do not contain, apart from servants) a man of 21 or over. This figure is not surprising, as the number of widows is given in King's Table III as 240,000,[2] and there were some households headed by spinsters.[3] We may assume then, that of the 1,360,586 families, some 200,000 (roughly one-seventh of the whole) contained no adult[4] male (other than in-servants). Hence, to convert the number of families to the number of adult males we must reduce by one-seventh.

It is not necessary to make this calculation for each of King's categories, but only for each of the classes into which we have to regroup his categories for our franchise purposes. We shall apply the same reduction of one-seventh to each of those classes (with certain exceptions, to be noted): this requires the arbitrary assumption that each class contained the same proportion of widows and spinsters at the head of households, but the difference made by varying that assumption would not be substantial.

We may now complete our estimate of the number of adult male servants. Adult male in-servants have already been estimated at 130,000. To get the number of out-servants we start with the 364,000 families of 'labouring people and out-servants', and convert this to the number of adult males by making the reduction of one-seventh; this gives us 312,000 adult males. We must then take in King's 'common seamen', for they were wage-earners.[5] But while we have assumed that all the male out-servants were aged 21 or over, we cannot make this assumption for the seamen.[6] We shall assume arbitrarily that 13,000 of King's 50,000 common seamen were under 21.[7] We thus have 37,000 adult male wage-earning seamen.

[1] King in Chalmers, p. 40. His 'those above 21 years old' appears to mean those who have reached their 21st birthday.

[2] Ibid., p. 39. Cf. Yarranton's remarks about the difficulty widows with children had in getting second husbands, even when the widows had some property (A. Yarranton, *England's Improvement* (1677), pp. 165–6, 167, 168, 172).

[3] In King's tabulation for the city of Gloucester the number of spinsters keeping house is 4·7 per cent. of the number of households (King in Chalmers, pp. 70–71).

[4] For brevity we shall hereafter use 'adult' to mean aged 21 and over.

[5] Davenant, ii. 201. Presumably this includes naval seamen as well as the merchant seamen whom Davenant mentions particularly; both may be treated as wage-earners.

[6] We do assume that each of the 'families' of seamen was headed by a male, i.e. we assume that seamen's widows' households would be included in King's categories of out-servants or cottagers and paupers.

[7] The assumption that about a quarter of the common seamen were under 21, although arbitrary, is not unreasonable. An adjustment of this magnitude brings the total estimated males of 21 years and over as calculated from King's main table, to approximately the same figure (1,300,000) as his total for them in his Table IV.

We assign also to the servant class King's 'common soldiers'. They would not ordinarily be described as servants, but their wages and expenditures put them in that class rather than the class above. Whether any of King's 35,000 soldiers had the franchise in his day is not important in our calculation, as we shall have to make a special estimate of the number of soldiers in 1648.[1] King's 35,000 'families' of soldiers may be reduced by the standard one-seventh,[2] giving a total of 30,000 adult male soldiers.

The total of adult male out-servants is thus 379,000. We thus have 130,000 in-servants and 379,000 out-servants, a total of 509,000 adult male servants.

(b) Alms-takers and beggars

We have still to consider the category of 'those receiving alms', or beggars. In their discussions of exclusions from the franchise, the Levellers referred indifferently to 'those receiving alms'[3] and 'beggars';[4] and in one place to 'those that receive alms from door to door'.[5] The grounds stated by the Levellers for excluding alms-takers from the franchise (that such men were dependent on the will of others and afraid to displease them) apply even more plainly to those who took public poor relief from the parish or were in alms-houses, than to transient beggars, for the families that were a charge on the parish were notoriously marked out as dependent. We shall accordingly take in to our estimate both King's vagrant beggars and his cottagers and paupers who were a charge on the parish.

King estimated only 30,000 single 'vagrants', which included 'hawkers, pedlars, crate carriers, gipsies, thieves, and beggars'.[6] Perhaps 10,000 of these might be counted as adult male beggars.

The number who were a charge on the parish is far larger. King, in his main table, shows as a single category, 400,000 families of 'cottagers and paupers'. This figure, we learn from Davenant's account of King's calculation, was reached by subtracting from the 554,631 cottages all those which had land about them and all those whose inhabitants 'get their own livelihood and are no charge to the parish'.[7] King's 400,000 families of cottagers and paupers include, therefore, only those who do not 'get their own livelihood', are a

---

[1] See below, pp. 291–2.

[2] As with seamen, we assume that each of the 'families' of soldiers was headed by a male, but allowance must be made for some under 21 years of age. A reduction of only one-seventh, instead of a quarter as for seamen, may be justified on the assumption that the sea was a more attractive wage-earning occupation for young men than the army.

[3] e.g. Putney debates, in A. S. P. Woodhouse, *Puritanism and Liberty* (1938), pp. 82–83; Second *Agreement*, ibid., p. 357; Third *Agreement*, in Don M. Wolfe, *Leveller Manifestoes* (1944), p. 401.

[4] e.g. *Letter* of 11 Nov. 1647, in Woodhouse, p. 452; *The Grand Designe* (8 Dec. 1647); *Petition* of 18 Jan. 1648, in Wolfe, *Leveller Manifestoes*, p. 269.

[5] Putney debates, in Woodhouse, p. 83.

[6] King in Chalmers, p. 36.　　　　　　　　　[7] Davenant, *Works*, ii. 203–4.

'charge to the parish', 'live chiefly upon others', and do not 'get themselves a large share of their maintenance'.[1] It is, of course, not to be inferred that even these cottagers subsisted entirely on poor relief. The rural ones might have an animal or two, and some rights on the common, and some of them would carry on some cottage industry, or be intermittently employed as day labourers;[2] but Davenant is clear that all these families were a charge on the parish.[3] And although some wage-labourers lived in cottages and might sometimes be a charge on the parish, no one is included twice in King's table: a man who could be described both as a labourer and as a cottager is counted as either but not as both.

The 400,000 families of cottagers and paupers must therefore have been considered to be all to some extent dependent on the parish. And there can be little doubt that these are the persons whom King describes, in three other tables, as 'receiving alms'. In an estimate of the yearly consumption of meat he shows '440,000 families who receive alms'.[4] In a calculation of the yield of the poll tax of I William and Mary he shows 600,000 persons (male and female, not children) 'receiving alms';[5] of these some 300,000 might be men. In a calculation of the yield of the duty on houses and windows in 1696 he shows 330,000 houses (out of the total of 1,300,000 inhabited houses) excused the tax as inhabited by 'those who receive alms'.[6] The order of magnitude of these figures, and the fact that the last one is based on the house and window taxes, make it clear that King's 'persons receiving alms' are not just the inhabitants of almshouses (whose total number is given in still another table[7] as only 13,400, men and women) but are in substance the 'cottagers and paupers'.

We may therefore accept King's figure of 400,000 families of cottagers and paupers as being roughly the number of families receiving alms. It cannot be assumed that these 'families' contained 400,000 men of 21 years and over, for in the category of 'cottagers and paupers', as in other categories of King's main estimate, allowance must be made for 'families' headed by widows. Making the same allowance as for other categories (one-seventh), we get a figure of 343,000 men aged 21 and over in the category of 'cottagers and paupers' receiving alms.

If then we add the estimated 10,000 vagrant male beggars to these 343,000 men receiving alms, we have a total of 353,000 men of 21 or over in the category alms-takers and beggars.

Summary. Servants and Alms-takers

Adding now the 509,000 male servants of 21 or over, the total for servants and alms-takers who are men of 21 or over is 862,000.

---

[1] Ibid., 203, 205.   [2] Ibid., 201.
[3] Cf. G. M. Trevelyan, *English Social History*, 1946, p. 274: King's cottagers and paupers 'represent, we may suppose, those who attempted to be independent of wages, and according to King made a very poor business of the attempt'.
[4] King in Chalmers, p. 55.   [5] Ibid., p. 57.
[6] Ibid., p. 59.   [7] Ibid., p. 73.

Classes 1, 2, and 3

The size of the remaining franchise classes can be estimated with less difficulty. It is simply a matter of distributing among these franchise classes the men of King's categories above the poverty line, i.e. those 'increasing the wealth of the kingdom'. Assumptions must be made about the proportions in which some of these categories of King's should be distributed among our franchise classes. The assumptions made below are not the only possible ones, but the use of any alternative assumptions consistent with what is known of the social and economic structure of the time would not significantly alter the order of magnitude of three franchise classes.

Class 1. Freeholders and freemen of corporations

We assume that all the members of King's ranks from the peers down to and including 'merchants and traders by sea' fall within this class. They amount to 28,500 families. Apart from these King classifies another 180,000 as 'freeholders'. We assume further that one-half of the members of the following ranks were either freeholders or freemen of corporations: merchants and traders by land, persons in sciences and liberal arts, shopkeepers and tradesmen, artisans and handicrafts, naval and military officers; this gives us a further 66,000 families in this class. The total number of families thus assigned to class 1 is 275,000. Of these we allow six-sevenths as the number of adult males, that is, 235,700.

Class 2. Ratepaying householders not in Class 1

We allocate all of King's 'farmers' to this class, being 150,000. Since King's farmers and his freeholders are mutually exclusive categories, his farmers are all the (non-urban) non-freehold tenants. We have assumed that these consist of (i) the copyholders and (ii) the leaseholders for years and for years or lives, i.e. the two categories of rural tenants that we have described in the text as excluded from the Putney freeholder franchise. In other words, we have assumed that both King and the Putney debaters were following the established legal distinction between freeholders and non-freeholders, and the legal usage as argued by Blackstone as to copyholders.[1] As this assumption may be challenged, we must notice the effect of other possible assumptions.

(1) If King included the 'free copyholders' among his freeholders (whereas we have seen that the Putney debaters probably did not do so), it would be necessary to move the number of free copyholders from our class 1 to class 2. It is quite possible that King did do so, for as we have seen there was no certain rule as to whether or in what respect these free copyholders or customary freeholders counted as freeholders. We have no way of estimating

[1] See above, ch. III, p. 112.

this number. If it was substantial, it would substantially increase the disparity between the freeholder franchise and the ratepayer franchise.

Three further possible assumptions may be considered, although none of these is as probable as the one just discussed, for these concern the status of tenants for life or lives, and for years or lives, about which there was no legal doubt.

(2) If King, against legal usage, treated tenants for life or lives as non-freeholders, we have two possibilities: (*a*) that the Putney debaters also treated them as non-freeholders, in which case our estimates are not affected; (*b*) that the Putney debaters treated them as freeholders, in which case we should have to move their estimated number from our class 2 to class 1. This would reduce the disparity between the freeholder and ratepayer franchises, but we do not know by how much.

(3) If King, against legal usage, treated tenants for years or lives as freeholders, we have two possibilities: (*a*) if the Putney debaters treated them as freeholders (which is quite possible, since the tenant for ninety-nine years or three lives had as much security as the ordinary freeholder, and security of tenure was the main criterion used by Cromwell and Ireton for eligibility for franchise), our estimates are not affected; (*b*) if the Putney debaters treated them as non-freeholders, it would be necessary to move their number from our class 1 to class 2, thus increasing the disparity between the freeholder and ratepayer franchises, but again we do not know their number.

(4) If King treated tenants for years or lives as non-freeholders and the Putney debaters treated them as freeholders, it would be necessary to move their number from our class 2 to class 1, thus reducing the disparity between the freeholder and ratepayer franchises.

In short, of these four possible assumptions, the most likely one (the first) would increase the size of our class 1 and reduce class 2; the other three assumptions would either have no effect on our estimates, or would in one case have the same effect as the first, and in the other two cases the opposite effect. But none of these four assumptions seems any more probable than the assumption we have made. We therefore leave all King's farmers in the non-freeholder class.

We assume one-half of the merchants and traders by land, persons in sciences and liberal arts, and naval and military officers fall in this class, being 16,500. We put in this class also all the persons in the law and the clergymen, being 20,000.[1] We assume one-quarter of the shopkeepers and tradesmen and artizans and handicrafts, being 25,000. The total families thus assigned to class 2 is 211,500. The number of adult males is 181,300.

Class 3. Non-ratepayers not in class 4

We assume in class 3 one-quarter of the shopkeepers and tradesmen and artizans and handicrafts, being 25,000 families. The number of adult males is 21,400.

[1] See Note S, p. 300.

The assumption that these, and only these, are to be put in class 3 may appear arbitrary. Two considerations may be suggested to justify it.

(1) King's 'shopkeepers and tradesmen, artizans and handicrafts' were all independent producers or traders; the journeymen and other wage-earners were not in this category but in one of the categories of servants. That being so, it seems reasonable to assume that only a quarter of these men were neither freemen of corporations nor ratepayers.

(2) The attribution of any more than a quarter of the shopkeepers, tradesmen, artisans and handicraftsmen to the non-ratepayer class would seem to be too high, in view of what we know of the total number of non-ratepaying families. We have no exact figures for the number of families that kept house but did not pay rates. But King's estimate of the yield of the duty on houses and windows affords some indication. Of the 1,300,000 inhabited houses, he reckoned that 330,000 paid no duty because inhabited by those who receive alms, and a further 380,000 paid no duty because inhabited by 'Those who do not pay to church and poor'.[1] These figures are for houses, some of which must have contained more than one family. While these figures are not entirely consonant with the distribution of families above and below the poverty line in King's main table, they do suggest that the whole number of non-ratepaying families was scarcely more than enough to account for all the families of housekeeping wage-earners and persons receiving alms.

It may be noticed finally that even if, in spite of these considerations, we allowed twice as many men in class 3 as we have allowed, the proportions between class 3 and the other classes would not be significantly altered, and the proportions between franchise C and the other franchises would be altered even less.[2]

Conversion of Estimates from 1688 to 1648

Having converted King's numbers of 'families' to numbers of adult males, and allotted them to the franchise classes we are concerned with, we now have estimates of the size of these franchise classes as of 1688:

Class 1. Freeholders and Freemen of Corporations . .	235,700
Class 2. Ratepaying Householders not in 1 . . .	181,300
Class 3. Non-ratepayers not in 4	21,400
Class 4. Servants and Alms-takers	862,000
Total	1,300,400[3]

It is now desirable to convert these estimates to the population of 1648. We shall assume that there was no significant change in the distribution of

[1] King in Chalmers, p. 59.

[2] Class 3 would be increased from 21,400 to 42,800; class 2 would be reduced from 181,300 to 159,500; classes 1 and 4 would be unaltered. Franchise C would be unaltered (438,000); franchise B would be reduced from 417,000 to 395,600; franchises A and D would be unaltered.

[3] The total males above 21 years old in King's Table IV is 1,300,000.

population between ranks in the forty years 1648–88. But there was one significant change in the distribution between our franchise classes: in 1647–8 the army was considerably larger than in 1688, and since all the soldiers in the parliamentary army in 1647–8 were included in the Leveller franchise,[1] those of them who as civilians would have been in class 4 must be raised to a higher franchise class. In view of this, it is necessary to convert our 1688 estimates, which might otherwise have been allowed to stand as a sufficient indication of the proportions between franchise classes, to a 1648 population base.

While population growth in seventeenth-century England was uneven, the net growth between 1648 and 1688 may be assumed to have been about 10 per cent. We shall accordingly reduce each of our estimates by 10 per cent. We thus have:

Franchise class	1688 No. of adult males	1648 No. of adult males (unadjusted for army)
1. Freeholders, &c.	235,700	212,100
2. Ratepayers not in 1	181,300	163,200
3. Non-ratepayers not in 4	21,400	19,300
4. Servants and alms-takers	862,000	775,800
Totals	1,300,400	1,170,400

We may now make the necessary adjustment for the army. The number of men in the parliamentary armies in the 1640's varied with the exigencies of the civil wars. In 1645 it was 60,000 to 70,000, of which 22,000 were in the New Model Army.[2] After the first civil war some of the forces were disbanded and others merged under the single command of Fairfax; at the time of the Putney debate the army must have amounted to over 32,000.[3] More men were raised in 1648, during the second civil war; at March 1649 there were some 47,000 in the army.[4] The army at the time of the franchise demands of Second and Third *Agreements* (December 1648 and May 1649) must have numbered at least 45,000.

We can estimate roughly the proportion of soldiers who would as civilians have been in the class of servants or receiving alms. The New Model Army was originally composed of 6,600 horse, 1,000 dragoons, and 14,400 foot.[5] The horse and dragoons were volunteers and lived like gentlemen; they may be assumed to have been all from the freeholder or ratepayer classes. The infantry,

[1] See below, Note K, p. 297.

[2] C. H. Firth, *Cromwell's Army* (1902), pp. 33, 34.

[3] Counting the New Model Army as 22,000 and the northern army as 10,000 (Firth, op. cit., p. 34).   [4] Firth, op. cit., pp. 34–35.

[5] Firth and Davies, *Regimental History of Cromwell's Army*, i, pp. xvii–xviii.

of whom more than half were raised by impressment, were largely illiterate;[1] it does not seem too much to assume that three-quarters of the infantry (i.e. just under half the army) came from the wage-earning or alms-taking class, and the other one-quarter of the infantry from the non-ratepayer class. If we assume that the enlarged army of 1648 was in roughly the same proportions as the original New Model Army, we have some 22,100 of the 45,000 men coming from the servant or alms-taker class.[2] The distribution of the whole army, by civilian classes, is thus estimated as follows:

Classes 1 and 2. Freeholders and ratepayers . .	15,500
Class 3. Non-ratepayers not in 4	7,400
Class 4. Servants and alms-takers . . .	22,100
Total	45,000

The estimated distribution of the whole adult male population now appears as follows:

Class 1. Freeholders and freemen of corporations . . .	212,100,	of whom	8,500	were soldiers
Class 2. Ratepayers not in 1 . .	163,200,	,,	7,000	,,
Class 3. Non-ratepayers not in 4 .	19,300,	,,	7,400	,,
Class 4. Servants and alms-takers .	775,800,	,,	22,100	,,
Totals	1,170,400		45,000	

We must now move the 22,100 soldiers whose civilian status was class 4 into class 3. The resulting distribution of the adult male population of 1648 among the franchise classes is as follows:

Class 1. Freeholders and freemen of corporations . . .	212,100
Class 2. Ratepayers not in 1	163,200
Class 3. Non-ratepayers not in 4, plus soldiers originally in 4 .	41,400
Class 4. Servants and alms-takers, less soldiers originally in 4 .	753,700
Total	1,170,400

The cumulative totals for the four different types of franchise that were in dispute in the Leveller literature are thus:

A. Freeholder franchise . .	212,100
B. Ratepayer franchise . .	375,300
C. Non-servant franchise . .	416,700
D. Manhood franchise . .	1,170,400

[1] Firth, *Cromwell's Army*, p. 40.

[2] This proportion may appear too high, though it is much less than the proportion of the whole population in that class. We might put the proportion lower, but to do so would increase the number of soldiers of franchise class 3 to a point scarcely consonant with the number of men of class 3 in the whole population.

NOTES

NOTE A. (1) *The Elements of Law Natural and Politic*, circulated in manuscript in 1640, published in 1650 as two treatises (*Human Nature*, and *De Corpore Politico*), edited and published under its original title by F. Tönnies, Cambridge, 1928 (references are to the Tönnies edition, cited as *Elements*).

(2) *De Cive*, 1642, an English version of which was published in 1651 under the title *Philosophical Rudiments concerning Government and Society*; the text of the 1651 English *Rudiments* has been edited and published under the title *De Cive or The Citizen* by S. P. Lamprecht, New York, 1949 (references are to the Lamprecht edition, cited as *Rudiments*).

(3) *Leviathan*, 1651 (references are to the edition of W. G. Pogson Smith, Oxford, 1929).

NOTE B. If we used the economists' highly abstract concept of a man's powers, mentioned in the preceding note, we could construct a model of a perfectly competitive economy in which some men own no land or capital, and could show that the wage-relation involved no transfer of any part of a wage-earner's powers, for his powers would be defined to exclude any access to land or capital. In such a model it can be demonstrated that wages equal the marginal net product of labour, although, of course, the marginal net product of labour bears no fixed relation to the amount of energy and skill contributed by labour, but varies with the ratio of supply of labour to supply of capital and land. Even in the economic model, with the narrow definition of powers, there may be a transfer (over and above what is a transfer on our definition of powers) if the assumption of perfect competition is relaxed. The further transfer arises from the less-than-perfect competition between buyers of labour which is apt to result from the buyers being fewer than the sellers; being fewer, they can proceed on a tacit and conventional understanding not to bid above a certain rate of wages or not to accept less than a certain price for their land and capital, and so can get for themselves a larger share of the product than they could otherwise get.

NOTE C. e.g. Thomas Nagel, 'Hobbes on Obligation', *Philosophical Review*, lxviii (1959), 68–83. Nagel holds that Hobbes did derive obligation from self-interest but that it is a mistake to call it, as Hobbes did, moral obligation. 'Nothing could be called a moral obligation which in principle never conflicted with self-interest' (p. 74). But, granting this proposition, and granting that Hobbes's obligation is derived from nothing but self-interest, it does not follow that it cannot be moral obligation. For in Hobbes's concept each man's self-interest contains its own contradiction: short-run self-interest conflicts with long-run self-interest. Hence, obligation derived from long-run self-interest does conflict in principle with short-run self-interest.

NOTE D. What Hobbes intended by his references to God as the author of the law of nature is not clearly known. But even the strongest advocate of the view that Hobbes probably intended to base obligation either on divine rewards and punishments or on divine will, allows that Hobbes's system may be based 'upon a body of natural law which bears its own authority' and that this 'makes it unnecessary to introduce the role of God at all into Hobbes's political theory' (H. Warrender, in *Political Studies*, viii (1960), 49). Cf. Warrender *The Political Philosophy of Hobbes*, p. 311, where the interpretations based on divine will and on divine rewards are both stated to be 'devoid of significant consequences for the deduction of men's duties, except that they provide a formal termination for the scale of authority'.

NOTE E. It may be thought that there is a middle way: a society in which men acknowledge an hierarchical inequality, without any man claiming *unlimited* superiority. That would meet the condition: if no one claimed unlimited superiority, all could be morally bound. But it is difficult to conceive of a society where all acknowledge that men are unequal in some respect of overriding social importance, yet where some men do not claim unlimited superiority, i.e. where all men accept finite limits on the superiority which they can claim on grounds of factual inequality. A functional hierarchical system, such as an idealized feudal system, might be thought to meet these requirements; but such systems in fact have always relied on supernatural postulates (and sanctions) for their differential moralities.

NOTE F. Firth, while interpreting both the First Agreement and the Leveller position in the Putney debate as being for manhood franchise (see p. 107, n. 1), also cites the Leveller exclusion during the debate (*Clarke Papers*, i, p. li) but sees no inconsistency; Gardiner, loc. cit.; G. P. Gooch, *English Democratic Ideas in the Seventeenth Century*, 1898, ed. Laski 1927, notes the exclusion (p. 131) but then refers to this as 'their plan of manhood suffrage' (p. 132); T. C. Pease, *The Leveller Movement*, 1916, says that the outcome of the Putney franchise debate was that the Levellers 'carried the proposition for the universal franchise' (p. 224), whereas the proposition that was carried was for franchise for all except servants and beggars [letter of 11 Nov. 1647, in Woodhouse, op. cit., p. 452]; Woodhouse, op. cit., describes this same vote as a resolution in favour of manhood suffrage, p. [29], and refers to the *Agreement* as providing for universal suffrage, p. [71]; D. W. Petegorsky, *Left-wing Democracy in the English Civil War*, 1940, refers to the Leveller demand for universal suffrage (pp. 96, 116, 118), while recognizing that 'wage-earners . . . were to be excluded from the scheme of universal suffrage they were advocating' (p. 109); Don M. Wolfe, *Leveller Manifestoes of the Puritan Revolution*, 1944, describes the vote at the end of the Putney franchise debate as a vote on manhood suffrage (p. 61), cites the *Petition* of Jan. 1648, as demanding manhood suffrage (p. 260), although the text of the *Petition* (p. 269) excludes servants and beggars, interprets the First *Agreement* as demanding manhood suffrage (pp. 14, 235), and describes *A New Engagement, or, Manifesto* of 3 Aug. 1648, as proposing manhood suffrage (p. 80), although the text asks only 'that the people be equally proportioned for the choyce of their Deputies'; Maurice Ashley, *John Wildman, Plotter and Postmaster* (1947), refers to the First *Agreement* as being in favour of manhood suffrage (p. 36), describes the Putney vote as an acceptance of 'the Leveller principle of manhood suffrage' (p. 43), and describes the *Petition* of Jan. 1648 as excluding beggars and criminals, without noticing its exclusion of servants; Perez Zagorin, *A History of Political Thought in the English Revolution*, 1954, presents the Levellers as advocates of manhood suffrage (pp. 30, 31), while noting the exclusion of servants and alms-takers in the Third *Agreement* and in the Putney debate (pp. 36, 37).

NOTE G. Eduard Bernstein, *Cromwell and Communism: Socialism and Democracy in the Great English Revolution* (1930; originally published in German in 1895), interprets the Leveller position in the Putney debate as for universal suffrage (p. 68 n.) and credits the Levellers with having championed 'the political interests of the contemporary and the future working class' (p. 86). He notes the exclusion of wage-earners and alms-takers in the Second and Third *Agreements* and reconciles it with his reading of Leveller principles by saying that journeymen 'were usually in the transition stage between apprentice and master' and that 'to extend the suffrage to the agricultural labourers would, in the then circumstances, have strengthened the reactionary party' (p. 87). While both these grounds must be allowed some weight, they fall short of a satisfactory explanation. The Levellers were zealots for principle, and had they ever embraced the full principle of universal suffrage they could scarcely have withdrawn it from all the agricultural labourers on such wholly expedient grounds. M. A. Gibb, *John Lilburne, the Leveller, a Christian Democrat* (1947), presents generally a manhood suffrage view (pp. 15, 139, 208), and describes the Putney vote as carrying 'the proposition for the universal franchise' (p. 209), while noting the Third *Agreement*'s exclusion of wage-earners. She offers an explanation, similar to Bernstein's, of 'this apparent departure from Leveller ideals' (p. 271); but an explanation which assumes that this was a departure from their ideals begs the question.

NOTE H. W. Schenk, *The Concern for Social Justice in the Puritan Revolution* (1948), finds a change from 1647, when the Levellers 'seem to have propagated unqualified manhood suffrage', to 1648 when they excluded almstakers and wage-earners. He cites, for this exclusion, the Second *Agreement*, without mentioning its further exclusion of all non-ratepayers; offers an explanation in terms of Leveller expediency; and concludes that 'in view of the Leveller theory it can be assumed that these restrictions were intended to be merely temporary' (p. 40, n. 48). The explanation and the assumption may possibly apply to the exclusion he does not mention (the non-ratepayers), but not to the exclusion he does mention (alms-takers and servants), which was consistently proposed by the Levellers at least from 29 Oct. 1647, to the end of their pamphleteering. Francis D. Wormuth, *The Origins of Modern Constitutionalism* (1949), presents the Levellers as advocates of manhood suffrage (pp. 75, 79), describes the Putney vote as for manhood suffrage (p. 81), notes that the Second *Agreement* excluded alms-takers, wage-earners, and non-ratepayers, and says that the Third *Agreement* restored manhood suffrage (pp. 83–84). Joseph Frank, *The Levellers* (1955), presents them as advocates of manhood suffrage from, at latest, Oct. 1646 (pp. 94, 123, 133, 151), until the Second *Agreement*, the wide exclusion of which is seen as a compromise (pp. 176–7), and notes without comment the exclusion of servants and paupers in the Third *Agreement* (p. 206).

NOTE I. The Levellers apparently never advocated woman suffrage. Gibb, op. cit., p. 174, draws attention to the fact that Lilburne, in his *The Freemans Freedome Vindicated*, 16–19 June 1646 (in Woodhouse, pp. 317–18), claimed that 'all and every particular and individual man and woman' were 'by nature all equal and alike in power, dignity, authority, and majesty, none of them having by nature any authority, dominion or magisterial power one over or above another' except 'by mutual agreement or consent'. Gibb infers that it follows that woman has political rights on an equal footing with men. But it does not follow, nor did Lilburne draw that inference. All that follows is that women as well as men must be assumed to have given their consent to the institution of government, and such consent may be 'given, derived or assumed . . . for the good benefit and comfort each of other, and not for the mischief, hurt or damage of any'. This would easily cover an assumed transfer of authority from women to their husbands. Lilburne's own wife, while very active in his defence, always deferred to his political opinions and decisions, and both of them appear to have thought this right and natural. The Leveller *Petition of Women*, 5 May 1649 (in Woodhouse, pp. 367–8), to which Gibb also refers, asserts the spiritual equality of men and women, and an equal interest in the liberties and securities contained in the laws (i.e. civil liberties) but does not claim equal political rights. (The same demand for relief from arbitrary legal proceedings for men and women is made in the Leveller *Petition* of Mar. 1647: in Wolfe, op. cit., p. 136.) The Levellers, men and women, seem rather to have taken for granted that women could be assumed to have authorized their men to exercise their political rights. And in an age when the typical employment relation was still considered similar to a family one, a similar assumed transfer of authority from servant to master would not be an extraordinary postulate. It is apparently Petty's postulate in the Putney debate: servants are 'included in their masters' (Woodhouse, p. 83, quoted above at p. 123).

NOTE J. Redistribution in proportion to the respective rates of counties is not only logically consistent with any breadth of franchise, but was actually proposed along with the narrowest freeholder franchise by Ireton in the Putney debate (Woodhouse, p. 83), and was endorsed by the Levellers in *The Case of the Army* (by virtue of their endorsement there of all the stipulations of the *Declaration* of 14 June; Haller and Davies, pp. 77, 61) along with, as I have argued, the non-servant franchise. The fact that two weeks later, in the First *Agreement*, the Levellers were proposing redistribution in proportion to population does not mean that they had changed their position on the extent of the franchise. Ireton and Cromwell, as we have seen, made much of this clause of the First *Agreement* during the Putney debate, but in doing so they misrepresented the position doubly, first by suggesting that the earlier redistribution in proportion to rates implied a property franchise (which it certainly had not done in the *Case of the Army*), and secondly by suggesting that the redistribution in proportion to population implied manhood suffrage (which, on the evidence of the Levellers' exclusion statements in the Putney debate, it did not do).

NOTE K. The right of the soldiers to a parliamentary franchise seems to have been assumed by the Levellers throughout the Putney debates: cf. Buff-Coat, i.e. Everard (Woodhouse, p. 7), Sexby (pp. 69–70), and Rainborough (p. 71). The Levellers also were presumably responsible for the franchise recommendation in the report of the Army Council's committee of 30 Oct. 1647, that 'all free-born Englishmen, or persons made free denizens of England, who have served the Parliament in the late war for the liberties of the kingdom, and were in the service before the 14th of June, 1645, . . . be admitted to have voices in the said elections . . . although they should not in other respects be within the qualifications' (Woodhouse, p. 450). The committee included Rainborough and Sexby as well as Cromwell and Ireton. The admission of soldiers otherwise not qualified appears as a concession by the army leaders, but not a serious one: the main recommendation, to which this was merely a desired addendum, left it to the present Commons to set the franchise qualifications 'so as to give as much enlargement to common freedom as may be, with a due regard had to the equality (? equity) and end of the present constitution in that point'. The vote taken at the end of the Putney debate, as reported in the *Letter from Several Agitators* (Woodhouse, p. 452), was on the proposition 'That all soldiers and others, if they be not servants or beggars' should have the franchise. As the *Letter* was addressed to all the soldiers, and as it claimed this vote as a victory for 'your native freedom', the proposition can only have meant that all the soldiers, and all those civilians who were not servants or beggars, should have the franchise.

NOTE L. e.g. Rainborough at Putney (Woodhouse, p. 53); Lilburne, *Free-man's Freedom Vindicated* (ibid., p. 317). It is doubtful if the Levellers thought even of this right as applying to those who were 'included in their masters'. Their idea of the social contract was never clearly formulated. Lilburne frequently referred to a 'maxim of nature' that no man can be bound

without his own consent, and used it to justify indiscriminately (*a*) the right
of everyone to be a party to the contract or deed of trust empowering a government, and (*b*) the right of everyone to choose the legislators. He used it in the
latter sense in *Rash Oaths Unwarrantable* (see above, p. 135) where, as we
have seen, it can only have been intended to mean every free man. He used it
in (chiefly) the former sense in *Regall Tyrannie discovered* (Jan. 1647): 'Reason tells me, I ought not to have a law imposed upon me, without my consent
. . . yea Reason tells me in this that no Soveraignty can justly be exercised, nor
no Law rightfully imposed, but what is given by common consent, in which,
every individuall is included . . .' (p. 10); and '. . . it is a maxime in Nature
and Reason, that no man can be concluded but by his own consent, and that it
is absolute Tyranny, for any what (or whom) -soever, to impose a Law upon a
People, that were never chosen nor betrusted by them to make them Lawes . . .'
(p. 46). Lilburne equates 'my consent' with 'common consent in which every
individual is included'; those already 'included in their masters' may thus be
included in the political consent at one remove. Cf. the reasoning of the
Petition, above, p. 124.

NOTE M. *Oceana*, pp. 99, 154; *Prerogative*, pp. 243, 247. It is not clear
what notion Harrington had of the size of the English population. At *Prerogative*, p. 247, he speaks of 'one million fathers of families', which appears to
include labourers as well as citizens. This is a reasonable estimate, not far from
Gregory King's figure of one and a third million 'families' as the total of all
classes in 1688. At *Oceana*, p. 154, the number of men over 18 is given as one
million, apparently heads of families; but it is not clear whether this is intended
to include 'servants' or not. For the total of one million is here reached from
the number of male 'elders' (age 30 and over) and 'youths' (age 18–30) 'on
the annual roll', which seems to mean citizens, not servants; but he immediately
uses the figure one million to include day labourers. At *Art of Lawgiving*,
p. 403, he speaks of England as a commonwealth of '500,000 men, or more',
the context implying, though not clearly, that this is men above the level of
servants. On the whole it seems likely that he thought of there being about
500,000 male citizens and an equal number of male servants. This also is not
far from King's estimate (see above, pp. 280, 286).

NOTE N. Laslett, in the Introduction to his edition of Locke's *Two Treatises
of Government*, while agreeing that Locke 'is perfectly willing to contemplate
the continuous or permanent appropriation of the product of one man's
labour by another', suggests that it is 'an over-interpretation to say that a man
can sell his labour in the sense of the propensity [*sic*] to work' (p. 104). What
is sold in a wage contract is a man's ability to work. The 'service he undertakes to do' (Locke's phrase) is no doubt limited in kind—the journeyman
baker does not undertake to do the work of a servant in husbandry—and it
may be limited in amount, but what is sold is the man's future labour, or

his supposed ability to perform in future the work which the employer has contracted for. A man's labour being alienable, it follows that Locke does separate life and labour: see above, pp. 219–20.

NOTE O. The articles of belief are essentially that there is a future life, and that salvation can only be had by believing that Christ was raised from the dead to be the divine saviour of mankind. Locke argues that this is a plain notion which, along with miracles, can readily be grasped by the illiterate in terms of their common experience: 'the healing of the sick, the restoring sight to the blind by a word, the raising, and being raised from the dead, are matters of fact, which they can without difficulty conceive, and that he who does such things, must do them by the assistance of a divine power. These things lie level to the ordinariest apprehension: he that can distinguish between sick and well, lame and sound, dead and alive, is capable of this doctrine' (ibid. ii. 580).

NOTE P. Laslett (Locke's *Two Treatises of Government*, Introduction, p. 105) in citing sect. 111 as an obstacle to any interpretation of Locke as essentially a bourgeois theorist, has failed to see this. The other obstacles Laslett finds to such an interpretation may also be mentioned here. His remark that one must explain away all Locke's statements about the origin and limitations of property has, I hope, been sufficiently dealt with in sect. 2, iii above. His statement that one must ignore all that Locke says about 'regulating' property is doubly curious. In the first place, if anyone's property, and right to acquire property, are to be secured, everyone's must be 'regulated', as Locke explicitly argued (*Second Treatise*, sect. 120). But presumably Laslett has in mind here the fact that Locke 'nowhere complains against the complicated regulations of his "mercantilist" age in terms of property rights' (p. 104). Locke was of course a mercantilist. But this is perfectly consistent with his being a proponent of capitalist enterprise and of capitalist appropriation unlimited in amount. The right of capitalist appropriation does not imply the absence of state regulation of the mercantilist sort; on the contrary it may require the presence of such regulation: see above, ch. II, pp. 57–58, 62, 98. Finally, as to Locke's insistence that the obligations of the Law of Nature hold in society, it is not at all necessary to deny that Locke meant this to apply to property. On the contrary, it is because Locke did mean it to apply to property that he took such care to show that unlimited appropriation was not contrary to Natural Law and was allowable in the state of nature (see above, pp. 203 ff., 218). Charles H. Monson, Jr., seems to have fallen into the same error about regulating property. 'It is simply not true', he writes (*Political Studies*, vi. 2 (1958), 125), 'that Locke sanctions unlimited appropriation and inalienable property rights'. Of course Locke did not sanction 'inalienable property rights'; nobody says he did. Locke's individual, in consenting to civil society, consents to state regulation of property as a way of securing his property. But this in no way controverts a right of appropriation unlimited in amount.

Unlimited capitalist appropriation, as I have shown, *requires* state jurisdiction over property, and is consistent with a great deal of state interference with individual property.

NOTE Q. sect. 21. This passage is not in the Everyman edition of the *Treatises* (ed. W. S. Carpenter), nor in the Appleton-Century edition of the *Second Treatise and Letter Concerning Toleration* (ed. C. L. Sherman, New York, 1937). Each of these follows, at this point, a printing of the first edition of the *Treatises* which did not contain any sect. 21, and each has covered up the deficiency by arbitrarily dividing another section into two. (Sherman divides sect. 20; Carpenter divides sect. 36, so that all the sections in the Everyman edition from 21 to 35 are wrongly numbered.) The particulars of the two printings of Locke's first edition, and of their handling by modern editors, are given in Peter Laslett's 'The 1690 Edition of Locke's *Two Treatises of Government*: Two States', *Transactions of the Cambridge Bibliographical Society*, iv (1952), 341–7.

NOTE R. Cox, *Locke on War and Peace* (1960), argues persuasively that Locke's real position was the second of these; that Locke took the first position at the opening of the *Second Treatise* in order 'not to shock the received opinions' of his readers; that having opened by disguising his real view he then undertakes a 'gradual, but precisely ordered, shift', and 'manages, unobtrusively yet systematically, gradually to reverse' the opening picture of the state of nature (pp. 72–73, 76). The reversal is not quite as gradual as Cox suggests, for Locke contradicts his pleasant version of the state of nature as early as sect. 21. But the real difficulty with Cox's interpretation is that Locke needed *both* versions of the state of nature (as I have pointed out, e.g. in the preceding paragraph above) in order to sustain his conclusions. It therefore still seems to me more probable that Locke genuinely held both views without being conscious of their inconsistency.

NOTE S. The 10,000 lawyers have all been assigned to class 2, and the 10,000 'persons in offices' all to class 1; each group might well have been equally divided between the two classes. Clergymen ought perhaps to have been omitted from the calculation entirely, since it is doubtful whether they had the franchise in 1648. As long as the taxes to be paid by the clergy were voted by Convocation (i.e. down to the beginning of the Civil War, and again for a short time after the Restoration), clergymen did not have the parliamentary franchise. In 1663 by agreement between Archbishop Sheldon and Lord Clarendon it was resolved thereafter to tax church benefices as temporal estates were taxed, 'in consequence of which . . . the inferior beneficed clergy have constantly voted for members of the house of commons' (Burnet, *History of His Own Time*, ed. 1823, i. 340). Many clergy 'voted at the first election after the Restoration; and by an Act passed in the session of 1664–5 [16 and 17 Car. II, c. I], which taxed the clergy in common with the laity, their own status as Parliamentary electors was confirmed' (Porritt, *The Unreformed House of Commons*, 1903, i. 3). But it was not only after 1663 that the clergy gave over the right of taxing themselves; from the beginning of the Civil War to 1660 the clergy 'either out of voluntary compliance, affectation of popularity, or for want of proxies to represent their body, had their benefices taxed with the laity in the pretended Parliaments' (Laurence Echard, quoted in A. Browning (ed.), *English Historical Documents* 1660–1714, p. 416). It is thus quite possible that the clergy might have been considered not disqualified for the parliamentary franchise during the Civil War period.

NOTE T. The simplest calculation of the number of full-time wage-earners is as follows: 260,000 male in-servants (King's Table III), 364,000 ('families' of) labouring people and outservants, 50,000 ('families' of) common seamen, 35,000 ('families' of) common soldiers (all from King's main table, reproduced on pp. 280–1, above): total 709,000. This is 45 per cent. of the 1,578,000 males over 16 years of age (King's Table IV). Other calculations, using the totals of King's main table and allowing for the existence of some 'families' without a male head (see above, pp. 284–5) give results between 43 and 45 per cent. If the 400,000 cottagers are added, the proportion is over two-thirds.

NOTE U. That 'servants' in 17th century usage meant all wage-earners is more fully documented in my 'Servants and Labourers in 17th Century England', *Democratic Theory, Essays in Retrieval* (Oxford, 1973), Ch. XII.

WORKS AND EDITIONS CITED

I. *Seventeenth-century Works*

1. HARRINGTON

References to all of his works are to the *Oceana and Other Works*, London, 1771.

2. HOBBES

Behemoth or the Long Parliament, ed. F. Tönnies, London, 1889.

De Cive, see *Philosophical Rudiments*.

Decameron Physiologicum, in *English Works*, ed. Molesworth, London, 1839–45, vol. vii.

Elements of Law Natural and Politic, ed. F. Tönnies, Cambridge, 1928.

Elements of Philosophy, the First Section, Concerning Body, in *English Works*, ed. Molesworth, vol. i.

Leviathan, ed. W. G. Pogson Smith, Oxford, 1929.

Philosophical Rudiments Concerning Government and Society. This, the English version (1651) of the Latin *De Cive* (1642), is published under the title *De Cive or The Citizen*, ed. S. P. Lamprecht, New York, 1949. References are to this edition, cited as *Rudiments*.

3. LEVELLER WRITINGS

Many of the significant Leveller writings are to be found in one or more of the following four modern collections:

William Haller (ed.), *Tracts on Liberty in the Puritan Revolution 1638–1647*, 3 vols., New York, 1934 (cited as Haller *Tracts*).

William Haller and Godfrey Davies (eds.), *The Leveller Tracts 1647–1653*, New York, 1944 (cited as Haller and Davies).

Don M. Wolfe (ed.), *Leveller Manifestoes of the Puritan Revolution*, New York, 1944 (cited as Wolfe).

A. S. P. Woodhouse (ed.), *Puritanism and Liberty, being the Army Debates (1647–9) from the Clarke Manuscripts, with Supplementary Documents*, London, 1938 (cited as Woodhouse).

References to those of the Leveller works which are printed in whole or in part in one of these collections are given, in footnotes, to the appropriate collection(s), cited as above; references to other Leveller works are to the originals, and, where they are reproduced in part in a modern work on the Levellers, to the appropriate modern work.

4. LOCKE

(a) Printed Works

An Essay Concerning Human Understanding, ed. A. C. Fraser, Oxford, 1894.

Essays on the Law of Nature, ed. W. von Leyden, Oxford, 1954.

The Reasonableness of Christianity, in *Works*, 6th edition, London, 1759, vol. ii.

Some Considerations of the Consequences of the Lowering of Interest and Raising the Value of Money, in *Works*, 6th edition, 1759, vol. ii.

Two Treatises of Government, ed. Peter Laslett, Cambridge, 1960.

(b) Manuscripts

Journal for 1678. As printed in H. R. Fox Bourne, *The Life of John Locke*, New York, 1876, vol. i, 403–4.

Civil Magistrate (1660). Bodleian Library, MS. Locke, c. 28 and e. 7.

Report on the Poor (1697). As printed in H. R. Fox Bourne, *The Life of John Locke*, 1876, vol. ii, 377–91.

Trade. Bodleian Library, MS. Locke, c. 30, f. 18.

II. *Modern Works*

The title, date, and place of publication if other than London, of each modern work cited or quoted, is given in the first footnote or Note in which reference is made to that work. See the Index, which gives for each modern author the page(s) on which his work or works are cited; in each of these Index entries, the first number (or the first two or more numbers, joined by '&', where more than one work by an author has been cited) gives the page on which the full reference first appears.

INDEX

Agrarian law, 182, 184–8.

Agreement of the People: First, 107, 108, 109, 119, 122, 124–5, 131, 145, 257, 294–5, 297; Second, 109, 110, 112, 114, 115–17, 138, 145, 295, 296; Third, 109, 114, 117, 125, 145, 295, 296; Officers', 114.

Alms-takers, *see* Beggars.

Apprentices, 108, 123, 130.

Aristotle, 246.

Artificers, Statute of, 282.

Ashley, Maurice, 295.

Audley, Capt. Lewis, 126.

Bacon, Francis, 171.

Balance, principle of the, 162–74, 188–92.

Baxter, Richard, 134; 121.

Baynes, Capt. Adam, 170.

Beggars: estimated number of, 286–7; excluded from Leveller franchise, 107–9, 121, 122–36, 144, 146–8; *see also* Poor.

Bentham, Jeremy, 2, 270.

Bernstein, Eduard, 295.

Birthright, 122, 123–9, 131, 136, 146–7.

Blackstone, Sir William, 112.

Bourgeois: defined, 162; assumptions in Harrington, 162, 174–81, 182, 187–8, 190, 192–3; assumptions in Hobbes, 62–68; assumptions in Locke, 221, 245–7; *see also* Possessive market society.

Bourne, H. R. Fox, 223, 239.

Bowle, John, 91.

Bracton, 113.

Brown, Stuart M., Jr., 12.

Burke, Edmund, 86.

Burnet, Gilbert, 300.

Campbell, Mildred, 282.

Capital, 54–57, 60, 293; in Levellers, 149; in Locke, 206–8, 217, 218, 234.

Carey, John, 282.

Carpenter, W. S., 300.

Case of the Army truly stated, 107, 124, 130–1, 297.

Chalmers, George, 279 ff.

Chaloner, Thomas, 170.

Charge of High Treason, 118.

Civil War, The: Harrington on, 175; Hobbes on, 64–67, 86, 94; Leveller franchise for participants in, 115–16, 135–6, 297; Locke on, 252, 260; size of army in, 291–2.

Clapham, J. H., 61.

Clarendon, Lord, 300.

Clarke, Capt. John, 126, 127, 139.

Classes: in Harrington, 166–7, 176, 182, 191–2, 268; in Hobbes, 89, 93–95, 98–99, 265; in Levellers, 152, 154–6, 266–7; in Locke, 216–17, 221–9, 243, 245–7, 248–51, 257–8, 261, 269–70; in 17th-century England, 279–92; in 20th century, 271, 273–4.

Clergy, taxation of, 300–1.

Coke, Edward, 112.

Coleman, D. C., 279, 283.

Commodity, labour as a: 48, 51, 55, 59–60; Hobbes on, 62, 66, 68, 91; Levellers on, 148–51, 153; Locke on, 214–20.

Community, Leveller sense of, 156–8.

Commutative justice, 63–64, 80.

Competition, 38–39, 50, 52–53, 54–57, 59–60, 293.

Consistency: hypothesis of, 7–8; Harrington's, 172, 188, 190, 192; Hobbes's, 9–15, 40–41, 100–6; Levellers', 109, 110–11, 117, 126, 129, 136, 145; Locke's, 194–7, 229–30, 238, 243–7, 250–62.

Copyholders, 112–13, 114, 121, 129.

Covetousness: Harrington on, 176; Hobbes on, 38, 154, 237; Levellers on, 154–5; Locke on, 236–7.

Cox, R. L., 7, 197, 300.

Cranston, Maurice, 253, 258.

Cromwell, 112, 113, 118, 119, 120, 121, 123, 124, 126, 127, 128–9, 138, 139, 148, 151, 297.

Cruise, William, 113.

Customary society, 49–51.

Davenant, Charles, 279, 285, 286–7.

Davies, Godfrey, 61 & 118 & 123; 291.

Declaration of Some Proceedings, 122.

Declaration or Representation, 14 June 1647, 297.

Delinquents, 115, 122, 124, 130.

Distributive justice, 63–64, 80.

Echard, Laurence, 301.

Equality, postulate of: in Harrington, 185–6, 188; in Hobbes, 74–80, 83–85, 87–90; in Levellers, 129, 138, 140, 144, 296; in Locke, 199, 231–2, 243–5, 247; necessary for deduction of right from fact, 83, 265, 272; in Stoic and Christian Natural Law, 88; in 20th century, 276–7.

Everard, Robert, 297.

Firmin, Thomas, 282.

Firth, C. H., 107 & 291 & 123; 109, 292, 294.

Franchise proposals: Harrington's, 181, 183; Independents', 116–17, 120–1, 126–7, 128–9; Levellers', 107–36, 144–6.

Franchise, types of: Freeholder, 112–14, 115, 117, 120, 128–9, 151–2, 288–9, 291–2, 297; Manhood, 107, 109–11, 115, 117, 118–19, 120, 122, 125, 126–7, 130–6, 292, 294–7; Non-servant, 114–17, 118–19, 129, 136, 279, 289–90, 291, 292; Ratepayer, 110, 114–17, 118, 279, 288–9, 291, 292; Soldiers', 115–16, 135–6, 291–2, 297.

Frank, Joseph, 133, 296.

Freedom: bourgeois, in Hobbes, 97–98, 100, 106; Leveller and Independent concepts of, 128–9, 130–1, 133, 134, 137, 139, 140–1, 142–58; in models of society, 51, 53.

Freeholders, 112–14, 121, 128–9, 173, 288–9.

Furniss, E. S., 229.

Galileo, 30, 77, 101.

Gardiner, S. R., 107, 294.

Gentry: in Harrington, 160–74, 177–81, 183, 186, 190, 193; in Independents' theory, 152.

Gibb, M. A., 295; 131, 132, 296.

Gooch, G. P., 294.

Gough, J. W., 196, 210, 253, 258.

Green, T. H., 3.

Grotius, 88.

Habbakuk, H. J., 258.

Haller, William, 118 ff.

Harrington, James: *The Art of Law-giving*, 163–91 passim, 298; *A Discourse Shewing that the Spirit of Parliament . . . is not to be trusted*, 174; *Oceana*, 65, 163–92 passim, 298; *Pian Piano*, 171; *Politicaster*, 191; *The Prerogative of Popular Government*, 91, 163–91 passim, 268, 298; *A System of Politics Delineated in short and easy Aphorisms*, 163–88 passim; *Valerius and Publicola*, 169, 183, 184; ambiguities in, 161–2; principle of the balance, 162–74, 188–92; England as bourgeois society, 174–82; proposals for England, 182–4; the agrarian, 182, 184–8, 192; concept of equality, 185–8; contradictions, 189–92; and Hobbes, 65, 91, 191, 193, 267–8; and Levellers, 268; and Locke, 248.

Harris, John, *The Grand Designe*, 124–5; 8, 108.

Hill, Christopher, 160, 227.

Hoarding, Locke on, 204–8.

Hobbes, Thomas: *Behemoth*, 64–66, 94; *De Cive*, 88 (see also *Philosophical Rudiments*); *Decameron Physiologicum*, 42; *Elements of Law Natural and Politic*, 11–103 passim, 293; *Elements of Philosophy, the First Section, Concerning Body*, 10, 103; *Leviathan*,

10–104 *passim*, 154, 220, 237, 293; *Philosophical Rudiments concerning Government and Society*, 11–96 *passim*, 293; alleged disjunctions of his political theory, from materialism, 10, from psychology, 10–19; state of nature, logical not historical, 19–21, not about uncivilized men, 21–29, inadequacy of, 45, 47, 68–70, 84; resolutive-compositive method, 30–31, 101–5; man as automated machine, 31–34; human relations as power relations, 35; power comparative and contentious, 35–37; value, honour, and power, as market relations, 37–40; innate and acquired desire for power, 41–46; his model of society, 61–68; political obligation, deduced from motivation, 70–72, claimed as moral, 72–73, 87, via postulate of equality, 74–78, 83–87, and materialist and market postulates, 78–81, 84–87; materialist postulate required, 76, 78–79; market postulates required, 79–80, 84–85; market postulates justified, 85–87, 88–90; deduction of obligation from facts valid, 87; self-perpetuating sovereign unnecessary, 90–93; source of his error, 93–95; sovereign necessary, 95–96; sovereign possible, 96–99; method reconsidered, 101–5; moral objections reconsidered, 105–6; and Harrington, 65, 91, 191, 193, 267–8; and Levellers, 141, 154, 156; and Locke, 91–92, 106, 197, 207, 219–20, 237, 239, 241, 245, 247, 256–7, 269–70.

Hooker, Richard, 197, 243, 245, 269.

Hume, David, 82, 270.

Independents: concept of freedom as proprietorship, 148, 150–1; position on franchise, 112–14, 116–17, 126–9, 138, 151–3; on right to property, 138–9; and the Second *Agreement*, 116–17; *see also* Cromwell, Ireton.

Individualism: Harrington's, 267–8; Hobbes's, 84–86, 93, 265; Inde-

pendents', 148–59; Levellers' 137, 142, 148–59, 266–7; Locke's, 231, 252–7; in the liberal tradition, 1–3; *see also* Possessive Individualism.

Ireton, Henry, 112, 119, 120, 121, 122, 126, 127, 128–9, 138, 139, 148, 150, 151–2, 250, 297.

Jacob, G., 113.

Joint-stock theory of state, 195, 251–2

Kendall, Willmoore, 195–6.

King, Gregory, 279–90 *passim*.

Labour justification of property: in Harrington, 179; in Locke, 200–21.

Labour, property in one's: Levellers on, 145–53, 266; Locke on, 200–2, 214–15, 219–21; *see also* Commodity, labour as a.

Labourers, *see* Wage-earners.

Laird, John, 10.

Laissez-faire, 58, 62.

Laski, H. J., 195.

Laslett, Peter, 198 & 300; 215, 298, 299.

Leaseholders, 112–14, 129.

Letter sent from several Agitators, 108, 297.

Levellers: explicit exclusions from franchise, 107–9; neglect of these, 109, 294–5; partial notice of these, 110, 295; faulty notice of these, 110, 295–6; types of franchise discussed by, 111–15; freeholder franchise, 112–14; ratepayer franchise, 114–18; non-servant franchise, 114–16; manhood franchise, 115; and the Second *Agreement*, 115–17; franchise position in Putney Debates, 117–29; franchise position before Putney, 129–36; right to property, 137–9; property in one's person, 139–42; case for civil and religious liberties, 142–3; case for economic rights, 143–4; case for limited franchise, 144–8; concept of freedom as proprietorship, 148–54; shortcoming from full possessive individualism, 154–8; sense of community, 156–8; radical liberals not radical democrats, 158; and Harrington, 268; and Hobbes, 141, 154, 156; and Locke, 141–2, 145, 152, 154, 156, 158–9, 257.

Liberal-democratic state, 1, 272, 274–5.

Liberal-democratic theory, 3, 271, 274–5.

Liberties, in Leveller theory: civil and religious, 142–3, 296; economic, 143–4; political, 144–6.

Lilburne, John: *The Charters of London*, 133–4; *Englands Birth-Right Justified*, 131, 137, 143; *Free-man's Freedom Vindicated*, 139, 157, 296, 297; *Ionah's Cry*, 135; *Just Defence*, 143; *Londons Liberty in Chains discovered*, 132–3, 157; *Rash Oaths Unwarrantable*, 134–5, 298; *Regall Tyrannie discovered*, 298; *Vox Plebis*, 137; *A Whip for the Present House of Lords*, 137.

Locke, John: *Civil Magistrate* (MS.), 258–61; *Some Considerations of the Consequences of the Lowering of Interest and Raising the Value of Money*, 205, 216–17, 223, 229, 230, 253; *Essay concerning Human Understanding*, 230, 239; *Essays on the Law of Nature*, 258; *Of Government, First Treatise*, 212; *Of Government, Second Treatise*, 91–92, 197–261 *passim*, 298–300; *Journal* for 1678 (MS.), 239; *The Poor, Report on* (MS.), 222–3; *The Reasonableness of Christianity*, 224–6, 229, 252, 299; *Trade* (MS.), 207; contradictions in his theory, 194–7; natural right to property, derived from right to life, 200, 213–14, and to labour, 200–21, and expanded to an unlimited right, 203–21; class postulates, 221–9; generalized into natural differentials in rights, 230–2, and rationality, 232–8; differential rights and rationality conflated with equal rights and rationality, 238–51; his joint-stock theory, 251–2; his majority rule theory, 252–5; his individualism, 231, 252–7, 261–2; his constitutionalism, 257–61; his liberalism, 262; and Harrington, 248; and Hobbes, 91–92, 106, 197, 207, 219–20, 237, 239, 241, 245, 247, 256–7, 269–70; and Ireton, 250; and Levellers, 141–2, 145, 152, 154, 156, 158–9, 257.

Logical *v.* historical canons of interpretation, 14–15.

Ludlow, Edmund, 170.

Machiavelli, 192–3; 166, 167.

MacIntyre, A. C., 82.

Market relations: Harrington on, 175–7, 186, 268; Hobbes on, 38–40, 62–67, 86–87, 89–90, 93–94; Levellers on, 266–7; Locke on, 204–10, 216–18, 235–6, 245, 268–70; in 20th century, 275–6; *see also* Possessive market society.

Marx, Karl, 48, 181.

Materialism: in Hobbes, 10, 76–79; in Locke, 243.

Mercantilism, 58, 62, 96, 205, 207.

Mill, John Stuart, 2–3, 275.

Money, Locke on, 203–11, 213, 218, 233–5.

Monson, Charles H., Jr., 299.

Mournfull Cryes, 155.

Nagel, Thomas, 293.

Natural Law: Locke's, 197, 199, 203, 218, 232, 235, 238–40, 242–7, 259–61, 269, 270; Stoic and Christian, 88, 243–5.

Natural Right: in Levellers, to franchise, 111, 125, 129, 136; to life, 138, 140–2; to property, 138–9, 154–6, 158; in Locke, class differentials in, 230–2, 251, 261, to labour, 199–221, to life, 199, 219–20, to property, 197–221, 251, 256.

Neville, Henry, 170.

New Engagement, or, Manifesto, 295.

Oakeshott, M., 11.

Obligation: conditions for deduction of, 272–5; derived from possessive individualism, 271; in Hobbes, 70–90, 97–98, 100–1, 265; possibility of new theory of, 276.

'Ought' from 'is', 13, 15, 81–83.

Overton, Richard: *Appeale*, 137–8, 139, 141, 156; *Arrow*, 139, 140–1; *Remonstrance*, 143.

Paternalism: admitted by Levellers, 146, 296; rejected by Hobbes, 66; rejected by Locke, 244–5.

Pease, T. C., 294.

Petegorsky, D. W., 294; 137, 143.

Peters, Richard, 42.

Petition of March 1647, 296.

Petition of January 1648, 108–9, 124, 154–5, 156, 294, 295.

Petition of 11 September 1648, 138.

Petition of Women, 5 May 1649, 296.

Petty, Maximilian, 108, 113, 122–3, 125–6, 127, 139, 146, 152, 296.

Petty, Sir William, 229.

Petyt, William, 228–9.

Plato, 77.

Pluralism, 3.

Pocock, J. G. A., 174–5.

Poor, The: Hobbes on, 66; Levellers on, 128, 146–7, 152, 154–5; Locke on, 217, 221–6; Puritan doctrine on, 226–7; Restoration views on, 227–9; *see also* Beggars, Wage-earners.

Porritt, Edward, 301.

Possessive individualism: defined, 3, 263–4; in Harrington, 267–9; in Hobbes, 264–5; in Levellers, 142, 154–6, 265–7; in Locke, 269–70; source of 17th-century strength, 270; source of 20th-century dilemma, 271–5.

Possessive market society: defined, 48–49, 53–61, 271–2; as condition for deduction of obligation, 89–90; freedom and compulsion of, 106; Harrington's recognition of, 268–9; Hobbes's awareness of, 62–67; and Hobbes's model, 59–67; Levellers'

oversight of, 266; Locke's recognition of, 269–70; need for sovereign in, 95–96; net transfer of powers in, 55–57; persistence of and change in, 271–5; possibility of obligation in, 100–1, 105; possibility of sovereign in, 97–99; power-seeking in, 58–59; role of state in, 57–59; and 17th-century England, 61–62; *see also* Market relations.

Poverty, not same as dependence, 134, 149; *see also* Poor.

Primary accumulation, 181.

Property: defined, 143; in one's labour, Harrington on, 179, Levellers on, 145–53, 266, Locke on, 200–2, 214–15, 219–21; in one's person, Hobbes on, 264–5, Levellers on, 139–54, 265–6, Locke on, 198, 200, 214–15, 219–20, 247–8; in things, Harrington on, 162–3, 179, Independents on, 138–9, 148, 151, Levellers on, 127, 137–9, 143, 149–53, 154–6, 158–9, Locke on, 197–221, 247–8.

Putney debates, 107–9, 113–15, 118–29, 134, 136, 138–9, 146, 150, 151–2, 296, 297.

Rainborough, Col. Thomas, 121, 126, 127, 128, 134, 150, 152, 297.

Ratepayers, 114, 288–9.

Reade, Lt.-Col. Thomas, 123.

Remonstrance of Many Thousand Citizens, 131–2.

Resolutive-compositive method, 30–31, 101.

Rich, Colonel, 128.

Robertson, G. C., 10.

Rousseau, J. J., 196.

Schenk, W., 295.

Servants, defined, 107, 282; *see also* Wage-earners.

Sexby, Edward, 121, 297.

Sheldon, Archbishop, 300.

Sherman, C. L., 300.

Simple market society, 51–53, 54, 55, 57, 59–60.

Social assumptions: often overlooked, 4; often unclear, 5–7; risks of imputing, 5–7.

Sombart, Werner, 48.

Sovereignty: in Harrington, 91; in Hobbes, 20–21, 69–72, 76, 89, 90–100; in Locke, 91, 195, 237, 239, 241, 255–61, 270.

State of nature: in Hobbes, 16, 18–29, 31, 45, 47, 68–70, 84; in Locke, 196–7, 208–11, 215–19, 229, 231–47, 251.

Status society, see Customary society.

Stephen, Leslie, 195.

Strauss, Leo, 7 & 10; 42–44.

Suffrage, see Franchise.

Supple, B. E., 62.

Tawney, R. H., 160 & 169 & 228; 174, 195.

Taylor, A. E., 10–12.

Tenants, see Copyholders, Freeholders, Leaseholders.

Trevelyan, G. M., 287.

Trevor-Roper, H. R., 169; 168–72.

Unwin, George, 282; 121, 283.

Utilitarian theory, 2, 270, 272.

Vaughan, C. E., 195.

von Leyden, W., 258.

Wage-earners: estimated number of, 282–6; excluded from Harrington's franchise, 181–2; excluded from Leveller franchise, 107–36, 144–6, 294–6; recognized by Hobbes, 66; recognized by Locke, 212, 215–17, 219, 221–30; recognized in 20th century, 272; see also Poor.

Wage relation: as net transfer of powers, 56–57, 293; Harrington on, 187; Hobbes on, 62–63, 66; Levellers on, 148–9; Locke on, 214–20; in 17th century, 61–62.

Walwyn, William, The Bloody Project, 155; A Manifestation, 157.

War, changed conditions of, 274; see also Civil War.

Warrender, Howard, 11, 15, 294.

Watkins, J. W. N., 30, 101.

Weber, Max, 48.

Wildman, John, 126, 295.

Winstanley, Gerrard, 157.

Wolfe, Don M., 108, 125, 133, 135, 294.

Women, rights of: Levellers on, 126, 143, 296.

Woodhouse, A. S. P., 108, 113, 130, 294.

Wormuth, Francis D., 296.

Yarranton, Andrew, 282, 285.

Yeomen, 121, 187, 202, 216, 257.

Zagorin, Perez, 295.